W9-DHM-929

Southern History
in the Making

Southern History in the Making

Pioneer Historians of the South

WENDELL HOLMES STEPHENSON

Louisiana State University Press : 1964

Library of Congress Catalog Card Number 64–21592

Manufactured in the United States of America by
Kingsport Press, Inc., Kingsport, Tennessee

Published with the assistance of a grant
from the Ford Foundation

For

ROBERT AND LOUISE WOODY

Genial and Generous Hosts

Acknowledgments

The writer's obligations in the preparation of this volume are chiefly three: to the General Education Board for a grant in aid of research; to the editors of historical journals for permission to reprint articles that appeared in their publications; and to sundry persons who performed valuable services in assembling material and in improving the manuscript.

Among the historians and archivists who in one way or another aided the writer were the following: Thomas P. Abernethy, Eugene C. Barker, Mrs. John Spencer Bassett, William C. Binkley, Peter A. Brannon, Lester J. Cappon, Henry Steele Commager, R. D. W. Connor, David L. Corbitt, E. Merton Coulter, Christopher C. Crittenden, Virginius Dabney, Fletcher M. Green, J. G. de Roulhac Hamilton, William Stanley Hoole, Herbert A. Kellar, Thomas P. Martin, Chase C. Mooney, Mrs. Marie Bankhead Owen, James W. Patton, George Petrie, Walter B. Posey, Charles W. and Mrs. Ramsdell, Alfred W. Reynolds, Alfred K. and Martha Dodd Stern, Earl G. Swem, Charles S. Sydnor, Nannie M. Tilley, and Walter P. Webb. The writer is especially indebted to David D. Van Tassel and Robert H. Woody for critical reading and constructive criticism of the manuscript. And finally, Hildagarde's patience and understanding were an indispensable factor; and so was her fortitude in providing an intelligent audience for oral rendition of the essays. To some of them she listened with avid interest, a commendable contribution; others induced drooping eyelids and nodding head; and the writer, sensing embarrassing therapeutic value that cured insomnia, endeavored to improve literary quality. Alas, the drowsiness never completely disappeared; neither did the causes that produced it.

Of the twelve chapters in the volume, two have not hitherto been published: VII ("William A. Dunning: Teacher, Humorist, and Scholar"), and XI ("Twenty-five Years of Southern Historical Writing"). The present editors of historical magazines who graciously permitted reprinting of articles that appeared originally in their reviews are Philip F. Detweiler, the *Journal of Southern History;* Oscar O. Winther, the *Mississippi Valley Historical Review;* William Stanley Hoole, the *Alabama Review;* E. Merton Coulter, the *Georgia Historical Quarterly;* Christopher C. Crittenden, the *North Carolina Historical Review;* and Richard Walsh, the *Maryland Historical Magazine.* The ten reprinted articles, with original titles, are as follows:

I. "William Garrott Brown: Literary Historian and Essayist," *Journal of Southern History,* XII (August, 1946), 315–41.

II. "Herbert B. Adams and Southern Historical Scholarship at the Johns Hopkins University," *Maryland Historical Magazine,* XLII (March, 1947), 1–20.

III. "William P. Trent as a Historian of the South," *Journal of Southern History,* XV (May, 1949), 151–77.

IV. "John Spencer Bassett as a Historian of the South," *North Carolina Historical Review,* XXV (July, 1948), 289–317.

V. "The Negro in the Thinking and Writing of John Spencer Bassett," *North Carolina Historical Review,* XXV (October, 1948), 427–41.

VI. "Some Pioneer Alabama Historians: I. George Petrie," *Alabama Review,* I (July, 1948), 164–79.

VIII. "Ulrich B. Phillips: The University of Georgia and the Georgia Historical Society," *Georgia Historical Quarterly,* XLI (June, 1957), 103–25.

IX. "Charles W. Ramsdell: Historian of the Confederacy," *Journal of Southern History,* XXVII (November, 1960), 501–25.

X. "Some Pioneer Alabama Historians: III. Thomas M. Owen," *Alabama Review,* II (January, 1949), 45–62.

XII. "A Quarter Century of American Historiography," *Mississippi Valley Historical Review,* XLV (June, 1958), 3–22.

A few of the reprinted essays have been revised a little; others have been modified only slightly. In some cases the problem of anachronism discouraged more extensive revision. Here and there some repetitiousness has been retained in order that each chapter might appear in its original completeness.

Contents

Southern History in the Making

Introduction: The Making of a Book

The essays in this volume acquired their initial impulse a quarter of a century ago, and they have been accumulating in the interim at a slow tempo as a busy life permitted or pressure from historical societies provided stimulus. The publication of a meritorious assemblage of letters served as incentive. A morning's mail in 1939 brought a copy of W. Stull Holt's *Historical Scholarship in the United States, 1876–1901,* and that evening the writer sat down after supper to peruse the volume. He did more than scan its content; he read every word of the impressive correspondence of Herbert Baxter Adams and his former Johns Hopkins University students before retiring at the usual hour of 2:00 A.M. *Isaac Franklin, Slave Trader and Planter of the Old South* had recently come from the press, and the writer was seeking another research project to occupy leisure time, for a nine-hour teaching load, the *Journal of Southern History,* the prospective ten-volume cooperative "A History of the South," the "Southern Biography Series," and the recently inaugurated Fleming Lecture program seemed insufficient to keep a sympathetic and generous administration on the other side of the campus. The new project did not move as fast as he anticipated.

The present book and its predecessor, *The South Lives in History,* are less ambitious than the goal the writer conjured up in his mind as he read the published letters of Adams and his neophytes in Johns Hopkins "colonies." At that moment he visualized a comprehensive history of southern history: colonial and antebellum writers who recorded local events and sectional problems; historians of the past century and their productivity in ever changing emphasis and interpretation; incentives that prompted colleges and universities to inaugurate courses in the region's history; activities of state and local historical societies; and the great repositories of southern research materials. That panoramic project could not be completed; hence the unfinished work presented in this and its earlier companion volume.

After reading *Historical Scholarship in the United States,* the writer visited Baltimore for a week to explore the unpublished Adams and Daniel C. Gilman papers. A year's leave of absence soon followed, and a generous grant from the General Education Board subsidized research in archives and libraries from Austin to Cambridge. The personal papers of historians, some of them still living at the time, provided human interest material to supplement their published works. Subsequent journeys added new evidence to the research of 1944–45.

The introductory chapter, "Southern Avenue to Now," in *The South Lives in History* will also serve as a preface to this supplementary volume, for the perspective and climate of opinion were essentially the same for the two groups of essays. The earlier work appraised William E. Dodd, Ulrich B. Phillips, and Walter L. Fleming. The new one presents Phillips in other activities than those emphasized in the basic essay. Adams and William A. Dunning were not southern historians, but their work in the education of young scholars from the South was so fundamental that their significant contributions could hardly be ignored. William Garrott Brown, William P. Trent, John Spencer Bassett, George Petrie, Charles W. Ramsdell, and Thomas M. Owen complete the roster of historians. Two interpretive essays are included to give perspective to recent performance in southern and American historiography.

The writer received conflicting counsel as to the scope of the book. The dozen historians whom he consulted suggested the following alternatives, arranged in ascending order of their frequency:

1. Omit everything between the title page and the index.
2. Delete four or five of the essays and parts of others in the interest of unity or central purpose.
3. Print all of them and permit the reader to demonstrate irritation by mutilating irrelevant sections or by tossing the whole thing into the trash can.

What a dilemma! Of one thing the writer could be certain. Whatever course he decided upon, he shouldn't have. After two years of reflection, he unwisely chose the third alternative. Encouragement by the author of *An Honest Preface* [1] was a deciding factor, unrestrained endorsement in other quarters was another, and his own invidious rationalization was a third.

As has been indicated, the writer started out with a blueprint, but circumstances defeated the original architectural design. The house was built a room at a time. Like some other series of essays, the segments accumulated; and the order of arrangement as well as the inclusion of peripheral studies may be designated accumulator's license. Title and subtitle combined may provide a protective umbrella, more from the sun than from the storm.

The essays differ in form as well as in substance, and if the volume has any merit, it may lie in this diversity. The nature of the materials may provide a part of the explanation. The writer consciously sought enlightenment in historians' correspondence files; as a result the participants' personal lives, thoughts, and actions appear on many pages. They were men as well as historians: human personalities who lived normal lives in their relationships with colleagues, administrators, students, and communities in which they resided. Frustrations, disappointments, sometimes physical infirmities affected their contributions to historical scholarship. The conditions under which they worked and their differing personalities often spelled the measure of success or failure. Surviving personal papers permitted them to think and talk and act through another medium than the inhibiting public record of books and articles.

The essay on Dunning is quite unorthodox—and purposely so. A strict conceptual approach would have excluded many pages and thereby omitted the attractive and magnetic qualities that made him effective as a teacher. Petrie made hay, so to speak, in his own back yard; yet within the limits of his circumscribed orbit the crop had more than local significance. Brown's talents and interests stand in a class by themselves, and an unusual set of values affected his life and work. Phillips as a historian in the national picture differed in more than reputation from Phillips the polemicist or reformer of local historical enterprise. Owen shared experiences and interests with many contemporaries, but no one of them attained the distinction in the one contribution he was capable of making. The essays may provide a cross section of the totality of historical activity, as diverse as the historians themselves. The ever present complexity and confusion of history find expression, though the writer hopes these attributes are partially hidden underneath a straightforward narrative.

I

Two of the historians treated in this work, Adams and Dunning, guided dozens of doctoral candidates through their degrees at the Johns Hopkins University and at Columbia University. The Adams-trained men—Trent, Bassett, and Petrie—carried their preceptor's concepts of historical activity into the South—to colleges in Tennessee, North Carolina, and Alabama. Phillips and Ramsdell represent the Dunning school, Ramsdell perhaps better than Phillips, for the Georgian owed nearly as much to his academic association with Frederick Jackson Turner, older colleague at the University of Wisconsin, as to his Columbia mentor. The other two historians, Brown and Owen, fit into no category: neither came out of a well-established seminar. They developed independently of any great scholar, though each profited immensely from informal association with stimulating minds. They, like Dodd, carved corridors to preferment at the century's turn without benefit of school of thought or persuasive influence. Fleming as well as Phillips, subjects of earlier essays, supplement the new volume's consideration of the Dunning school.

The historian in the present group who excited the writer's warmest enthusiasm and highest esteem was William Garrott Brown. He produced no magnum opus; in fact, his publications with the possible exception of *The Lower South in American History* have passed into oblivion; and even that work has been largely relegated to unconsulted parts of bibliographies or buried in footnote citations. But in the decades on both sides of 1900, eminent historians and editors of well-known periodicals commended his work in superlative language. In a generation when much historical writing degenerated into formless monography, Brown gave life and meaning to his biographical and historical essays, pulsating narratives that attracted readers beyond the province of professional students of history. The subject matter of America's past, he thought, belonged to all the people, not alone to the guild. Without distorting facts or resorting to sensationalism, he wrote with felicitous style and impressive vitality. If his *Stephen Arnold Douglas,* to cite only one other work, has become a forgotten classic, it is only because less worthy essays have crowded from faithless memory sterling merit of sixty years ago. The great literary and public affairs magazines of two generations past eagerly sought his essays which combined the virtues of a vigorous and perceptive mind with the artistry of a gifted writer.

Contemporaries saw in Brown's distinguished prose, qualities that foreshadowed a worthy successor to Francis Parkman. The Alabamian began his productive career in the 1890's just as the romantic genius ceased his labors, and for three decades he wrote historical and philosophical essays that provided readers of the *Atlantic Monthly* and other reputable magazines with thoughtful and penetrating sketches of men and measures and movements. Both men attended Harvard, with Brown probably profiting more than Parkman from his studies at the elite New England school. Each tried his hand at novel writing: Parkman, *Vassall Morton* and Brown, *A Gentleman of the South;* neither succeeded well in the endeavor. Parkman often spoke of the Enemy with whom he battled for almost the whole of his productive career. Still, he survived threescore years and ten, with inherited wealth a relief from financial worry. Brown's two Enemies—deafness and tuberculosis—plagued him unmercifully, the first for twenty years of his brief life-span of forty-five, the second for the final decade. An analysis of his career might well be called a study in courage. Parkman found an epic theme in the hundred-year triangular conflict among English, French, and Indians for the possession of North America. Brown's Enemies handicapped him so early that he could not, or did not, concentrate upon an obsessing subject, though he searched for one before a second tragedy interposed its fateful hand.

Here the analogy begins and ends. Brown was in no sense a romanticist. He lived in a world of reality, ever conscious of the sea around him, intent upon improving its political structure and of elevating its intellectual quality. His limited achievements merit study: they may inspire young historians of today to find an absorbing theme and a vehicle of expression that lifts the written word above monotonous and commonplace pedestrianism.

If Brown had an unrealized ambition, it was a career in politics and a seat in the United States Senate. His fellow Alabamian, Thomas M. Owen, succeeded as a politician though he held no political office. He played the game skillfully with state officials and legislators who appropriated funds for the establishment and maintenance of a department of archives and history. No southern state in Owen's period succeeded half so well in founding a reputable service institution necessary for preserving and making accessible historical records. He was a pioneer in archival organization and administration, but before he embarked upon his major accomplishment, he acquired stature in the historical guild by compiling comprehensive bibliographies of Alabama and Mississippi. His ability as compiler and organizer was recognized by officialdom of the American Historical Association. Other states, particularly in the South, followed the Owen pattern of preserving and servicing state records; and while the Alabamian did not "patent" his plan, he insisted that other states recognize Alabama's priority in originating a practicable and workable model. In this field of activity, historians recognize also that credit should be assigned to Wisconsin, where Lyman Copeland Draper and his successor in the state historical society, Reuben Gold Thwaites, built a functional organization that succeeded even better in combining a historical society and a state archives and in effectively relating both to historical activity at the state university. In his efforts to lift his native Georgia out of its historical lethargy, Phillips, who observed both systems at firsthand, preferred the Wisconsin to the Alabama pattern.

The two universities represented by Adams and Dunning made immeasurable contributions to the origin of interest in southern history, the Johns Hopkins University before 1900, Columbia University after that year. Adams attracted to his history, political science, and economics department a larger clientele from North and West than from the South, but southerners were so important a segment that they convinced themselves at least that it was a southern university in a southern city. The "great Captain of Industry, a captain in the field of systematic and organized scholarship," as Woodrow Wilson characterized Adams, welcomed recruits from the South, encouraged them to investigate southern institutions, fitted up a southern room in the department's quarters, established a collection of printed and manuscript southern materials, provided courses that presented southern institutions and the first systematic survey of the history of the South, and opened the *Studies in Historical and Political Science* to their dissertations and postdoctoral studies. Little wonder Johns Hopkins became a mecca for graduates of southern colleges and universities who sought postgraduate education in history.

The aptitudes and objectives that Johns Hopkins students carried into the South were of course never identical. Despite certain uniformities for which the Adams influence was responsible—assembling of records, mediums of publication, courses in local and eventually southern history, and physical arrangements of the seminar or "laboratory"—the personality and special interests of each Johns Hopkins product lent variety, and so did the local problems that faced "colonial" administrators. Trent and Bassett were exponents of southern liberalism, and they founded the *Sewanee Review* and the *South Atlantic Quarterly* to provide opportunity for liberal expression as well as for scholarly and creative contributions. Petrie, Franklin L. Riley, and John H. T. McPherson exhibited no great enthusiasm for liberalizing thought in the states to which they were "accredited," except as truth in history served that worthy purpose. Petrie's long service at Alabama Polytechnic Institute enabled him to inspire able students with a love for history and an ambition to acquire the doctorate at reputable graduate schools. In this sense he may have succeeded better than any other Johns Hopkins man in the South, albeit his overall reputation suffered in comparison with the spectacular performances of Bassett and Trent who became more widely known in the North as well as in the South.

With the retirement of Adams in 1900, the center of interest in southern history shifted to Dunning and Columbia University. A few southern scholars with great potential, like Douglas S. Freeman and H. J. Eckenrode, subsequently sought the doctorate at the Johns Hopkins; but Dunning's growing reputation as an authority on the Civil War and Reconstruction, his kindly and genial disposition, and supporting strength in other fields of history and in allied subjects made his seminar a rendezvous for aspiring young historians from the South.

This does not mean that Dunning and Columbia enjoyed the monopoly that Adams and the Johns Hopkins maintained during the past quarter century. Other graduate schools, in the East and in the West, developed stature and reputation as increasing enrollment required expansion of personnel and the flow of Americans to European universities slackened in the twentieth century. Elite eastern schools, particularly Harvard, and middle western universities such as Chicago and Michigan, were more than minor meccas for doctoral candidates in history. Perhaps the University of Wisconsin, where the Johns Hopkins-trained Turner was building a strong department and a stronger personal reputation as an authority on frontier and sectional history, acquired preferred status over most other schools in the East and the West. Inauguration of the School of Economics, Political Science, and History in the 1890's, with Richard T. Ely as its director, brought acclaim and prestige. The addition of Phillips and Carl Russell Fish to the history staff after 1900 gave added strength to an already well-established department.

The fact remains that in the field of late nineteenth-century American history (the recent era of that day), Dunning provided an unusual opportunity for graduates of southern institutions of higher learning if they were interested in the Civil War and its aftermath. The magister's dynamic teaching gave them confidence in the significance of history. His growing reputation rested firmly upon what was then considered to be an impartial attitude toward a controversial epoch.

The basic article on Phillips in the earlier publication left a residue of relevant data, for the first essay found little room for a consideration of his educational experiences at the University of Georgia, his interest in the Georgia Historical Society during his years in Wisconsin, or his determination to improve southern economy. The new essay lacks the significance of the appraisal previously published, yet it illustrates Phillips' early emphases: the importance of local history and the efforts to strengthen his native state's moribund historical society along lines marked out by the Wisconsin and Alabama organizations. A third study of Phillips, withheld from the present volume, presents his views on economic adjustment in the New South.

His interest in reform has all but been forgotten, if indeed it survived the memories of his contemporaries. He participated actively in discussions of controversial issues, whether in or outside the profession. He became spokesman for all contributors to the *Documentary History of American Industrial Society,* in which he published the two-volume *Plantation and Frontier,* in their fight for recognition on its title pages. Later he entered the dispute over reform of the American Historical Association, an activity that chagrined "Uncle" Worthington C. Ford.

At the beginning of the century, the plight of the South engaged his attention. Phillips' rural Georgia background, his experience in growing a crop of cotton, and his observation of southern labor gave him more than an academic interest in southern history. The agricultural and labor problems of the South focused attention on the present. He advocated the "New History" a decade before the idea was proclaimed in definitive form. It may be concluded with some justification that Phillips became interested in the Old South with its plantations and slave labor in order that he might better comprehend southern problems of his formative years. He would study the past to understand the present to reform the future. As a corollary he espoused an economic interpretation of history.

The lure of the Old South seems now to have been his absorbing interest from the beginning. The discovery of so many plantation records with their plethora of material on staple economy and the subsidiary history of the Negro in slavery provided a never ending task; and what began as a preparation or background for an understanding of the present actually became the major objective. His unrealized dream of a three-volume magnum opus on the history of the South from colonial times to the twentieth century remained unfinished. *Life and Labor* appeared in 1929; the second volume, published posthumously as *The Course of the South to Secession,* was an incomplete venture. It is significant that he planned a third volume on "War and Peace," and this was the era toward which he had been pointing ever since he began delving into the records of antebellum history.

In the literature of controversy in which Phillips engaged—in newspapers and magazines—he belabored two themes: diversification of agriculture and the future of the rural Negro laborer. As to the first, he spoke words of wisdom: the South must abandon one-crop economy, for its reliance on cotton was an unhealthy dependence. Here he was forward-looking as he urged limitation of cotton production to keep its price profitable and attention to a better balanced and diversified economy, including manufacturing as well as agriculture. In the matter of Negro labor, his eyes turned toward the past. Phillips had little confidence that Negroes would ever be capable of accepting responsibility as independent farmers, and he therefore proposed a modification of the antebellum plantation regime that would continue regimentation in large-scale agricultural economy. He saw little promise for an "inferior race" outside the relations that had always existed between whites and Negroes. One of his last speeches—in the early 1930's—indicated a persisting belief in Negro racial inferiority.

Historians lamented at Ramsdell's death in 1942 that so much Confederate and other southern history perished with his passing. That he knew much history, all conceded; that he put only a modicum on the printed page, everyone recognized. But unlike

Phillips, who held throughout his life to concepts formed at the beginning of his career, Ramsdell grew with study; and a changing climate of opinion found him in maturity, if not apace with new interpretation, at least not far behind. His dissertation on Texan Reconstruction conformed generally to the conservative pattern of the Dunning school; his writings of the 1930's left little trace of the earlier concept expressed in his first research venture. Pages in print were limited in number; and some of his interpretive articles were not universally accepted, but he made other contributions to the development of historical scholarship in the South. He assembled records in the Littlefield collection at the University of Texas, he worked assiduously in behalf of historical societies, he helped to plan the cooperative "A History of the South," and he conscientiously guided many students through graduate degrees.

II

The making of a book is not all lonely drudgery in accumulating evidence, or monotonous syntax in processing it. The investigator encounters a variety of unexpected sources of help that encourage his quest for knowledge. Sometimes they yield indispensable ingredients from which a book is made; often they are mere incidents that provide only color and atmosphere and a spirit of good will, trivial in isolation, significant in their cumulative effect. A few that aided the traveler of some years ago may be worth the reader's attention. They are the human touches that make descent from the ivory tower into the world of pleasant realism an enjoyable experience.

The historian is searching for a past, and if that past is not too remote, he can recapture its spirit from men who experienced it even though their historical contributions have been outdated. The new age has not treated them kindly; too often the cumulative portion of today's chronicle of the past goes unrecognized while only the innovative receives acclaim. One such person with whom the writer had the privilege of conversing in the fall of 1944 was George Petrie.

An interview with that venerable historian was a rewarding event. For an hour and a half the Auburn octogenarian, whose teaching experience began in the 1880's and whose vivid memory carried him back to his youthful years in Baltimore, enlightened the visitor with intimate glimpses of his Johns Hopkins University mentors, Adams, J. Franklin Jameson, and Woodrow Wilson. He recalled his pioneering efforts at Alabama Polytechnic Institute where so many sons of the South found a stimulating academic oasis in a period that antedated the southern renaissance, of an era when history was regarded as a science taught by the "laboratory" method. He radiated a wholesome, forward-looking faith in the younger generation of college students; and he underscored the need of a sense of humor that in his case continued undiminished despite his fourscore years. Hastening to his hotel room, the eager interviewer recorded in his diary a faithful account of Petrie's reflections on a significant past.

Who could fail to profit from fireside chats with those two North Carolinians, R. D. W. Connor and J. G. de Roulhac Hamilton, the best initialed men in the profession according to their Columbia mentor Dunning. Both gave the researcher access to their personal papers, and both regaled him with stories from their past as archivists and collectors of southern materials at Raleigh and Chapel Hill. Colorful characters in divergent ways, Hamilton seemed to recall more combative incidents from his unmellowed years. He delighted to tell stories of sectional rivalry in Dunning's seminar. A contemporary at Columbia, Paul Leland Haworth, older damnyankee from the writer's neighborhood in Indiana, baited southern members as they studied in the room at off hours. Tiring of northern jibes, Hamilton hurdled the seminar table to have at him, but other members intervened to prevent a renewal of clash and conflict a generation after Appomattox.

An experience perhaps unique among researchers occurred in the spring of 1945. For some months the writer had been seeking access to the William E. Dodd Papers, recently transferred from Round Hill farmhouse in Virginia to the country estate of Alfred K. and Martha Dodd Stern near Ridgefield, Connecticut. The Stern family generously offered the researcher the hospitality of their luxurious house, unoccupied at that season except for the butler who worked the swing shift at a war plant in New Canaan. For three weeks the writer lived the life of a hermit in splendid isolation on a beautiful lake in an enchanting valley, the radio and the New York *Times* his only contacts with the outside world. A well-filled larder, replenished daily by some unseen pixiecrat, satisfied gustatory propensity with delectables of the hermit's own devising. The precious papers were stored in a spacious barn that had been converted into a summer lodge, the hundred letter boxes guarded by a huge lion, stomach as flat as the floor, feline incapacitated for further fight, yawning mouth evidence of former ferocity, lightning flashes recreating eerie shadows of African jungle. Note cards accumulated at the rate of a hundred a day, laboring hours beginning at seven in the morning and continuing until after midnight, writer's cramp a sorry infirmity, pot of coffee in constant readiness, crackling wood in big fireplace, pursuit of Clio a pleasant vocation.

Emerging from the valley of isolation, a contrasting fortnight's sojourn awaited the traveler in the home of the aged widow of John Spencer Bassett at Northampton, Massachusetts. The gracious lady offered the researcher the use of the Bassett Papers—and also accommodations including "kitchen privileges" if he had the requisite qualifications for taking advantage of them, which he had. The hospitable hostess also provided opportunities to meet the elite of Northampton: for a week she entertained at tea every afternoon at four, with guests from the Smith College faculty and from the community, and with Mrs. Coolidge an honoree. Other visitors were women from the local historical society who invited the researcher to its quarters at the Parsons Home. So he sat down to tea in Northampton's oldest house, built in 1658, with four ladies who added maturity to the atmosphere. After tea the president took him on a tour of the time-honored museum to acquaint him with relics of other ages, a tour that he tolerated with genuine appreciation: ancient pewter dishes, cups and saucers that came over on the *second* Mayflower voyage, spinning wheels and churns, pots and pans hanging in massive fireplace, fancy dresses of preceding generations, a great collection of dolls dating from colonial days, attire contrasting strangely with Smith College raiment. Then back to the Bassett Papers, fully convinced that something was lacking in his historical training.

Of Bassett's habits of life and work, the researcher learned much from his genial hostess: that his greatest ambition, dating from pre–Johns Hopkins days, was to write history; that in preparing *The Federalist System* and several other books he organized, drafted, and polished as he went along; that much of his writing was composed at the typewriter; that he was enticed to Smith College and remained there largely because he had a light teaching load and a reader for examination papers; that he accepted the position in 1906 at a salary of $2,500, eventually received $6,500 and perhaps $7,000 his last year, the same as the president was paid; that his annual income after he became well established amounted to $18,000 to $21,000; that the *Short History of the United States* yielded royalties of $5,000 to $6,000 a year over a period of time, and that the royalty was still considerable; that Bassett worked incessantly, rarely getting over five hours of sleep a night; that he did not appreciate dull company and might go to sleep if the conversation were uninteresting, an embarrassment to her; that he was a good businessman—safe investments and no speculations; that criticism did not worry him as he always had important things to do; that during the "Bassett incident" of 1903 he received hundreds of letters, some of them threatening, but that he did not read all of them, only those that she thought he ought to see; that she managed the household so that he would not be disturbed when he wanted to work; that in the Bancroft-Jameson controversy of 1915 he thought Jameson correct, and that Bancroft who had been his intimate friend never spoke to him again.

Not all benefactors were historians or members of their families. Two in particular contributed to the making of a book, though neither sensed his important role. Arriving in busy Baltimore one afternoon, the researcher inquired of a kindly lady at the Travelers' Aid desk for help in finding quarters. Sundry telephone calls brought no results. As a last chance she told him of a friend who lived two blocks from the station but who had no telephone; he betook himself and baggage to the rooming house. The landlady was "full up" or nearly so; she had a double room in the attic with only one occupant. Who was he? Mr. Canfield. His occupation? Policeman. The distressed traveler would take a chance with the arm of the law. As it turned out, the patrolman was on the night force, and before ascending the two flights of stairs at five in the morning, he read the landlady's note apprising him that he had a roommate. Possessing the instincts of a gentleman, the sentinel of security undressed in the dark so as not to awaken his cohabitant. The researcher arose an hour later and shaved and dressed in the dark so as not to awaken his considerate friend. These arrangements continued during the sojourn in Baltimore: never did the two meet or see each other. The temporary occupant profited from the patrolman's library. Shelves were piled high with murder stories, tangible evidence that he kept abreast of his profession by reading the latest literature in the field. Imaginatively, the writer contrasted respective callings: the patrolman was interested in tricks on the living; the historian in tricks on the dead, or so Carl Becker said.

Parkman and Brown battled with Enemies much of their lives, and perhaps the only thing the writer shared with those eminent historians was one of his own: a friendly Enemy with whom a plan of coexistence ripened into understanding—but not without an occasional unprovoked attack. One cold, drizzly morning when he was a guest at the Harvard Faculty Club while researching in the Widener Library, he waited too long, after a shot of elixir that Banting and Best made famous, before going out to breakfast. Coma overtook him as he sought a restaurant on Harvard Square, mental faculties fading to the point of failure to distinguish cafes and shops. Realizing that he must sit down or collapse, he entered a door and somehow found a seat at a counter.

A sympathetic gentleman with keen perception and ripe experience diagnosed the case immediately and placed a tall glass of orange juice before his visitor to produce a sobering effect. As if by instinct, the ailing suppliant drank it without pausing for breath. In a moment he was himself again.

"There, that helped, didn't it?" said the portly bartender. "I recognized your trouble as soon as you staggered in. Ordinarily they ain't so well dressed."

With kindly feeling, the would-be researcher thanked his benefactor and asked for his check.

"Forget it. Glad to help a man in trouble. You must have had a rough night. Better take it easy."

The writer was so grateful that he tossed a dollar bill on the counter and with more thanks started to leave.

"Put the money back in your pocket," the bartender insisted. "You may be flat broke if you give me that. Come back and see us when you're feeling better."

Despite a late start, research went well at the Widener that day.

III

Reflecting upon the careers of men presented in these essays, it seemed appropriate to set down some of the attributes of the ideal chronicler for the consideration of historians in the making. In doing so the writer has turned historical novelist; he has painted a composite by creating a fictitious character and superimposing upon his person all the desired qualities that produce the man who rises above his fellows. But the novelist must keep his hero and heroine human, else he fails in his task of reflecting accurately a segment of society. No one realizes better than the historian that we live in an imperfect world, or that the historian himself cannot attain entirety. It is well to remember, however, that the guild has produced a Parkman, a Beard, a Turner.

The making of a first book does not begin when the researcher finds a subject worthy of investigation and starts the long and arduous task of assembling data. For a book is built upon foundations that have their origins many years before the future author becomes aware of his high calling. Research and writing in the field of history presuppose a comprehensive knowledge of the area and its related fields. The student's research project may be a limited segment in time and place, but he can handle it more effectively if he has a broad background of learning to give it perspective. Historical research involves a mechanical process that must be mastered if the student is earnestly seeking a graduate degree and hopefully anticipating a career as a scholar. A mastery of mechanics is secondary to a more fundamental achievement, for an uneducated writer cannot aspire to attainment in the world of scholarship.

There is nothing new or profound in the statement that the historical scholar should be liberally educated as well as technically trained. It is another way of saying that freedom and bondage are happily combined in the labor of those who build the "bridge which arches the stream of Time and links the Past and the Present together"; freedom to explore the limitless record of human experience, bondage to measure and weigh it objectively; freedom to master our social and humanistic heritage, bondage to use judgment and perspective in making it meaningful. Freedom promotes a broadening and deepening of learning, bondage obligates the historian to simple rules and honest purpose. Because many students of history lack one or both of these qualifications, it may be advantageous to examine and illustrate them.

Basic to the mechanical process are certain fundamentals: the habit of reading, the art of writing, and a talent for thinking. Another, the ability to speak, is dispensable if the scholar contemplates a hermit's existence, but the openings for a hermit are limited in an articulate society. This ability is not closely related to theses and dissertations, although it is observable that some students who speak fluently also write precisely.

The habit of reading is absolutely essential for anyone who aspires to compete successfully at the graduate level. It is a habit that few undergraduates acquire; most seniors leave college without sensing its importance, and many students enter graduate school with the habit still unformed. Teachers may inspire, guide, and impart a modicum of knowledge. Books are great teachers, too, and they have professors outnumbered at least ten thousand to one. A page from the life of the novelist Thomas Wolfe points a lesson, though an extreme one. When he entered Harvard, he assaulted shelf after shelf of books, insatiable appetite pitiably unappeased. "Within a period of ten years he read at least twenty thousand volumes . . . and opened the pages and looked through many times that number." One student who came under the writer's tutelage possessed no such overpowering curiosity for knowledge; yet, she read at least a book a day in every one of her graduate courses. And if some teacher posed a question that she couldn't answer adequately, she lost no time after adjournment in searching library resources until she found the information, her knowledge of several peripheral subjects enriched as an additional reward. The next day she would seek the professor in his office to report findings that sometimes surpassed his own command of the subject. Another student was a chain reader. The assigned book would lead him voluntarily to a second treatise for comparison of interpretation, and that one to a third for a different philosophy, and all three to the principal documents to discover for himself the fountainhead of evidence. This ultimate resort to the raw materials of history gave him a sense of maturity, of transition from the ranks of the novice to membership in the historical guild.

That sense is also promoted by reading the great masters of history from other ages. The student cannot acquire the "feel" of the ancient period unless he reads Homer and Herodotus, Polybius and Thucydides, Plato and Aristotle. Edward Gibbon, Thomas B. Macaulay, Edward A. Freeman, W. E. H. Leckey, Theodor Mommsen, Leopold von Ranke, Benedetto Croce, William H. Prescott, Francis Parkman, and scores of other historians with sundry interpretations and philosophies offer opportunities for the study of historical thought and for comparison of it with present-day scholarship. And some of them, whose pens were poised and polished, are worthy of emulation as masters of graceful style.

The student who has learned to write before he enters graduate school is the exception to the rule. Ordinarily it requires more time and effort for master's and doctoral candidates to learn good

English than to understand methodology. Furthermore, we think in language; and fuzzy thinking is inseparably associated with fuzzy writing. If the student has not learned the art of writing before he enters graduate school, precise craftsmanship must be one of his immediate goals.

Many years ago the dean of American historians, J. Franklin Jameson, who served for many years as editor of the *American Historical Review,* deplored the "want of attractiveness" in historical writing. "As to smoothness of expression and consequent ease of reading," he wrote, "it often seems impossible that the writer can have read a single paragraph aloud, else he would have perceived that he was driving over corduroy and not concrete." He observed that "cultural subjects" and "contacts with the world of letters" would have an improving effect. To young historians who sought to publish their papers in the review, Jameson gave wise counsel about hastily constructed sentences and paragraphs. One of them who profited by his gentle chiding and who became a literary artist was advised: "Secure reputations, valuable when a man is fifty or sixty, are not to be had but by taking a good deal of pains and time for the execution of everything that a man prints over his name while he is young." [2] He might have added that candidates for graduate degrees would more often attain them if they gave meticulous attention to the cultivation of literary style.

Pedestrianism can be overcome, even belatedly, and the art of attractive presentation acquired if the student has incentive and patience. He should not be content with his chapters until he has examined every sentence microscopically; he should not be satisfied with his product until he has achieved a lucid, unlabored style, pliantly responsive to the exact pressure of the thought he seeks to convey. There are words with exact shades of meaning that fit the context of his thought. There are arrangements of words in sentences and of sentences in paragraphs that provide the writer with an attractive vehicle of expression and the reader with the sensation of riding over a smooth pavement rather than bumping over an old-fashioned corduroy road. Students who have not pondered for an hour or two the proper structure of a single sentence have never experienced the thrill of creative craftsmanship. Those who do not have the "gift" of writing should form the habit of drafting their work eight or ten times to achieve precision.

A writing knowledge of English is more important than a reading knowledge of foreign languages—significant as they are—and it may take longer to acquire it.

Deficiency in writing simple, straightforward English is often paralleled by inability to speak effectively. The profession requires articulate members. A quarter of a century ago Guy Stanton Ford, dean of the University of Minnesota graduate school, gave wise advice. Addressing the Association of American Universities, he acknowledged the existence of "mute geniuses and glib charlatans," but he would have all students learn to convey their ideas in well-chosen words. They should be able "to talk, and to talk clearly, readily, and articulately. Too often their spoken words, whether in a classroom or in their employer's office, fall mouthed and maimed on their side of the desk. Such speech never reaches the battle line where mind meets mind, and the victory is to the master of incisive, expository speech." [3]

Basic to reading, writing, and speaking is the capacity to think. Breadth of learning is a goal of the undergraduate college; breadth plus depth are the desiderta of the graduate school. The graduate student must take time to ponder what he reads, to think reflectively. It matters tremendously what he thinks about. For thought can be no deeper than subject matter, no broader than the range of one's interests. Critical, constructive thought that avoids the extremes of unwholesome skepticism on the one hand and too ready acceptance on the other; thought that penetrates the surface to discover imagery and symbolism that artists fashion into rhythmic prose; thought that senses the relationship of forces that yield understanding of the past; thought that skirts the unknown to discover what lies on its farther edge—such thought is worthy of the educated mind. The highest compliment that can be paid a member of the guild is to say of him: he is an educated man; he is also a historian.

Deficiencies in the four fundamentals account for many casualties; possession of them does not assure arrival at historianship. Another factor contributes largely to successful graduate work. The essence of study beyond the bachelor's degree may be expressed in the one word "graduate-mindedness." In simple language, the student studies to learn. He declares his independence of the registrar's office. The accumulation of credits and the assignment of grades no longer have meaning; mastery of knowledge acquires new significance. This does not mean that a student ever completely masters areas he studies; it does mean that he strives constantly to broaden and deepen his knowledge of them. Thoughtful reading beyond assignments, browsing in library stacks, attention to professional journals, awareness of new projects in the historical world, membership in national and regional associations—these are some of the tangible evidences of graduate-mindedness. But the "mindedness" itself is an intangible thing, an undefinable spirit or atmosphere.

It is a concept of study that approximates the task system. Time work—desultory residence in the shadow of an institution of learning—is relegated to limbo. In its place develops an unquenchable thirst for knowledge. The will to learn, as well as the ability, is essential. For those who have the ability and the will, the new life becomes a challenge. The twelve to fifteen hours a day cease to be drudgery. The hours pass swiftly; the unburdensome task becomes life itself.

Open-mindedness is an important ingredient of graduate-mindedness. There are so many philosophies and interpretations of history that the young scholar should take time to determine his own position with relation to the verities of the past. He should avoid discipleship—carbon copyism—drink at many fountains, temper criticism with wholesome respect, and refuse to toss existing scholarship into the wastebasket until he is sure that it has no value. For thought is cumulative as well as innovative, and new thought is more often modifying than substitutive. Understanding the past is basic to criticism of its delineators.

Closely related to open-mindedness is humility. Once in a while an arrogant scholar leaves an impress, but most of the great minds have an awareness of their own infinitesimal contribution to the sum total of learning. The vast body of knowledge in such areas as literature and history should convince the neophyte that he faces a tremendous task in endeavoring to comprehend segments of it. Humility, if not possessed in overdose, is a genuine trait of the sincere scholar. If he makes an unusual contribution, others will discover it without the contributor's prompting.

Competence in reading, writing, speaking, and thinking, and the possession of graduate-mindedness, are positive expressions of requisites for successful graduate work. A negative factor, procrastination, may defeat the student who possesses all of them. Procrastination produces the great alibi: everything except the dissertation has been completed. In many cases it has not even been started.

Sculpturing the capstone is a process that parallels the building of the arch. The longer it is postponed, the less likelihood it will ever be completed.

The inability of some students to understand the immediacy as well as the significance of the research problem is one of the most disheartening aspects of graduate work. Sometimes a mental block, more often lack of industry, preclude an approach to the formidable task. Reading books and comprehending their meaning is one thing, but an assault on the records for a contribution to knowledge often staggers students with good minds. Others find in research and writing a welcome and exhilarating experience.

Many years ago a newly appointed assistant arrived on campus a week early. Could he begin research on a thesis subject before the semester officially opened? That one question inspired confidence in his capacity for graduate-mindedness. He found a topic for investigation that promised a contribution to knowledge; and before classes formally began, he accumulated two or three hundred note cards. A publishable master's thesis was completed by the following June—without neglecting courses or paper-grading responsibilities. Elsewhere, he continued research in the same field and made his dissertation into a meritorious book. Another student discovered a copious collection of records, and with unsuspected talent for research and writing, converted them into a prize-winning master's thesis that soon found its way into print. In the interim between graduate degrees, while working to support his family, superior capacity paid off in papers read before historical associations, in published articles, and in generous foundation aid to finance work for the doctor's degree. A German *emigré* with an Old World grasp of mankind's past and its meaning, studied journalism at an American university to complete requirements for the bachelor's degree begun at a school in his native land. The transition to history was not difficult, and an unusual master's thesis promptly found a publisher. Intellect, industry, a well-ordered mind—and the book—won a generous fellowship at an eastern school; and attainment of the doctorate there led to an appointment in a reputable state university.

If anyone believes that the only road to education lies in an orthodox pattern of instruction, let him recall that some very learned men from ancient times to the present reached enviable stature by other means. One of today's well-known historians declared his independence of high school and college classrooms and sought knowledge from books and from great teachers on unofficial time. Research was an obsession, and by the time many students are entering college, he was publishing articles in historical journals. His first effort was twice returned for further research and improvement in composition. The published piece was in no sense a second "Significance of the Frontier" performance, but it demonstrated a willingness to learn and a determination to succeed. One of his two published volumes served as a master's thesis when he finally decided a union card was prerequisite to a university position. The following year he packed a manuscript dissertation in his briefcase and entered another graduate school in quest of the doctorate. The thesis became a third book, published at the ripe age of twenty-three. Other volumes of substantial quality followed regularly during the next ten years.

Such instances, except the last, are not uncommon, but they are all too rare. Every director of graduate study has been privileged to work with students possessed of the spark that ignites latent talent and provides incentive to excel. But the director cannot create the spark, though he can recognize its presence and guide it into channels that lead to historianship.

IV

Some students may sense the fundamentals of learning without the stimulating influence of a great teacher who presides over a seminar. More often a dynamic scholar inspires them. In either case the learner is indeed fortunate if choice, or fate, leads him to an Adams, a Walter Webb, a Fletcher Green, or some other director of graduate study whose name is synonymous with quality education.

Seminars are as highly personalized as the men who direct them. At the head of one table sits a professor of great erudition who has little interest in creating scholars of tomorrow out of untutored and uncultivated minds. They bore him; and after two hours of wasted time, his own and theirs, he is off to the library or his study and leaves behind only an iota of impress. In another seminar room a man of less knowledge points the way to light and learning that he could not achieve; and students, who recognize his limitations, profit from the self-confidence he stirs in them. In a third, an "employee" who knows little and cares less detains students for the time prescribed in the catalogue, and then they go out into the sunshine. In a fourth, a man of much learning is so full of his subject and so eager to share the fullness thereof with young students, that he looks forward to the privilege of taking them on an exploring expedition that leads to Mount Olympus.

The Adams seminary at Johns Hopkins captivated men who participated therein, and they felt themselves enriched by the experience. With one significant change, a modern-day historian could make its basic concept a more effective device. A departmental seminar that encouraged students to concentrate on the production of one superior paper rather than scattering time and thought on so many busywork term reports of questionable value, might yield publishable articles by the best of them. The quality of the papers would be enhanced if they were multigraphed and distributed to all members at least a week in advance of presentation to prompt meticulous preparation and critical discussion. The completion of an impeccable paper, exhaustive in research, sophisticated in craftsmanship, and verified for accuracy, would contribute toward the making of a book by providing a model segment. Thereafter, the path to destination would be considerably eased for student and director.

Walter Webb's seminar at the University of Texas, described so delightfully in his presidential address before the Mississippi Valley Historical Association, is worthy of emulation—by anyone who has the rare qualities of that teacher. Bearing little resemblance in outer shell to the Johns Hopkins seminary, its inner purpose was achieved through two original ideas of the master. These eventually found public expression in *The Great Plains* and *The Great Frontier*. In each instance the seminar with changing personnel continued to follow the leader for several years—until each idea materialized as a book.

Some other seminars with genuine inner life have had a purpose other than producing books from a central seminal idea of the teacher. The director of one at the University of North Carolina since the 1930's cannot identify the spark that sets members on the road to historianship. "I agree," he says, that they "must have the burning desire to learn, to teach, and to write, but under what circumstances and why they come by that zeal I cannot say." Members of the seminar and observers of its fruits may know the answer even if the modest director does not. Numeration does not explain it, though it may serve as an index. One hundred and fifty have completed the master's degree, nearly ninety have attained the doctorate, and twenty-five more are working on their dissertations. A few of the hundred books and two hundred and twenty-five articles in historical journals have been awarded prizes. Thirty former members have won Guggenheim, Ford, Rosenwald, Social Science Research Council, Fulbright, and Institute for Advanced Study fellowships. They have taught in half of the states and in England, Germany, Japan, and India. This record equals, if it does not surpass, that attained by Johns Hopkins students under Adams' tutelage.

There is another type of seminar from which some postdoctoral students profit, if they have vision enough to understand that completion of the degree is only the beginning of wisdom. Among the thousands of letters in the writer's files are many from young scholars who are contributing the first article to a scholarly journal. The elation is justified: they are entering the Republic of Letters. The accepted manuscript is returned with pages interlined to improve sentence structure, quotations and spellings corrected, footnotes modified beyond recognition to achieve standardization and accuracy, irrelevant material deleted, and additional evidence to make the thesis more convincing suggested.

Occasionally a completely rewritten manuscript comes back to the editorial office. Author has surpassed editor as a revisionist. With many apologies for a half-finished product, he adds an appreciative sentence that makes the hard life of the editor worth living: "Contributing an article to the *Journal* is the best seminar I have ever taken." In striking contrast, another doctor of philosophy writes that he has contributed two chapters to Professor Titan's monumental history, and that what is good enough for him is surely good enough for the *Mississippi Valley Historical Review.*

Humility and Arrogance! The first made his subject into a book, and a good one. The second, perhaps fortunately for the guild, decided to make a career of the navy. It is quite unlikely that his major professor, a superior scholar who writes distinguished prose, would have approved his neophyte's irritation at constructive criticism.

Where does responsibility for shabby performance of young historians lie? Well, partly with themselves. The essential facts of historical life are not hard to come by. Some seminar directors must share the blame. Their own careless work breeds the same trait in their students. The responsibility lies, too, in a faulty concept of education. We place too much confidence in periodic revisions of technical requirements for graduate degrees: what courses and how many and in what combination shall stand guard over high standards in the registrar's office. We are slow to learn that students at whatever level cannot be legislated into an education. Graduate Dean Ford had something worthwhile to say on the subject of great teachers versus less significant factors. "Making budgets is necessary," he said, "and tinkering with curriculums is busywork; but getting together a real faculty is the only thing that makes a great institution." [4] Specifically, great scholars rather than petty legislation will improve graduate learning.

The fragmented fabric labeled "Southern History in the Making" may suggest, even though it does not achieve, the high standards of the calling that seeks to recover the past. In an age when athletes break track and field records every season and science asserts the limitless horizons in man's quest for the unknown, young historians face a challenge that may inspire improvement in teaching and researching and writing. The teacher expects his students to do better than he did. Ample evidence indicates advancing standards and better performance—and a large residue of complacent mediocrity.

CHAPTER I

William Garrott Brown: Literary Historian and Essayist

In the early years of the twentieth century, William Garrott Brown acquired an enviable reputation as a literary historian, philosophical essayist, and political paragrapher.[1] Publishing houses and literary magazines competed for the provender from his prolific pen. Men of letters and professional historians commended his articles and books in superlative language, and practical politicians heeded his pungent paragraphs on contemporary issues. William R. Thayer thought he "possessed ampler gifts for producing history of the highest rank than anyone who has come out of Harvard during the past 25 years—may I not say that he was easily first of the younger men from anywhere in America?" This appraisal was penned three years after Brown's death, but Thayer had already lauded his young protégé. "You have a real gift of story-telling," he wrote after reading *Andrew Jackson;* and again, "That was a graceful article you wrote in the *Historical Review* on Rhodes." * Albert B. Hart asserted that Brown was "one of the few men in the country who has both got something to say and can say it." After listening to a paper he read at a meeting of the American Historical Association, Hart was envious of his "power of language and statement! Everywhere I hear the same story—that W. G. Brown is one of the few men in the country who can actually write history." [2] Quoting Charles F. Adams to the

* William R. Thayer to John S. Bassett, December 14, 1916, William Garrott Brown Papers (Duke University Library, Durham, N.C.) ; Thayer to William Garrott Brown, November 27, 1900, November 12, 1905, Brown Papers. The Brown Papers were assembled by Bassett, 1916–17, with the intention of writing a biography of Brown. He contributed a brief article, "My Recollections of William Garrott Brown," to the *South Atlantic Quarterly,* XVI (April, 1917) , 97–107. After Bassett's death in 1928, Mrs. Bassett presented the papers to the Duke University Library through the courtesy of William K. Boyd.

effect that "learning, judgment, and the literary sense" were historical prerequisites, Jeremiah Smith thought Brown's writing happily combined all of them. "Your 'sense of proportion' seems to me perfect." [3] Soon after his election to the speakership, Champ Clark told a dinner group: "The best piece of political biography of the past twenty years is a book on Stephen A. Douglas by William Garrott Brown." [4] Brown's power of expression impressed J. Franklin Jameson, chairman of the committee to arrange the American Historical Association's program for 1904, who observed that "the attractive form which you know so well how to give to a brief paper would be as welcome as it is unusual in our proceedings." [5] Andrew C. McLaughlin, managing editor of the association's review, wrote Brown regarding an article on Oliver Ellsworth: "You have very skilfully woven your facts together and given to the dry details gathered from the journals a living interest, all this coming from the alchemy of a writer with literary instinct and power." [6]

I

What was the background of the man who impressed his contemporaries so favorably? [7] His life spanned the brief period from 1868 to 1913. Born in Marion, Alabama, with Virginia, North Carolina, and Connecticut ancestry, he was educated at various preparatory schools in his native town, and attended Howard College, 1883–86. Excelling in scholarship as well as in activities of the philomathic society, he graduated with honor, devoted a year to independent study and writing for the Montgomery *Advertiser,* and taught English for a biennium at the Marion Military Institute. Brown contemplated graduate study at the Johns Hopkins University, but correspondence with a former schoolmate at Howard College, Francis G. Caffey, resulted in both of them entering Harvard as juniors in the fall of 1889. Brown graduated in 1891, *summa cum laude.*[8] Awarded the Ozias Goodwin Fellowship, he continued at Harvard during the following year to work for the master's degree in history. The teacher who impressed him most favorably was Charles E. Norton,[9] whose course on Roman and medieval art gave him a permanent interest in the subject and prompted a visit to Italy some years later.[10] In the department of history he studied Western Europe from the Germanic Invasions to the Treaty of Verdun with George Bendelari, the Reformation with Ephraim Emerton, and he enrolled in Edward Channing's seminary in American history.[11] His research problem was "The Genesis of the Southern Confederacy," and on this topic, Brown wrote a few years later, "I had the nerve to deliver several lectures when I visited my old home in Alabama, in the winter of 1892–93. Some of my audiences were sprinkled with ex-Confederates, but I escaped with no bones broken." [12]

In 1892 Brown was placed in charge of the Harvard University archives, and four years later he was made Deputy Keeper of University Records.[13] In both of these positions his work was supervised by the librarian, Justin Winsor, whose learning the young scholar deeply appreciated. Under Winsor's direction he prepared *A List of Portraits in the Various Buildings of Harvard University* (1898). The director of the project died before it was completed, and Brown wrote: "How much better it might have been if he had lived can be conjectured by those who knew his tirelessness and his marvelous familiarity with the minute details of the lives of many men. I once asked him a question about a New England family of no national importance, and his reply was a hasty pencil sketch of a family tree, showing the births and marriages of a century; it was the work of a minute, without a glance at any source of information." [14]

It is quite likely that Brown's ambition was a career in politics, but for a time at least he hoped for an academic connection. Increasing deafness prevented either from materializing, although he was appointed lecturer at Harvard for the year 1901–1902 and gave a course on the political and constitutional history of the United States since the Civil War.[15] Perhaps it was Brown's political ambition that led him to study history; at least that was the conjecture of Charles M. Thompson, intimate friend and the editor of *Youth's Companion,* to which Brown was a frequent contributor. Thompson wrote, "The men he admired were the early statesmen"; "the great subject he was interested in was the future of the South"; the career he preferred was "national politics. I think he had all the Southerner's traditional liking for them and that he studied history primarily to make himself competent in political ways." [16]

Whatever the reason for taking up history, Brown had his own concept of how it should be written. He was one of the first to protest against the monographic, dry-as-dust product that emanated from historical seminars. When a new professorship was established at Harvard in 1900, he saw an opportunity for a radical departure from the current method of teaching and writing. Professors in the American universities, as in the German, had reduced method and motive to a science, eliminating imagination, sympathy, and conjecture. The "human element" had been subordinated to institutions, customs, and laws; indeed, "men are important chiefly as affecting these, not these as affecting and revealing men." With emphasis upon facts that admitted of definite proof, professors frowned upon "a sympathetic and imaginative treatment." The monographic method did not permit the painting of pictures; but there could be no "living republic" until passions, ideals, and instincts clothed the framework of the nation's development.[17]

Some of the requirements set down by Brown, though by no means all, were considered by him to have been met by Woodrow Wilson in his *History of the American People* (1902) . Wilson was, according to Brown, a brilliant writer. With "the quickest and keenest mind now at play on our American past," he considered "scholarship as a means, not as an end," and looked upon "history as a branch of literature rather than of science." He had successfully resisted the dominance of the document when German influence invaded the United States, and European and American universities were attempting " 'to develop learning at the expense of writing,' and to elevate history by subduing the historian." Free of partisanship, spacious in conception, intelligent in presentation, there was nothing "profoundly philosophical and sagacious" about his recent work, nor did it "stir, absorb, elevate, depress." A truly great work is the devotion of a lifetime; Wilson's fell far short of the standard set by John R. Green and Francis Parkman.

Comparing Wilson and John Fiske, whose *Essays, Historical and Literary* (1903) had just appeared, Brown thought that Fiske had succeeded better, if one considered all his works, than had the president of Princeton. Analyzed in detail, Wilson's writing was more felicitous and impressive. "That is why we call it brilliant. It shines." But it failed to "hold the reader," for "the continuous flow of skillful sentences actually tends to draw one's attention from the matter in them. They sometimes come between the reader and the story which they tell; and, after all, it is the story, not the English, which one means to read." With Fiske there was no artifice, no affectation—"the style is as unmistakable as his voice or his handwriting." *

Two years later Brown reviewed for the *American Historical Review* the fifth volume of James F. Rhodes' *History of the United States from the Compromise of 1850* (1904). His critique was in reality an appraisal of the first five volumes. They impressed the reviewer favorably. Together they constituted "the best history of the Civil War." He would go further: the project was "clearly entitled to the first place among the various enterprises in historiography now in progress in this country." And, with the passing of Green, William Stubbs, Edward A. Freeman, and Mandell Creighton, there was now no one in England whose work could compare with it. Rhodes assembled all the evidence, provided ample citations to prove his statements, and arrived at the truth. He avoided the "constant temptation to overstate and overcolor," a restraint that demanded firm resolution. As to style, he "is never brilliant"; his "prose is not imaginative. Fancy, grace, tenderness are wanting. . . . The pace is slow, and it never changes." Despite these criticisms, he continued, the work is, "after all, decidedly readable. The author's candor and sincerity and thoroughness, his great appetite for truth, his deep, masculine interest in his subject—these things far outweigh his mainly negative infelicities. . . . May he not have been wise to choose for himself the style and manner which he finds most natural, most expressive of his own everyday standards of judgment and taste?" Brown was hopeful that the author would eventually publish a popular work, stripped of scholarly paraphernalia, that would attract readers "whom the very air and method of scholarship affrights." [18] He

* William G. Brown, "The Problem of the American Historian," *Atlantic Monthly*, XCII (November, 1903), 649–61. In addition to the works by Woodrow Wilson and John Fiske, this article also considered briefly *The United States* (New York, 1903), volume VII, in "The Cambridge Modern History" (13 vols.; New York, 1903). Brown used the three works as a point of departure in expounding his own concept of history. After reading Brown's article, Frederic Bancroft wrote to Bassett: "His *Atlantic* article has many good touches & also a good deal of vague long-windedness that he & [Bliss] Perry consider style. Dunning & I think just the same of his work: it's very clever & very superficial. If he would only work, meditate silently & ripen! His (I fear fatal) mistake is that he would be judge before he has fully mastered the routine learning to the making of a good lawyer. . . . He's too self-conscious, & because he sees many below him he imagines that he is at the top. That's the amiable weakness of the typical Southerner, especially of 'the old school.'" Bancroft to Bassett, November 9, 1903, John Spencer Bassett Papers (Manuscript Division, Library of Congress, Washington, D.C.).

would, as he wrote Rhodes, plead "that we ought always to keep the untrained reader in mind, since the past is his as well as ours." [19]

Lest it be supposed that Brown was artist and nothing more, it should be emphasized that he recognized truth as the primary aim of historical literature. The historian's "imagination must serve, not control. He must tell what actually happened in former times." [20] Brown was aware that a search for facts was absolutely necessary; this was done at all universities. But history had not attained its goal if it went no further. To vitalize the record, someone must breathe the breath of life into it. With one notable exception in his own writing, Brown was content to draw heavily upon the inquiries of others. His *Life of Oliver Ellsworth* showed considerable delving into the sources; elsewhere his contribution embraced a modicum of research, artistry of expression, proper balance, and a measure of meaningful interpretation. Success as a writer, whether as historian or essayist, stemmed from a lucid and unlabored style.

II

The brief period from the turn of the century to 1905 witnessed the publication of a half-dozen books. A textbook *History of Alabama* appeared in 1900. To Houghton Mifflin and Company's "Riverside Biographical Series," Brown contributed two volumes, *Andrew Jackson* (1900) and *Stephen Arnold Douglas* (1902). Then came his greatest work, *The Lower South in American History* (1902), a collection of lectures and essays, some of which had already appeared in a literary magazine. *The Foe of Compromise and Other Essays* was published in 1903. The *Life of Oliver Ellsworth* (1905) was the last of his books, except for a posthumous assemblage of articles, *The New Politics and Other Papers* (1914). He had, however, tried his hand at writing a novel, *A Gentleman of the South; A Memory of the Black Belt* (1903); and he also wrote a play depicting planter politics in the Lower South which did not command a publisher.[21] In the midst of his productive period, irreparable tragedy overtook him, although it was not until 1906 that doctors diagnosed his illness as tuberculosis. He had already projected other historical studies, on some of which he had done considerable work, but declining health prevented a continuation of any of them. He did not lay down his pen, however, until six weeks before his death, for he was a regular contributor to newspapers and periodicals. During the last two and one-half years, his writing was done mainly in bed.

Brown's *History of Alabama* was written for school children entering their teens. Because of its elementary nature, it need not concern us here except as it indicates a wholesome balance between sectional background and a spirit of nationalism. As Brown was chronicling the history of his "own people," he "escaped the temptation to set down aught in malice"; he did not think "it right or necessary to abate one jot of reverence for the great captains of a long lost cause." But he wrote "also as an American, ardently attached to my whole country, and determined from the first that no word of mine should ever weaken in any child's mind that devotion to the great Republic which in me is grown into a passion." [22] One of Brown's favorite expressions was, "The South is my Mother but New England is my Sweet-heart." [23] In this spirit he wrote to John S. Bassett in 1907, soon after the Trinity College (North Carolina) professor transferred to Northampton, Massachusetts: "I am interested in the evolution of Johnny Rebeldom by you[r] contact with New England civilization. If you keep on living up there, you will go through many oscillations of the scales, but if, after a while, you are shipped off as I have been, you will find Southern kindliness mighty agreeable. But I should be the last to forget how many fine enthusiasms one can catch in New England." [24]

Andrew Jackson, a little volume of some twenty thousand words, was the first of the "Riverside Biographical Series," and undoubtedly set a proper pattern for succeeding numbers. Written in clear and simple but forceful English, its style has no monographic flavor. It is doubtful if the author consulted many primary sources. With James Parton's *Life of Andrew Jackson* and a few general histories before him, supplemented by knowledge of recent monographs, he could easily have written the book without going to original materials except for verification. In doing what was expected of him, Brown performed with considerable merit. In small compass he wrote in an entertaining and readable manner of the outstanding events of Jackson's career. It is a book of highlights, with facts and illustrations ably selected. In portraying Jackson's character, his points of strength and his weaknesses, Brown is at his best. He balanced positive against negative, virtue against fault, in superior fashion. One puts the book aside with the feeling that he knows Jackson the man intimately. In one respect the author succeeded far better than many biographers and political historians: his political terminology is correct.[25]

In *Stephen Arnold Douglas,* as in *Andrew Jackson,* Brown selected his facts and illustrations carefully and exhibited fairness in dealing with Douglas' contemporaries. He found no such faults in the Illinois statesman as he discovered in Jackson; his detachment is revealed, however, in his portrayal of the two great Illinois leaders, "The Rivals." [26] In a chapter on "Leadership," his description of Senate scenes as Douglas defended himself and the Kansas-Nebraska bill by putting his critics on the defensive is superb. Brown had some of the qualities of the successful fight announcer: he saw the dramatic, the wild thrill of enthusiasm as the match warmed into skillful boxing and hard-hitting slugging. There are in this work, as in his life of Jackson, a few minor errors; but never is accuracy sacrificed for dramatic effect.[27]

Oliver Ellsworth stands in sharp contrast to Brown's briefer portraits of Jackson and Douglas. It is less readable, yet its dullest portions represent craftsmanship of a higher order than the typical monographic study attained. The difficulty was with the subject: the Connecticut jurist was a drab character, and the author had no more than launched the project before he questioned his capacity to produce an interesting narrative.[28] Despite Brown's self-depreciation, critics received it generously. McLaughlin accepted two of the chapters for publication in the *American Historical Review* and complimented the contributor on his literary ability.[29] He also appraised the book for the review, and concluded that Brown had made his subject "a living personality." The "mere advocate of measures . . . [had] become a man and an impressive one." [30] Documentary material was scarce, for Ellsworth wrote few letters and seldom drafted a speech. Brown used to good advantage the Jonathan Trumbull Papers, manuscripts prepared by Oliver Ellsworth, Jr., and biographical sketches written by Joseph Wood and Abner Jackson, who married respectively Ellsworth's daughter and granddaughter. To a large extent he depended upon such printed sources as the writings of his subject's contemporaries, Senate records, and Supreme Court reports, and there are frequent citations to the Continental Congress journals. With few exceptions he spoke definitively only when reliable evidence was available; then he gave bold and vigorous interpretation to the facts he found.[31]

Brown's reputation as a historian of the South rests largely upon his *Lower South in American History*. As one critic put it, "if he had written nothing else, that alone should perpetuate his memory." [32] In evaluating the book, it should be remembered that he was pioneering in a new field, for only a few substantial treatises on any aspect or period of southern history had appeared by the turn of the century. His native Alabama provided disproportionate illustration; yet he demonstrated that, in a general way, he saw the deep South as a whole, though he offered "apology for the thin and fragmentary effect." [33] Like most collections of papers prepared for different purposes, the work lacks unity and design. The first three essays, which give title to the volume, were lectures delivered at Harvard and at several colleges in the South. Three others—"The Orator of Secession [William L. Yancey]," "The Resources of the Confederacy," and "The Ku Klux Movement"—were published originally in the *Atlantic Monthly*.[34] "A New Hero of an Old Type [Richmond P. Hobson]" and "Shifting the White Man's Burden" appeared in public for the first time.

Speaking for southerners of his day, Brown could "not recognize the picture" of the Cotton Kingdom painted by outsiders, though he esteemed the reasoning of John E. Cairnes and the observations of Frederick L. Olmsted. They and other doctrinaires and travelers had told only a part of the story; the whole truth revealed a less distorted portrait. He could not agree with Cairnes that the institution of slavery was solely responsible for the " 'idle and lawless rabble' " of poor whites, "since under freedom they have not changed or disappeared." [35] Brown antedated Ulrich B. Phillips by a quarter of a century in stating the fundamental basis of the latter's "Central Theme of Southern History." A generation under freedom, he asserted, had demonstrated "that the real cause of all the trouble was not slavery, but the presence of Africans in the South in large numbers." And he added that southern leaders of the last two antebellum decades "were trying to do just what the leading men of the South are trying to do now, viz.: to discover some way or ways by which a society made up of whites and blacks in almost equal proportions can keep pace with a society made up of whites only." [36]

Commending Alabama's government, Brown insisted that it rested on a broad base, for many self-made men reached political office, and planters did not dominate as much as tradition recorded. While the author cites no authorities, he was probably following Daniel R. Hundley's *Social Relations in Our Southern States*

(1860) in finding classes that critical antebellum travelers did not see. In Congress representatives of the Lower South stood for "the whole social organism," not just slavery and staple-crop agriculture. Reminiscent of William P. Trent's *William Gilmore Simms* (1892), he spoke of "a primitive industry, a primitive labor system, and a patriarchal mode of life" southerners struggled to maintain "in the most progressive country in the world." Economically, leaders demanded unrestricted exchange of agricultural staples for foreign commodities and unhampered expansion into new territory; politically, they sought "protection from criticism and from social and humanitarian reforms and changes." To secure these ends, they must assume the offensive—"they must rule." [37] Brown's statement of the challenge they faced merits quotation: "And it was the belated concern of the Northern mind about the things of the spirit, not its absorption in material enterprises, that boded ill to the plantation system. It was the North's moral awakening, and not its industrial alertness, its free thought, and not its free labor, which the Southern planter had to fear. The New England factory made no threat, the town meeting did. The Northwestern wheat farms and pork packeries and railways were harmless; but Oberlin College and Lovejoy's printing press and the underground railway were different. . . . The true danger from without was in the moral and intellectual forces which were at once the cause and the result of the North's progress." [38]

Many of the facts in "The Orator of Secession" were drawn from John W. Du Bose's *The Life and Times of William Lowndes Yancey* (1892); Brown gave them historical life and intelligent interpretation. Overgenerous in assigning the Alabama leader "a place among the half-dozen men who have had most to do with shaping American history" in the nineteenth century, he correctly evaluated his tremendous success in influencing people—an "impassioned invective" that swayed the masses. Foe of compromise in a generation of indecision, single-minded in devotion to the goal of a separate southern confederacy, his oratory appealed to the political and religious assemblages of antebellum years. His mastery of the spoken word was complete: "The sentences sometimes rush like charging cavalry. There are phrases that ring out like bugle calls. It is the language of passionate purpose; of an orator bent on rousing, convincing, overwhelming the men in front of him." [39]

As to the Confederacy's resources, John C. Schwab and Ernest A.

Smith had arrayed facts and figures but had left many questions unanswered, for their researches were "set forth too abstrusely, or too cautiously, or too minutely," albeit their unimaginative and restrained findings whetted the intellectual appetite by arousing curiosity. As reasons for the defeat of the Confederacy, Brown cited a defective financial policy, laws that violated sound economy, a retarded industrial development, paucity of practical statesmen, and weakness of the Confederate Congress.[40]

For proper perspective, a statement of the conditions that brought forth its existence, and an appraisal of results obtained, Brown's essay on "The Ku Klux Movement" is a superior piece of work. It is no disparagement of Walter L. Fleming to say that, in treating the Klan, he built upon the excellent foundations laid by Brown, delved deeper into the sources, filled in significant details, but left the framework much as he found it. Drawing upon childhood memories of stories heard from "fast friends of the kitchen and the quarters," later conversations with the older generation of whites, written memoranda of participants, the twelve volumes of testimony taken by a congressional investigating committee and its one-volume report, Brown reconstructed the movement in all of its essentials. Enormous as "mismanagement" of state governments was under carpetbag control, he saw greater evils in local communities. He concluded that the movement was successful, implied that, with conditions as they were, it was justifiable, but perceived its continuing ill effects on southern political and social life.[41]

Love for his country had, as Brown put it, "grown into a passion." With the coming of the Spanish-American War, he volunteered his services and even sought the influence of Congressman Joseph Wheeler from his native state in his quest for military duty. But alas, a physical infirmity precluded acceptance, and, in a depressed state of mind, he remained at Harvard to record the exploits of other graduates and to follow with avid interest the fortunes of other Alabamians.[42] His heart swelled with justifiable pride as he read of the heroic deed of young R. P. Hobson in sinking the *Merrimac* in Santiago harbor, for Brown had known him as a boy "among the Alabama cotton fields" and on the baseball diamond, and had followed his record at Annapolis. Son of a Confederate father, growing up in an impoverished South, he was of the same type as Lucius Q. C. Lamar and Henry W. Grady, representing that class of southerners who had faith in the future.

But he was "A New Hero of an Old Type"; of the same stock as Stephen Decatur and Sir George Somers and W. B. Cushing. His prototype might be seen in Paul Jones, or even in Walter Raleigh and Francis Drake. Less historical than the other essays in the volume, it illustrated Brown's intense patriotism, and perhaps his remorse that he could not have shared in the glory of war.[43]

In "Shifting the White Man's Burden," he revealed an awareness of current political problems in the South: the legal and constitutional disfranchisement of the Negroes since 1890, the effect of Populism upon southern politics, the contests between white and black counties for supremacy, the shifting of influence from the plantation to the industrial South, and conflicting views of southern whites as to a proper solution of the race question. As Brown saw it, "The main thing is not what to do for the negro, but what to do for the white man living among negroes." The accomplishments of Tuskegee and Hampton institutes were tangible evidences of improvement among southern blacks. Illiterates of both races should be educated "up to the limit of their capacities," but he could speak with more assurance of the results of "educating white men of English stocks." As they had greater capacity, as well as greater tolerance, in dealing with illiterate as well as educated Negroes, Brown concluded that the improvement of "the whites is the safest, the easiest, the wisest first step to take." [44]

If Brown needed outside stimulus to convince him that he should try his pen at a novel, it was provided in 1900 by Walter H. Page, who recommended "a straight-forward, rip-roaring, exciting historical novel on the war between the States." The proverbial romance could be built around "the great dramatic events" of the war, and the story should depict social conditions and domestic life. Through this medium Brown could present the history of the Confederacy to millions who could be reached in no other way.[45] He wrote the novel, but gave it an antebellum rather than a war setting, and published it with Macmillan rather than with Doubleday, Page and Company. He entitled it *A Gentleman of the South: A Memory of the Black Belt, from the Manuscript Memoirs of the Late Colonel Stanton Elmore* (1903). The manuscript was, Brown said on the title page, "edited without change," and he explained in the preface that he discovered it among Elmore's papers.[46] It would not be difficult to detect Brown's subterfuge from a reading of the novel even if there were no other evidence that he was author rather than editor. It would have been better if he had performed only editorial duties. Fortunately, he was convinced that he should stick to history.

One of Brown's severest but kindliest critics was William R. Thayer, editor of the *Harvard Graduates' Magazine,* to which Brown frequently contributed. He appreciated Brown's gift and kept him conscious of the need for precision in his writing. After commending *Andrew Jackson,* Thayer wrote: "Go on! and when your hand has complete mastery over language, take some great subject, and put your best into it." [47] With the uninspired *Oliver Ellsworth* completed, Brown informed Thayer that he was contemplating a life of Robert E. Lee and that there was a possibility he could have access to the voluminous material on the Virginian assembled by George F. R. Henderson, "Stonewall" Jackson's biographer. "Admiration for Lee grows on me," Brown wrote, but a successful "biographer should have the very rare kind of literary art that is most like a sculptor's." Thayer's reply is not available, but Brown wrote again a week later: "I understand perfectly, I think, & appreciate highly, your wishing me an obsession by a great theme, but does that kind of thing ever happen after disillusionment? . . . I agree that the biographer should be fascinated, absorbed, convinced, from the start." [48]

The "Lee" did not materialize, nor did various other projects Brown had in mind. At Albert B. Hart's invitation he contracted to write a volume tentatively entitled "Elements of the Civil War" for the "American Nation Series," but for some unknown reason he asked to be relieved of the assignment in the fall of 1903.[49] He planned a biography of Ulysses S. Grant for the Macmillan Company,[50] and the editor of the *American Illustrated Magazine* offered him $300 an installment for twelve to fourteen articles on Grant for serial publication.[51] He also contracted with Macmillan to write a history of the United States since the Civil War, but this volume had to be abandoned, though several essays on the Reconstruction period appeared in the *Atlantic Monthly.**

* Caffey to Brown, December 23, 1910, Brown Papers. For the series of Reconstruction articles, captioned "The Tenth Decade of the United States," see *Atlantic Monthly,* XCV (May, 1905), 577–94; (June, 1905), 766–80; XCVI (July, 1905), 31–39; (September, 1905), 359–76; (December, 1905), 760–75; XCVII (April, 1906), 465–88.

In 1903 Frederic C. Howe invited Brown to contribute a biography of John Jay to a five-volume series, "The Lives of the Chief Justices." Howe to Brown, November 18, 1903, Brown Papers. In the same year Alexander Jessup asked Brown to write a volume for the "American Men of Action" series. Jessup to Brown, December 8, 1903, Brown Papers. J. Henry Harper, of Harper and Brothers, invited Brown in 1905

The man who knew Brown most intimately was uncertain "whether 'man of letters,' 'essayist,' or 'historian' more nearly describes him." [52] Three of his books—*The Lower South, The Foe of Compromise,* and *The New Politics*—appeared first, either in whole or in part, as contributions to periodicals. The list of magazines in which he published articles is in itself an eloquent tribute to his genius as a stylist. Perhaps his best essays were published in the *Atlantic Monthly,* but he contributed also to the *Century,* the *North American Review,* the *Fortnightly Review,* the *Independent,* the *Outlook, Youth's Companion, Harper's Weekly, Harper's Bazaar,* the *Dial,* the *Critic,* the *Nation,* the *South Atlantic Quarterly,* and the *Harvard Graduates' Magazine.* Articles and reviews also appeared in such professional magazines as the *American Historical Review* and the *American Journal of Sociology.* In addition to a series of letters from a southern tour published in the Boston *Evening Transcript,* he contributed to the New York *Evening Post* and the Montgomery *Advertiser.* An *Atlantic Monthly* article on "Golf" was subsequently published as a booklet. Few writers have received so wide an acceptance of their literary output. Fewer still have been able to make a living with their pens, but this, Brown accomplished most of the time from 1906 to 1913 despite the fact that tuberculosis not only sapped his strength but also increased his financial obligations.*

---

to prepare a biography of George William Curtis "that shall tell the story of his work, both political and literary." Harper to Brown, September 25, 1905, Brown Papers. Earlier, in 1903, the Baker and Taylor Company of New York had written Brown: "We have noted with very great interest the success of your recent books, and wish that we might confer with you regarding any forthcoming work which you have either in process or in contemplation." Baker and Taylor Company to Brown, November 21, 1903, Brown Papers. There were scores of requests for contributions to magazines, encyclopedias, and other cooperative works.

* For book royalties, which were rather small, see Caffey to Brown, December 23, 1910, Brown Papers; Macmillan Company to Brown, April 30, 1912, Brown Papers. It is probable that Brown received $200 per month from *Harper's Weekly,* 1908–1913, though the amount may have been increased to $250. From *Harper's Bazaar* he was paid $40 for "a monthly synopsis (2,000 words) of the most important questions before the public, discussing each topic briefly for the special interest of the women." This arrangement continued from February, 1910, until April, 1912. Elizabeth Jordan to Brown, January 21, February 10, 1910; April 22, 1912, Brown Papers. From the spring of 1912 until shortly before his death in 1913, Brown contributed two articles of from 300 to 700 words each per month to the *Youth's Companion,* for which he received $15 per article. Thompson to Brown, March 21, 1912, Brown Papers. For his *Atlantic Monthly* articles on "The Seventh Decade of the United States," Brown received $150 each. Bliss Perry to Brown, May 5, 1905, Brown Papers.

Some of Brown's essays which appeared in book form have already been analyzed. The subject matter of some others is unrelated to history and cannot concern us here, though method and reception may be illustrated. The best of them, "The Foe of Compromise," uses a historical springboard—the Compromise of 1850, with Rufus Choate as the orator of compromise and William L. Garrison as its foe—but it employs abstractions to point a thesis. Its publication in the *Atlantic Monthly* stirred a mild sensation on both sides of the Atlantic. An English woman who had spent a dozen years searching "for Truth, and a reliable theory of Life & Duty," studied it "with impassioned interest" and transcribed it in a notebook. "Almost every sentence in it found a thrilling response in my consciousness," she wrote, "and some parts of it stirred the very 'deeps' of my experience and hope & aspiration. . . . The whole of it swayed me: I rose & fell with its thought & feeling. . . . It is to me like a supreme vision of the tragedy & the *greatness* of the *seeing* soul's passage through the immeasurable mystery.[53] In phraseology that anyone can understand, Paul E. More, literary editor of the *Independent,* caught a "glimpse of greatness in pure literature"; he praised it as "a rarely excellent piece of literary work." [54] And a Chicago friend wrote that "this rings the bell. Haven't liked anything so well since Virginibus Puevisque and there are places where you have Stevenson—but we shant blaspheme. Please write some more like it." [55]

Although only an intellectual can comprehend "The Foe of Compromise," any "honest duffer" can fathom "Golf." [56] This essay, inspired by his own love for the game, elicited commendation at home and abroad. It reveals in the author a sense of humor, a grasp of human nature, a philosophical comprehension, an appreciation of the relationship between the animate and the inanimate, and a vocabulary approaching an artillery of words. It is a masterpiece of diction, accomplished without verbal topping, hooking, or slicing.

III

In the winter and spring of 1904, Brown made a tour of the South to report conditions for the Boston *Evening Transcript.* His Alabama background, frequent vacations in various parts of the South from Virginia to Texas, the excellence of *The Lower South in American History,* and his penetrating analyses of southern problems in sundry periodicals brought him to the attention of the

Evening Transcript publishers as a person capable of competent observation and impartial reporting. The arrangement stipulated a compensation of $400 for twenty articles, plus railroad and pullman transportation.[57] For some reason Brown desired anonymity, and all of them were published over the pseudonym "Stanton." [58] In introducing the series of letters, captioned "The South at Work," the newspaper identified the correspondent as "a Southern man with Northern education and residence," who was "peculiarly well equipped to make an exposition as well as an interpretation of the development of the industrial South." [59] There was only one point of disagreement between correspondent and editor: as 1904 was the fiftieth anniversary of Frederick L. Olmsted's journey, Brown desired to make "pretty constant reference" to the New Yorker's observations by way of contrasts and comparisons, but this approach was discouraged. "That is going rather too far back," the editor wrote. "What we want to know is how the South is picking up now and how it has improved in the last ten years." The *Evening Transcript* was no longer "a repository of reminiscences"; it was interested in "*news*—new things, new enterprises, new aspects of old problems and prospects for the future." [60]

Brown adjusted his method to meet the desires of his employers, although conformity to a journalistic pattern sacrificed historical perspective and compromised a graceful and charming style. He could not forget that he was a historian, however, and despite editorial policy he occasionally alluded to events of the antebellum and postwar generations.* While he undertook the tour with certain definite notions about the South, he did not hesitate to change his mind if he found new evidence. His attitude toward the Negro was still an Alabama point of view, slightly liberalized by northern residence and schooling. Like Olmsted, Brown began his itinerary at Washington, D.C., and between the last of February and the middle of May he traversed the seaboard states from Virginia to Texas.[61] As a newspaper reporter, he interviewed governors, legislators, businessmen, laborers, farmers, consuls,

* With few exceptions, Tracy was pleased with Brown's articles: "Your Durham letter is a tip-top one and is quite a model. I think, however, that a few statistics put into these letters will assist them. . . . The Richmond letter was a trifle scattering, although interesting and good. . . . These little touches that you put into your letters in regard to shooting quail in this or that place, etc., are very attractive and show that you are familiar with your surroundings." Tracy to Brown, March 8, 1904, Brown Papers.

commissioners of agriculture, commerce, and immigration—hundreds of persons, he said, "from mill men to ranchmen, from governors to teamsters." He purposely sought out the South's "busiest men rather than people of leisure," and on the whole tour he did not experience "a single rudeness, a single incivility." [62]

Brown emphasized half a dozen major southern problems in his letters and wrote briefly about many others. His visit to Durham provided grist for a report on the tobacco industry and its central figure, the Duke family. A letter from Columbia treated the cotton textile mills and conditions under which their white laborers worked. From Orlando he described the Florida citrus industry. The Birmingham article concentrated on the city's iron and steel business. The Jackson stopover gave opportunity to discuss reactionary politics as exemplified by Governor James K. Vardaman's administration; the Greenville sojourn provided a proper setting to describe the tenant system in the Delta region and the preference for Negro labor; and his stay at Vicksburg prompted a story of the levees and the need for further flood control. From Houston he wrote of rice cultivation; from College Station, Texas, cotton production and the boll weevil menace; from Austin, the University of Texas; from Santa Gertrudes Ranch, cattle raising; from Cleburne, the southern caste system. He discussed the manufacture of locomotives at Richmond, the historical significance of graveyards, the Theodore Roosevelt–Booker T. Washington episode, experiments with Italian and Chinese laborers on cotton plantations, the New Orleans cotton exchange, by-products from cotton manufacture, the evil effects of the Civil War and Reconstruction, and the Bassett affair at Trinity College.

He made it clear in the first letter that "the present and true 'Southern Question' is the question of how to make money out of the South's resources," not the Negro problem. In determining why the region lagged industrially, the Negro was only a part of the picture. "The lack of competent and persistent labor among the whites is the matter. A low standard of living is the matter. Ignorance and illiteracy is the matter." [63] He did not penetrate far into the South before he concluded that there was little support for an opinion, expressed at the beginning of his tour, that the "lowest point in the efficiency of Negro labor has been reached and passed." Governors Andrew J. Montague of Virginia, Charles B. Aycock of North Carolina, and Duncan C. Heyward of South Carolina, as well as many other individuals in those states, agreed "that the Negro as a laborer is deteriorating." The prevailing southern attitude was that "it is 'up to them to make good' under freedom," and the verdict of the first three states he traversed was that they had failed.[64] In New Orleans he found that the Negro was steadily "losing ground" as a laborer, and most of Texas got along very well without him.[65] But in Florida he discovered a "feeling of satisfaction with the Negro and with Negro labor," and the Delta region still preferred him.[66] Summarizing his findings near the end of the tour, he painted a discouraging picture. Free Negro labor in 1904 was ineffective for the same reasons that slave labor was inefficient half a century before. Absenteeism prevailed; Negroes quit jobs without notice, as they absconded in slavery days; the "fear of punishment" was still the only effective discipline; and theft and waste "were besetting sins" of freedmen as they were of slaves. Slave labor was expensive in the Old South; "Negro labor in the South is still, I am convinced, more costly than white labor in the North." [67]

It was reassuring to note that the caste system did not forbid manual labor by whites. This not only encouraged immigration but also made the white man's standard of competence the controlling factor. When this situation obtained to a greater degree, the South would offer less inducement to the Negro, for he remained largely because a living was possible "without hard, intelligent work, without habits of foresight and saving." [68] Despite his pessimistic view of the Negro, Brown was encouraged about the prospects for both industrial and agricultural development of the South. Everywhere he saw men at work as never before. A central theme of his report on "The South at Work" was "the advancing South."

IV

Mention has been made of the fact that Brown was interested in politics and perhaps was ambitious for a political career. He carried with him from Alabama to Cambridge a predilection for the Democratic faith. He joined the Young Men's Democratic Club of Massachusetts, helped to organize the Democratic Campaign Club of Harvard University in 1892, and took the stump for Grover Cleveland in Rhode Island and Massachusetts. During the next few years he frequented Democratic state conventions, served on his party's state committee, and in 1896 attended the

Democratic National Convention. In the same year he became a prime mover in organizing the William E. Russell Club of Cambridge and served as chairman of its executive committee. At the turn of the century he wrote: "Still call myself a Democrat, but the title is disputed by acquaintances of the silver persuasion." [69] William J. Bryan's third candidacy in 1908 drove Brown into the Republican camp, and he labored to carry North Carolina for William H. Taft.[70]

At the same time opportunity came to write political articles for *Harper's Weekly,* then under the editorial direction of George Harvey. As a contributor he was associated with Edward S. Martin, another Harvard graduate, although Brown was forced to do his writing wherever he happened to be sojourning at the time, whether at some eastern summer residence or at a southern sanitarium in winter. No longer able to write books because of his inability to gather material or to maintain sustained effort, he could, except in physical crises, follow political trends, analyze issues, and occasionally write longer articles for other magazines.

Brown's special assignments included tariff, monetary reform, and southern politics, and most of the "Comment" that appeared in *Harper's Weekly* on these subjects during Taft's administration and the early years of Woodrow Wilson's came from his pen. Aside from following these issues, he published full-page feature articles on the retiring and incoming presidents in 1909 and again in 1913. Under the captions "To Theodore Roosevelt: Greeting!" and "To William H. Taft: Greeting!" [71], he addressed them in such delectable analyses that readers lifted their eyebrows. They so impressed Mark Twain that he penned his "congratulations"—mistakenly to Harvey. They surpassed all other "bowings of the one President out & the other one in. . . . Yours are certainly masterpieces, in fitness, fairness, wisdom, depth, candor, compactness, lucidity, grace of style, felicitous expression . . . composure, the gravity & the fine dignity meet for the occasion." [72] The performance was repeated in 1913 with "Greetings" to Taft and Wilson.[73] Armed with an advance copy, Colonel Edward M. House presented the Wilson article to his dinner guest on the evening of February 28. The President-elect read it aloud and exclaimed, " 'it is a classic' and again 'it is a noble utterance.' " Wilson was so favorably impressed that he suggested publication in capital newspapers as a "companion piece to his Inaugural Address. . . .

He also wanted to know if it were possible to distribute several thousand copies among the assembled crowds." *

Much as Brown was interested in tariff and monetary reform, his desire to improve political conditions in the South transcended all other motives in his contributions to the publication. Until 1911 he depended upon presidential aid. He lauded Taft's southern policy as announced in his inaugural address, praised his independence in appointing non-machine Republicans and Democrats to office, and commended his timely and tactful speeches at Atlanta and Charlotte. He characterized Taft as "a President whom the South is beginning to like"; no President since Abraham Lincoln had exhibited such fairness; not even the Democratic Cleveland "has accomplished so much to break down sectional barriers and fully reannex eleven States to the Union." [74]

It was Brown's ambition to convert "The Thinkless South" into a two-party region by reforming Republican organizations which had long been cliques of federal officeholders.[75] To promote a normal and healthy political activity, the machines in the several states must be destroyed. The politician presently responsible for them was Postmaster General Frank H. Hitchcock, whose "referee" in each state, usually the head of the Republican machine, controlled federal patronage. Reform activity might well begin in North Carolina, for that state had cast 115,000 votes for Taft in 1908 and elected three Republican congressmen. The contest there, Brown wrote, "is for the control of the State Committee, but the real issue is between the pie-counter and the men who want a party that shall stand for something other than the pie-counter." [76] Two such North Carolinians were Congressmen John M. Morehead and Thomas Settle, who urged Brown "to come to Ashville and *'get in the game.'* " [77] Brown did not get to the convention, but he wrote the platform which was adopted without serious modification. It was a thoroughly "anti-pie-counter" document, which "utterly and emphatically repudiates that notion of . . . [the party's] character and function which would make of it a mere

* Edward M. House to Brown, March 1, 1913, Brown Papers. In this letter House continued: "Our friend, Martin, has kindly arranged for this through Colonel Harvey. Three thousand leaflets of it will be sent to Washington on Monday night and I am arranging with the Secretary of the Inaugural Committee to have them properly distributed. Martin thought your name should be placed on the article and I hope this will be done for, in my opinion, you have contributed a permanent piece of literature." Harvey changed his mind, concluding that "distribution would seem like butting in for an advertisement." Martin to Brown, March 3, 1913, Brown Papers. See also House to Brown, March 9, 15, 1913, Brown Papers.

machine for distributing Federal offices and electing delegates to national conventions. We proclaim ourselves a true party, and no machine. We need no dictator, and we will submit to no dictation." [78] But although the reform Republicans captured control of the party in North Carolina, they did not succeed in electing any members to Congress in 1910. [79] It was a Democratic year.

Through the instrumentality of A. Piatt Andrew, Assistant Secretary of the Treasury, Brown was invited to Washington to confer with Taft and the Secretary of the Treasury on the Republican party in the South. Because Brown was physically unable to make the trip, an interview was arranged with the President in New York City, but apparently it did not materialize.[80] A communication to the President's secretary reached Taft, who wrote Brown: "I have never read an article that is so illuminating and satisfactory on the Southern situation as your letter. I agree with you in every particular." [81] Other correspondence followed, and on May 30, 1911, Brown strongly recommended that the President, as the head of the party, should make an unequivocal declaration that federal patronage should not be used to secure support for his nomination by the Republican National Convention, that officeholders must not neglect their responsibilities to engage in party activity, and that political bargains should be considered as disqualifying an applicant for the office he sought. Brown fully realized the significance of the step he was proposing, and he anticipated the reaction of politicians toward it. He provided the President with valid reasons why the move was expedient: Taft's nomination was a foregone conclusion, the real contest would be in the election; the President's position before the electorate would be strengthened, particularly with advocates of civil service reform; total destruction of the "pie-counter" system would complete a praiseworthy southern program; and such action would destroy practices that were "wrong and mean and dangerous to our institutions." [82] Copies of Brown's letter to Taft were sent to the Treasury Department, Henry C. Lodge, and Samuel W. McCall, imploring their aid in promoting reform,[83] but Brown soon learned from Taft's secretary "that the President has considered the matter and has decided to take no action. It is receiving his attention, but he will not act on it impulsively, for it contemplates a revolution in a venerable system which operates in fourteen or fifteen states." [84] The political reformer understood that he could expect no support from the administration.

Meanwhile, anticipating such an eventuality, Brown had been contemplating a searching investigation of Republican politics in the South. Early in 1911 he approached the New York *Times* on publishing a series of articles on the subject. He would prepare a statement on the historical background of the Republican machines, and data from the several southern states would be assembled by a competent newspaper reporter with Washington and southern experience but without muckraking proclivities.[85] But the New York *Times* would not sponsor the project; *Harper's Weekly* and the New York *Evening Post* also declined. Rollo Ogden of the latter explained that if Brown himself could "make the investigation, and . . . send us some letters, the case would be different." [86]

Disgusted with Roosevelt and disappointed in Taft, Brown hoped that some acceptable Democrat would be presented. Wilson did not appeal to him. In the spring of 1909, when George Harvey was grooming the Princeton president for the governorship, Brown asked Edward S. Martin if he could not "coax the Colonel down off that moribund Wilson hobby? I know President Wilson, & admire him, but—! You and I are in the running if he is." [87] With Wilson in the governorship, Harvey pushed him for the Presidency, and encouraged *Harper's Weekly* contributors "to say something helpful." [88] Brown, who had been promoting the work of the Commission on Monetary Reform, read Wilson's Texas speech with alarm and determined to set him right before endorsing his candidacy. A five-page letter, urging careful study of the commission's report, asked Wilson not to "throw away what Cleveland kept, what Roosevelt lost—the confidence of men of your class." "And don't," Brown begged him, "do as Taft did recently, after inviting my advice about his Southern policy—pat *me* on the back with a compliment and disregard my advice." [89] The letter "made a great impression upon" Wilson. Admitting that he "went off half cocked" because he distrusted everything with the Aldrich stamp, he promised "dispassionate and open-minded treatment" of the issue. He lamented that the actual business of government left no "time for careful investigation. I seem almost obliged to form conclusions from impressions instead of from study." [90] This frank confession completely disarmed Brown, and he notified Martin that Wilson's reply had "simply made me his'n." He would back Wilson to the limit even if he had "to hire the *Outlook* to do it with." As paper writing would not insure a nomination, Harvey should immediately "get Wilson's boom into responsible hands for systematic management." [91]

Wilson's advisers were soon in touch with Brown. House wished he could meet with a small group in New York City—Wilson, Martin, Page, David F. Houston, William F. McCombs, and himself. Could he supply the names of Massachusetts Democrats who should be contacted? McCombs, campaign manager, invited suggestions as to proper men for the Wilson organization, particularly in the South.[92] And then, early in 1912, the bubble burst. Wilson decided that the support from *Harper's Weekly* was hurting his candidacy, and asked Harvey to withdraw it. As Martin explained it to Brown, the impression had got abroad in the West that the publication was John P. Morgan's mouthpiece. Brown agreed that Harvey had been treated shamefully, offered to help refute the charge, and concluded that fear of William Jennings Bryan had caused the move.[93]

It was at this stage that a friend wrote Brown to learn if he were still "a Republican or are you back with us Democrats?" [94] Brown replied that he was not a Republican, but that his first obligation had been "to smash Roosevelt." He hoped he could "support a Democrat this time. My greatest fear is that somebody with Bryanite notions of finance will be named." Judson Harmon and Oscar Underwood were trustworthy, but "Champ" Clark and Wilson were not. The latter "has been making some pretty wild speeches, & Clark's antecedents are thoroughly bad. Some personal correspondence with Wilson has failed to reassure me." He admitted that Wilson's nomination had improved the "political outlook . . . but I can't think much better of Bryan for it. The platform is pretty bad, & he is responsible." [95]

Brown was, as has been indicated, interested in currency reform. He had entrée to the Treasury Department through the assistant secretary, who wrote him that "no one in the country is working for the monetary legislation to more purpose than yourself. It is truly splendid." * Beyond articles in *Harper's Weekly,* Brown's contribution consisted mainly in promoting conferences and correspondence between administration men and leading Democrats

* Andrew to Brown, December 5, 1911, Brown Papers. See also Andrew to Brown, September 19, 1910, Brown Papers, in which Andrew wrote: "I have for sometime come to feel that your editorials in Harper's Weekly are the most sensible as also the most entertaining that are being written. In fact I have constituted myself a sort of press agent for the Weekly and go about telling everyone not to miss what you are saying from week to week."

such as Wilson, Underwood, and House. During and after the campaign of 1912, House plied Brown with innumerable questions on the monetary problem. "I feel that you know more about the Aldrich Bill," he wrote, "than anyone else in whom I have confidence." [96]

Displaying a lively interest in Wilson's appointments, Brown had a "deep design" to effect Charles W. Eliot's assignment to the State Department. "Think . . . what a figure Eliot would make in the approaching centenary of the Treaty of Ghent—& of Eliot & Bryce put in charge of the Panama controversy! For I believe a hint of the appointment would keep Bryce in Washington." [97] After learning that Bryan would be named, he wrote Martin: "It's going to be distasteful work defending the administration with a patent-medicine statesman at the head of the table." [98] Cabinet selections were "extremely disappointing—the weakest in my recollection." As to Josephus Daniels, "There would have been some excuse for giving him Frank Hitchcock's job—one smart Alec succeeding another." [99] Page was "not up to the place" as ambassador to England. "He is an expert hatcher of other birds' eggs; . . . Besides, Wilson is appointing too many Southerners." He could not accept House's explanation that able northern Democrats were as scarce as competent southern Republicans. It "simply isn't so. I've mentioned a few life-long Democrats in Massachusetts whom Wilson apparently hasn't considered." [100]

V

Brown did not long survive the return of the Democrats to power; and his death at the age of forty-five, on October 19, 1913, at New Canaan, Connecticut, terminated his efforts to contribute "a little towards making things go right in public affairs, which have been my life-long passion." [101] What he might have accomplished in the brief life-span allotted him had he not been handicapped by deafness and tuberculosis can only be conjectured. Although keenly aware of his condition and its effects on his career, he seldom complained of the isolation which it imposed. Writing to a friend in 1910, he expressed his pleasure in working for *Harper's Weekly,* but added: "The work comes too near being the only pleasure I get. Without the relief of a free body, the solitude of my life is at times about all I can stand for. . . . I know of course it's exile for mine to the finish; I am, I think a good deal deafer, and haven't the vitality for any sustained effort to get at the strangers and semi-strangers about me. But from a child I have foreboded precisely this closer and closer shutting-in of the world! It does not seem to me really manly or honest to try to make believe that work and thought and books are enough. One must be candid with life—most of all with one's own life." * But in spite of his isolation, he had managed to make an impression in the conduct of the Wilson campaign, and it is inspiring to speculate on how he would have performed as a United States senator or in some other public office. Regardless of these unrealized potentialities, however, his writings, both historical and political, represent a substantial contribution to the literature of his time; and through them his capacity for literary craftsmanship was firmly established.

* Brown to Thompson, May 20, 1910, Brown Papers. This pathetic note stands in sharp contrast to a telegram in reply to an invitation to attend a dinner in honor of his friend Caffey, who had been appointed solicitor in the Department of Agriculture: "Deeply regret inability to be present at dinner to Colonel Caffey. I raised him from a pup. Only trouble encountered was due to his notion that he was raising me. Submit to the company the question which of us did the better job. I can testify that he is a genuine farmer & true representative of Lowndes County [Alabama]. He may not tell us what is pure food but he can certainly tell us what is whiskey. Before deciding, he will sleep on it. He can sleep on anything. . . . I respectively suggest a toast to Wilson, Caffey, cut plug tobacco, real whiskey, and the principles of the Democratic party." Brown to Thomas W. Slocum, probably May 6, 1913, Brown Papers.

CHAPTER II

Herbert B. Adams: Southern Historical Scholarship at Johns Hopkins

In the last quarter of the nineteenth century the writing of history in the United States was undergoing profound changes.[1] The great literary historians, whose craftsmanship brought recognition of their wares, were passing from the scene; and a new era, with the college professor in the ascendancy, witnessed a radical departure in the treatment of the past. Monographic history became the order of the day. The new approach was supposedly impartial and scientific; the result was history that approximated truth but which, as critics said, was formless and dry-as-dust. Researchers consulted a multiplicity of sources in investigating local institutions and other minutiae, critically evaluated the evidence, cited authorities, and cast their findings in unliterary molds.

Other chroniclers than the literary masters antedated the "scientific" school and the dominance of the document. History was largely the avocational interest of clergymen, doctors, lawyers, and soldiers. They recorded both fact and fancy—a medley of reality and tradition. In the South in particular there were few if any literary luminaries preserving the past for posterity.[2] Histories of several southern states appeared in antebellum years, and some historical societies were established, a few of which began to assemble and publish records. But, for the most part, southerners were too busy defending their institutions and political and social creeds to become seriously interested in preserving records and in writing history. When the Civil War became a lost cause, sundry participants endeavored, through memoirs, reminiscences, and apologias, to justify the secession and to parade the military achievements of the Confederacy. State historical societies were revived or newly established, and Confederate veterans organized the Southern Historical Society which began a series of monthly publications.[3] A renaissance in state histories as well as in historical societies developed in postwar years. Yet postwar historical activity, like antebellum, was amateurish and unsystematic.

I

Critical and systematic study of history in the United States, it has long been recognized, began in the closing years of the nineteenth century, with the founding of the American Historical Association in 1884 as one of the early landmarks. Historians have also recognized Herbert Baxter Adams and his activities at the Johns Hopkins University as factors in the origin of a "scientific" school. Only recently have they come to appreciate the contributions of Adams and the university to the beginnings of southern historical scholarship.[4]

In a broader perspective Johns Hopkins was a significant factor in promoting a southern revival of learning in sundry fields of knowledge. While its influence on educational development in the South was recognized at the turn of the century, it has all but been forgotten in recent years. The editor of the *Southern History Association Publications* observed in 1901 that the school was "*The Greatest Southern University,* if we understand by that term an institution devoting a large part of its strength to postgraduate instruction." [5] Upon the retirement of Daniel C. Gilman as president of the university about the same time, the *Sewanee Review* said that the southern states' "educational history for the past quarter of a century has been largely that of the Johns Hopkins University. It is rare, indeed, to find at the South any college of note whose faculty has not been drawn largely from Baltimore, to say nothing of the impetus given everywhere to original research and to the publications of the results of such investigations." *

* Burr J. Ramage, in *Sewanee Review,* IX (July, 1901), 379. It is possible that the first part of this statement is an exaggeration. By 1896 sixteen colleges and universities south of Mason and Dixon's Line had the following numbers of Johns Hopkins students on their faculties: Woman's College of Baltimore, 10; University of the South, 8; Vanderbilt University, 6; Davidson College, 5; Louisiana State University, St. John's College, and Wake Forest College, 4 each; Central University, Georgetown College, University of Georgia, Richmond College, University of South

The South recovered slowly from the disastrous effects of the Civil War and Reconstruction. Despite a few signs of an educational renaissance, institutions of higher learning, many of them dating from antebellum days, were still bound by the chains of poverty. The founding of the generously endowed Johns Hopkins in 1876 provided an academic haven for students from the impoverished South. As one writer put it in 1900, while "the old and dismantled universities of the South were struggling to regain their vigor," the "newly created and fresh young leader, whom they soon learned to regard not as their rival, but as their inspiration and examplar," found her great opportunity.[6] The donor recognized the southern need for assistance, and requested in his will that the trustees establish scholarships for candidates from Maryland, Virginia, and North Carolina who possessed "character and intellectual promise." [7]

By 1886, a decade after the school was established, 235 men from these states had received free tuition, and 150 of them had been honored as Johns Hopkins Scholars. According to the president's report of that year, 419 students were enrolled from Maryland—nearly half of the student body. Virginia sent 26, North Carolina 24, Kentucky 18, the District of Columbia 15, and other southern states lesser numbers. "Very few Baltimoreans," it was asserted, "now go away from home to obtain a college education." [8] During the first twenty-three years of the university's life, Maryland contributed 1,455 students, and the whole South approximately 2,000 out of a total of 3,600. Dr. James C. Ballagh, instructor in the department of history, politics, and economics, exulted in 1900 that the founding of the Johns Hopkins had "checked the exodus of youth to foreign universities—a custom dating from colonial times at the South—by offering them not only equal facilities, but a training more American and more suited to our Southern needs." He pointed out that during "the past year 239 out of a total of 465 advanced students have been enrolled from the South." And, by the end of the century, some two hundred Johns Hopkins-trained men were teaching in southern states, and a like number were engaged in other professions or in business.[9]

Carolina, University of Texas, Trinity College, Tulane University, and the University of Virginia, 3 each. "A Survey of the Resources of the Johns Hopkins University in 1896," a forty-page supplement to the *Twenty-First Annual Report of the President of the Johns Hopkins University . . . 1896* (Baltimore, 1896), Supplement, 12–15.

The original faculty of the university drew heavily from the South, and by 1900 at least forty members—approximately a third of the whole—were "of Southern origins or connections." "This result, though without design," Ballagh asserted, "shows the broad liberality that governs the administration, and the creative work the University is doing for the South as well as for the rest of the country." [10]

If these expressions of indebtedness were true for the university as a whole, they were just as valid when applied to history and allied fields in particular. In appraising Adams' work near the close of his career, the *Sewanee Review* emphasized "the interest he has everywhere aroused in American history, and the publications which may be traced directly to his inspiration." While all parts of the nation had profited in these premises, no section "owes to the accomplished Director of the Historical Department of the Johns Hopkins University a heavier debt of gratitude than the Southern States. It is scarcely too much to say that the present interest this section manifests in history is contemporaneous with Dr. Adams. . . . And the occupant of many a chair of history at the various colleges of the South must always remember Dr. Adams as one who first taught him the true meaning of human progress, as well as the vital necessity of unceasing toil and publication." [11] Burr J. Ramage, Johns Hopkins doctor of philosophy and professor of law at the University of the South, declared in 1901 that the growing interest in southern history paralleled Adams' stimulating influence, "and in this regard that section owes him a lasting debt of gratitude. He never failed to call attention to the importance of preserving ancient records and letters, whilst the tardy activity of more than one commonwealth south of the Potomac in such matters as manuscript commissions, as well as the growing number of books devoted to southern history, may be traced in no small measure to . . . [his] influence." [12]

II

There was nothing in Adams' nativity or training to foreshadow a contribution to southern historical scholarship. He was born in 1850 at Shutesbury, Massachusetts, not far from Amherst. After graduating with honor at Phillips Exeter Academy in 1868, he entered Amherst College and received the bachelor's degree as valedictorian a quadrennium later. His fate was decided, he said, by a lecture on the philosophy of history by President Julius H.

Seelye who remarked "that history was the grandest study in the world." Following a year as teacher of classical history, mathematics, Latin, and Greek at Williston Seminary, Adams began an eventful three-year period abroad. He studied French at Lausanne, tarried a few months at Rome and Paris, and entered Heidelberg University in January, 1874. He mastered the German language in the home of Dr. Emil Otto, studied politics with Heinrich von Treitschke, Roman history with Wilhelm Ihne, and German philosophy and literature with Kuno Fischer. Treitschke's removal to the University of Berlin probably caused his own migration there for the winter semester of 1874–75. A necessity for economy required a return to Heidelberg where he completed the doctorate under the direction of Johann K. Bluntschli. This eminent political scientist exerted a profound influence upon his student. Scientifically trained by able German scholars, Adams returned to the United States in 1876 to accept a postdoctoral fellowship at the newly established Johns Hopkins University.[13]

For the next quarter of a century Adams labored at the Johns Hopkins to train students in scientific methodology, to inspire productive scholarship, to assemble collections of historical materials, and to locate Johns Hopkins men in responsible positions where they could establish colonies of the parent school. All of these objects were related in a mosaic. As so many southern men received their graduate training under Adams and his colleagues, it is appropriate to describe both mental stimulus and physical properties.

The hub of the department was, of course, the director, whose office served as editorial headquarters of the *Studies in Historical and Political Science* and the *Contributions to American Educational History* and whose prestige in the historical guild was enhanced by his position as secretary of the American Historical Association. As a productive scholar his major interest was institutional history. Two of his more significant monographs lay in the southern field: *The College of William and Mary* (1887) and *Thomas Jefferson and the University of Virginia* (1888), published in the contributions series. These studies of institutions of higher learning in Virginia provided a pattern for other scholars in evaluating educational development in the United States.

What were the qualities of the man responsible for the systematic study of American history and for the first graduate work in that subject that attracted southern scholars? Colleagues and students at Johns Hopkins, almost without exception, spoke of his inspiration and infectious enthusiasm. John M. Vincent, who succeeded him as head of the department, said that Adams' success did not emanate from profound lectures, though they were "sound and interesting." Rather his genius lay in "continually pointing to more work to be done, more fields to be cultivated and more reputations to be made." The successes of former graduate students, whether in publications or promotions, were paraded before their successors with hortatory effect. "Such things as these men did were within the reach of the young aspirant, and the effect was to spur every man to do something worthy of that company. . . . The results were unequal, but the inspiration was universal and lasting." [14] Adams' colleague in economics, Richard T. Ely, "soon discovered that capacity for leadership, for rallying men about him"; he gave Adams "credit for inventiveness in large plans and boldness in the execution of them"; he spoke of "his insight, his genius, in discovering talent where others did not see it." [15]

Student appraisals were in substantial agreement. A provocative statement by Adams in 1888, indicating that former Johns Hopkins students had exhausted local institutions, "the chief remaining opportunity for constructive work in American history," and that the European field would now provide topics for investigation, was a factor that prompted Frederick Jackson Turner to write "The Significance of the Frontier in American History." [16] But he conceded that Adams gave him "an added enthusiasm for historical research and a definite desire to relate history to the present. . . . His greatest power did not lie in keenness of scholarship nor in the critical character of his investigations; but I have never seen a man who could surpass him in inspiring men with enthusiasm for serious historical work." [17] Virginia-born Woodrow Wilson took the doctorate at the Johns Hopkins and later returned annually to give a series of lectures. Despite a critical attitude toward his mentor, Wilson sensed his points of strength. "If I were to sum up my impression of Dr. Adams," he recalled, "I should call him a great Captain of Industry, a captain in the field of systematic and organized scholarship. I think all his pupils would accord him mastery in the formulation of historical inquiry, in the suggestive stimulation of research, in the communication of methods and ideals. His head was a veritable clearing house of ideas in the field of historical study, and no one ever seriously studied under him who did not get, in its most serviceable form, the modern ideals of work upon the sources. . . . The thesis work done under him may fairly be said to have set the pace for university work in history throughout the United States." [18]

In evaluating Adams' contributions after the lapse of half a century, it should be noted that he was one of the American pioneers who employed the seminar or laboratory method. Instruction was given in various fields of history, politics, and economics through series of lectures by resident professors and visiting scholars, but the system's core was the "Seminary of History and Politics," often referred to as "Adams' Seminary." Embracing the department's teaching staff and all graduate students, it assembled on Friday evenings for two hours in the Bluntschli Library, a room on the third floor of McCoy Hall fitted up with cases, tables, and desks. The physical properties of this "laboratory" promoted a scholarly atmosphere. Tables were covered with magazines of history, economics, and politics; cases contained books and manuscripts of Bluntschli, Edouard Laboulaye, and Francis Lieber; and cases and walls were lined with busts and pictures of statesmen and historians. A special shelf was reserved for publications of former seminar students, and there was a complete file of the university *Studies in Historical and Political Science* and the *Contributions to American Educational History*.[19] Motivation was a work of genius: with classes "friendly conferences amid an environment of books," with portraits of eminent scholars to emphasize "the character of a family gallery or the congenial familiarity of a social club," and with the stimulating effect of books published by predecessors in the seminary—it is entirely understandable how students at the Johns Hopkins were fired with enthusiasm.[20] Usually an evening would be devoted to a single report, followed by discussion. Occasionally, a bifurcated program would be arranged, particularly when an off-campus scholar was available. Ordinarily a student made but one report a year, though an unusually industrious researcher might give two, and once, in 1887–88, William P. Trent reported three times on southern subjects. The secretaryship of the seminary rotated among the members, and the carefully transcribed minutes recorded the findings of embryo scholars.[21]

The Adams seminary was a unique organization. Walter Webb began a scintilating address on "The Historical Seminar: Its Outer Shell and Its Inner Spirit" by quoting the director: "It is easy . . . to outline a few external characteristics of the seminary, but difficult to picture its inner life." The outer shell at Johns Hopkins resembled a miniature social science association rather than Webb's small group of students gathered around a table engaged in the pursuit of a single idea. Eventually members totaled half a hundred with interests as diverse as the callings that awaited them. Among the heterogeneous participants were future historians, political scientists, economists, sociologists, philosophers, librarians, archivists, social workers, clergymen, attorneys, statisticians, editors, journalists, diplomats, public officials, high school teachers and administrators. More than a hundred received the doctorate during Adams' quarter century at the university; forty or fifty more remained for a year or two without acquiring the degree; and at least sixteen transferred to other schools in the United States or in Germany for completion of the doctorate.

An appraisal of so intangible a thing as the influence of Adams and the seminary is a difficult problem, though a roll call of students includes some well-known men. Among them were J. Franklin Jameson, Charles M. Andrews, Woodrow Wilson, Frederick Jackson Turner, Charles H. Haskins, James A Woodburn, Charles D. Hazen, John Holliday Latané, James A. James, John Dewey, John M. Vincent, Westel W. Willoughby, Jesse S. Reeves, Davis Rich Dewey, Albion W. Small, Frank W. Blackmar, Albert Shaw, and some of the southern men discussed in this chapter.[22] Thornstein Veblen completed the doctorate at Yale; Trent and John R. Commons terminated formal study without the doctor's degree.

If any seminal idea pervaded study at the Johns Hopkins, it was Adams' concept that institutional life in America descended principally from the "germs" of political forms prevalent among Teutonic tribes. How many of his students accepted the concept cannot be determined. Those who had not developed questioning minds must have done so, at least temporarily. Some of them, with Andrews and Turner notable examples, saw flaws in the idea and emphasized other controlling factors in the development of American institutions. Such men may have been a small minority. Students in any age are inclined to accept prevailing notions with only slight modification.

That Turner appreciated and also questioned the value of training at the university is apparent from contemporary and later correspondence. Letters to his mother and his fiancée reveal enthusiasm for the work he was doing. Turner was "growing like a plant in the sunshine"; he had "caught a little of the spirit of genuine scholarship." He singled out such men as Ely and Wilson for special commendation, but there is no reason to believe that he discounted the overall contribution of Adams, "a wonderfully energetic man—able to get work out of a crowd." His formal appraisal of the director in 1901 has already been quoted. Writing to Joseph Schafer thirty years later, he did "not think that the title, 'Fur Trade as an Institution,' was a gloss to Professor Adams," but rather an expression of his own desire "to conform to the institutional side of the Hopkins papers" and to provide institutions with "a wider interpretation than the purely civic or political conception that was so prevalent at that time." [23]

As one peruses the pages of the seminary minutes, it is difficult to conclude that many sessions attained Olympian heights, though secretaries may have done an inadequate job of reporting through failure to sense high-level thought. If published dissertations are a key to proper appraisal, it is quite likely that many seminar papers were routine performances. Only a modicum of discussion followed presentation of reports, though Adams always participated, often to commend.

No significant germinal books with Adams as author came out of the seminary. His forte lay in organizing, directing, suggesting, and encouraging, not in developing an overarching synthesis of an idea for posterity. The external characteristics were apparent, then as now. Did it have an inner life? Some students thought so. It was the capstone in the minglement of elements that gave them a sense of historianship; a spirit, an atmosphere, an *esprit de corps* that lifted them into the realm of understanding. Looking backward from the vantage point of successful attainments in their colonies, they recognized that intangible, undefinable thing known as graduate-mindedness.

III

The seminary was constantly at the focus of Adams' attention, but the director also provided supporting pilings for the superstructure. Rooms in McCoy Hall were arranged for students in European history, economics, jurisprudence, and comparative politics, each with appropriate books and portraits of outstanding scholars. A main lecture room served larger classes and also housed the department's archeological museum: collections of ancient implements, Lake Dwellers' relics, Egyptian antiquities, and Greek and Roman coins. Corridors housed government documents,

Alaskan artifacts, and assemblages of barbaric weapons and Indian relics.[24]

Of more significance to the present essay was the southern history room.[25] Southern scholars found the university a hospitable academic environment, and Adams sought materials on the literature and history of the southern region. The year 1891 witnessed the acquisition of two valuable collections. Books and pamphlets relating to slavery, assembled by James G. Birney and his son, General William Birney of Washington, were presented to the university. At the time this was said to be the largest collection of material on the subject.* Probably as a result of the Birney gift,† and following close on its heels, Colonel J. Thomas Scharf of Baltimore gave the university his collection of Americana. It consisted of "some 50,000 pamphlets especially on Southern history, the files of fifteen or more Confederate newspapers for all or portions of the Civil War period, 3000 broadsides, a large assortment of the papers of important private citizens, and a mass of official Maryland records." [26] "I have long noted with regret," the donor wrote in presenting his gift, "how imperfectly the history, general and local, of the Southern States has been written, and the fact that this imperfection has been largely due to the absence or inaccessibility of material. No great collection of Southern historical documents exists. It is my hope that the Johns Hopkins University, founded by a Southern man in a Southern city, may see the way to do for the South what Northern universities have done for the North, and become the general repository for Southern history." [27]

Adams himself added to the southern collection by contributing from his personal library sundry books and pamphlets on literature as well as history, on one occasion in the late 1890's donating a hundred volumes. About the same time a former student, Stephen B. Weeks, presented some works on North Carolina history. In

* William Birney thought of giving his collection to the American Historical Association but correspondence with Adams resulted in presentation to the Johns Hopkins University library. See William Birney to Herbert B. Adams, January 12, 1891, Herbert Baxter Adams Papers (Johns Hopkins University library, Baltimore, Md.).

† Birney to Adams, May 8, 1891, Adams Papers. Birney wrote: "I am glad to learn that Col. Scharf has presented his historical collection to the Johns Hopkins University, and I am much gratified by your assurance that my donation may have led to his. Let us hope that the two examples may be followed by many owners of historical papers and documents." He added that he was aware of Scharf's reputation "as a very good rebel."

1900 Adams gave the university his whole library, comprising some 3,600 bound volumes and an equal number of pamphlets. At the turn of the century the Johns Hopkins library exceeded one hundred thousand volumes and housed about that number of pamphlets. What proportion of its holdings represented history cannot be known, but a few years earlier the library boasted 18,000 volumes and 50,000 pamphlets in that category.[28] By the end of Adams' period there must have been a few thousand volumes on the South, in addition to manuscripts and pamphlets.[29] Interest in this field soon lapsed, and several years passed before other universities in the South began to build up southern collections.

Although Johns Hopkins had been in existence for over a score of years before formal courses in southern history were organized, from the very beginning of Adams' seminary students had been investigating local institutions and political and economic problems in the South.[30] They reported upon them in the seminar, and many of their monographs were published in the university studies series. As interest in the southern region grew, Adams provided special lectures in that field. In the 1890–91 session, J. Franklin Jameson, who received the doctorate at the university in 1882, gave ten lectures on "the Constitutional and Political History of the Southern States." A decade later David F. Houston, then of the University of Texas, lectured upon aspects of the doctrine of nullification, and in 1901 John S. Bassett gave a series of three lectures on the Negro.[31]

Meanwhile, in the second semester of the 1897–98 session, Ballagh inaugurated the first systematic course in the history of the South. It was described as "*Southern Economic History,* with eight graduate students, one hour weekly. . . . The economic development of the South from 1607 to 1860 was illustrated by special lectures on Agriculture, the Land System, Labor System, Staple Products, Extensive Cultivation, the Plantation System, and the Industrial Organization of each of the Colonies. The influence of customary and statute law, physical environment, political and commercial relations at home and abroad was also indicated." This course was supplemented by a weekly "*Conference on Southern History,*" with an enrollment of seven graduate students. They were instructed in the use of the Birney and Scharf collections and materials available in the Peabody Library, the Maryland Historical Society, and the Enoch Pratt Free Library. The purpose of the conference, Ballagh said, "was to encourage coöperative research in the southern field."[32] Under his direction students not only investigated topics in the history of the South but also compiled, over a period of years, "a descriptive bibliography of manuscript sources and research work in southern history."[33]

From 1898 until 1903 Ballagh gave either the course or the conference, sometimes both. In the 1900–1901 session he taught southern history to eight graduates. "The lectures were the result of original research," the description indicated, "and discussed the development of the land and labor systems of the American colonies; the peculiarities of Southern economic development and their bearing upon political history in the questions of the tariff, slavery, public lands and improvements; the creation and material development of the territory in the Southwest and West attached to the Old South; the influence of Southern agriculture upon incipient commerce and manufactures, etc. . . . The sources for original work in this field were pointed out to the class, and researches in phases of the history of Alabama, South Carolina, Virginia, and North Carolina were prosecuted by members of the class."[34]

Beginning in the fall of 1903 and continuing until 1913 when he resigned to accept a professorship at the University of Pennsylvania, Ballagh alternated a course in the history of American slavery with another in the history of secession in the United States.[35] In his seminar in American history, students investigated southern topics, and some able men, as Douglas S. Freeman and H. J. Eckenrode, presented dissertations in that field. With Ballagh's departure from the university, interest in southern history disappeared. Presentation of courses on the South in the 1890's and the early years of the twentieth century were an important integrant in the development of southern historical scholarship. Offerings in southern history began to multiply, slowly at first and then more rapidly, until by the 1920's thirty or forty schools were presenting aspects or periods of the history of the South.[36] By 1940 more than a hundred colleges and universities offered one or more courses in southern history.

It should be noted also that, with few exceptions, Adams-trained men were productive scholars. He himself established a modest publication record, but productivity was not responsible for his reputation among a growing clientele. His contribution lay in the spirit of scientific research that permeated Johns Hopkins students. They became saturated with an enthusiastic zeal for research and writing. Of the scores of former students—many of them in southern institutions—who corresponded with Adams, a large proportion wrote about the projects they had under way, the discovery of source materials that would promote research, or the problem of publishing completed manuscripts. Frequently they apologized for lack of productivity, with heavy teaching loads and other routine duties as an explanation.[37] "In the field of Southern historical writing," said the editor of the *Southern History Association Publications,* "it would not be far from accurate to say that Doctor Adams gave that great and greatly neglected subject almost the first well directed impulse that it had ever received." [38]

One has only to peruse the volumes of the Johns Hopkins University *Studies in Historical and Political Science* from their origin in 1883 to understand the importance of southern history as a field of research. Perhaps half a hundred monographs in the first nineteen volumes treated southern subjects, with an increasing proportion of space devoted to the field as time passed. A complete bibliography of the writings of students and faculty members during the last quarter of the nineteenth century is even more revealing. The astounding factor is the volume of productivity. It required 158 printed pages to list articles, monographs, and books of the group, together with brief academic notes about the authors.[39] Of the total output a larger proportion than one might suppose dealt with the history of the southern region. Analyzing the compilation in 1902, William K. Boyd, then a graduate student at Columbia University, found that "fifty-three Southern members of the Department of History have written 748 monographs, books or articles, of which 316 have been specifically on the South, while non-Southern men have written 51 articles in addition upon the South." He concluded that "such a record is one to be honored in any field of research, especially in one so important and long neglected." [40]

IV

Despite the volume of productivity by Johns Hopkins men in the southern field, historical scholarship in the South was still in its infancy. Much of the writing down to 1901 was superficial; many of the articles were extremely local in nature and represented little investigation; and a considerable proportion of the monographs published in the studies and elsewhere were based upon meager sources of information. Like their colleagues in the North, southern men belonged to that incipient "scientific" school that emphasized historical accuracy rather than acceptable diction. If they presented little interpretation or avoided legitimate use of imagination, they were following inexorable precepts of the new technique. If they utilized limited sources, it was partly because there were few great manuscript or printed collections for them to draw upon. If they misquoted or miscited authorities, they were guilty of the same faults that still afflict the profession. In evaluating their work, it should be remembered that they were pioneers in a new approach. But when all these imperfections are indicated, the fact remains that a serious beginning had been made toward systematic and critical treatment of the South's past.

The increasing number of Johns Hopkins graduate students in history, political science, and economics from the South resulted from several factors, among them the conviction that Baltimore was a southern city, the objective approach to the study of the subjects, and the large number of fellowships available to residents of Maryland, Virginia, and North Carolina. The most tangible of these factors was, of course, financial aid; the most substantial, the opportunity to study local institutions and other problems under competent and impartial direction. A roll call of southerners trained in history and allied social studies at the Johns Hopkins suggests the university's significant influence on the South. Among those who received the doctorate before Adams' death, and then did creditable work in the South, were Benjamin W. Arnold, James C. Ballagh, John S. Bassett, Charles H. Brough, Julian A. C. Chandler, William S. Drewry, Samuel E. Forman, Guy C. Lee, Alvin F. Lewis, Henry R. McIlwaine, John H. T. McPherson, Colyer Meriwether, George Petrie, Burr J. Ramage, Daniel R. Randall, Franklin L. Riley, Lawrence F. Schmeckebier, Enoch W. Sikes, St. George L. Sioussat, Francis E. Sparks, Bernard C. Steiner, Charles C. Weaver, and Stephen B. Weeks. Still other southerners enrolled who did not complete work for the doctorate but whose names are written, some large and some small, in the register of southern historical scholarship. Some of them were Henry E. Chambers, Shirley C. Hughson, Edward Ingle, Charles E. Jones, and William P. Trent. Walter H. Page held a fellowship from 1876 to 1878 and studied the classics with Basil L. Gildersleeve, but his publications were listed in the bibliography of Adams' department.

And because of their influence on the South and their interest in the region, the names of Jameson and Woodrow Wilson should not be ignored.

Several of these Johns Hopkins students left a considerable impress upon historical scholarship in the South.[41] Bassett and Trent were the most versatile in their interests and accomplishments. Both were southern liberals, extremely dissatisfied with intellectual backwardness in the region, and each founded a quarterly magazine to provide a forum of liberal thought and literary criticism. While serving as professor of history and English at the University of the South in the last decade of the nineteenth century, Trent wrote some notable books on southern leaders, inventoried the South's belated beginnings in preserving records and in writing history, and gave the *Sewanee Review* a character and reputation that made it a dynamic magazine. For a dozen years, beginning in 1894, Bassett served as professor of history at Trinity College, where he labored to promote state and regional development. He published monographs on North Carolina history, assembled southern materials in the college library, inaugurated courses in the history of his state, founded the *Historical Papers of the Trinity College Historical Society* and the *South Atlantic Quarterly,* and impressed upon his students a detached and critical historical attitude.

A great teacher who emerged from Adams' tutelage was George Petrie, whose fifty-five years of service at Alabama Polytechnic Institute inspired a score of southerners with a genuine love for history and an ambition to pursue graduate study. The list is impressive. If he had done nothing more than incite an interest in history in men the caliber of Walter L. Fleming, Frank L. Owsley, Watson Davis, Albert B. Moore, Alfred W. Reynolds, Herman C. Nixon, and Charles S. Davis, his contribution would be worthy of recording. With limited resources in an agricultural and mechanical college, he presented history by the "laboratory" method, found ample illustration in southern leadership, and vitalized local history by dignifying Alabama in the curriculum.

Perhaps Franklin Riley's greatest contribution lay in a revival of the Mississippi Historical Society and in the inauguration of its series of publications. Here he was emulating the example as well as the method of Thomas M. Owen of Alabama. But Riley's own service as editor and contributor provides a permanent place for him in southern historiography. Nor should it be forgotten that he inaugurated at the University of Mississippi, where he taught from 1897 to 1914, one of the early courses in the history of the South. His subsequent career at Washington and Lee University did not yield the constructive accomplishments of his Mississippi tenure.

Other editors of historical series who also served as librarians were Bernard Steiner and Henry McIlwaine. After teaching history and English at Hampden-Sydney College for a number of years, McIlwaine became librarian of the Virginia State Library. In that capacity he edited the *Journals of the House of Burgesses of Virginia* (a work begun by John P. Kennedy) and the *Legislative Journals of the Council of Colonial Virginia.* Steiner, librarian of the Enoch Pratt Free Library of Baltimore, taught history at the Johns Hopkins and elsewhere, wrote some meritorious monographs, and produced biographies of such Maryland statesmen as Reverdy Johnson, Henry Winter Davis, Roger B. Taney, and James McHenry. He served as editor of the *Archives of Maryland* in 1900 and again in 1916 until his death a decade later.

As editor of the *Southern History Association Publications,* Colyer Meriwether performed a commendable function for an organization which, with limited resources in a period when southern scholarship was still unfledged, struggled to preserve a record of the South's past. He was one of the earliest critics of the "scientific" school of monographers and took its devotees to task for writing history that no one read, not even those who attempted syntheses. Beyond his editorial function, he produced a valuable biography of Raphael Semmes.

Two Baltimore journalists, Edward Ingle and Guy Lee, made creditable contributions to history and near-history. Ingle is remembered chiefly for his *Southern Sidelights* (1896), a notable work that pictured antebellum economic and social life, but he also published books on the District of Columbia Negro and southern material progress, and he contributed sundry articles to the *Southern Farm Magazine* and other periodicals. As a publicist, Lee edited the Baltimore *Sun* and some nonhistorical series of books. For a time he taught history at Johns Hopkins and comparative politics at George Washington University, and he also wrote some history and biography, including a study of the Civil War and a life of Robert E. Lee.

After a tour of duty at Smith College, St. George Sioussat was appointed professor of history and economics at the University of the South in 1904, and he served as professor of history at

Vanderbilt University from 1911 until 1917. During his last two years at Vanderbilt he edited the *Tennessee Historical Magazine*. His early monographs were on phases of Maryland history, and several of his articles dealt with the history of the South. In 1917 he accepted a call to a northern university.

In the early 1890's Stephen B. Weeks taught history and political science for a biennium at Trinity College, where he founded the Trinity College Historical Society. He was also one of the founders of the Southern History Association. His monographs on North Carolina and southern history were serious pieces of investigation; his indexes to the North Carolina census of 1790 and to the commonwealth's colonial and state records were a tangible service to researchers. For several years he served the United States Bureau of Education as editor and historian. His contributions to southern educational history were particularly significant. These included histories of public school education in Arkansas, Alabama, and Tennessee, a bibliography of Confederate textbooks, and a study of the origins of southern common schools. Weeks assembled an extensive collection of Caroliniana, comprising ten thousand books and pamphlets, acquired after his death by the University of North Carolina.

At least four Johns Hopkins men of Adams' period attained college presidencies in the South: Julian Chandler at William and Mary, Enoch Sikes at Coker and Clemson, Charles Weaver at Rutherford, Davenport, Emory and Henry, and Martha Washington, and Franklin Riley at Hillman. Chandler had previously taught history at William and Mary and at Richmond College and had written some monographs on Virginia history; Sikes had served as professor of history and political economy at Wake Forest College and had produced some studies in North Carolina history; and Charles Weaver had been little interested in research and writing.

The only Hopkinsian of southern origins to attain political distinction in the national picture was Woodrow Wilson. Of the southerners who remained in the South, Charles Brough achieved most recognition in the political arena. He became professor of economics at Mississippi College and wrote monographs on taxation, banking, and transportation in his native state. In 1903 he became professor of economics at the University of Arkansas, attained prominence as a lecturer on economic and social problems, sponsored Wilson's candidacy for the presidency in 1912, and served as governor of Arkansas, 1917–21.

The accomplishments of a few other Johns Hopkins men may be considered briefly. After a year as instructor at the University of Michigan, John H. T. McPherson served for half a century as head of the history and political science department at the University of Georgia. Burr J. Ramage became dean of the law school at the University of the South, associate editor of the *Sewanee Review,* and author of articles on southern subjects. Henry E. Chambers was interested primarily in secondary education and participated in Chautauqua and Normal work. As a historian, his study of the Mississippi Valley in its early years and a three-volume history of Louisiana brought considerable recognition. Early writings of Samuel E. Forman treated Thomas Jefferson and Philip Freneau; later he concentrated upon general American history and civics. Lawrence F. Schmeckebier's dissertation dealt with the American party in the state of Maryland, and Daniel R. Randall, a Baltimore attorney, published some studies in Maryland history.

V

These and other Johns Hopkins-trained men who passed through Adams' seminary in the last two decades of the nineteenth century wrote and taught southern history, established historical societies and mediums of publication, gathered the raw materials of southern history into libraries and archives, administered southern colleges, and otherwise contributed to the origins of historical scholarship in the South. Adams' premature death in 1901, at the age of fifty-one, was an irreparable loss to historical activity at the Johns Hopkins. Where could the university turn for a recognized scholar to succeed him, especially one who would continue to attract students from the South?

Ira Remsen, who succeeded Gilman as president, sought the assistance of Bassett and Frederic Bancroft in inducing William A. Dunning to accept the directorship of the department. The Columbia University professor had already acquired a reputation as an impartial authority on the Civil War and Reconstruction periods, and graduates of southern colleges and universities were manifesting confidence by enrolling in his classes. Early in 1903 Bassett and Bancroft approached Dunning on the possibility of transferring to Baltimore, a suggestion which "flattered and honored" the man who was soon to be affectionately regarded as the "Old Chief" by a growing southern clientele. A definite offer was made the following summer which Bassett thought superior to the position at Columbia "because of its larger opportunity, the greater freedom of personal control and its somewhat increased salary." As late as August 25 Dunning assured Bassett that he would accept the call because of the "excellent prospect for good scholarly work" at the Johns Hopkins. It soon developed that a decision would depend upon the state of his health. Returning to New York from a summer vacation in New Hampshire, he took "the opinion of two high grade (& of course high priced) physicians," who said he "would incur grave risks in undertaking a task involving unaccustomed and nerve-straining duties." He would therefore have to "settle down in the old rut" and even relinquish the editorship of the *Political Science Quarterly*.[42] With Dunning at the helm the Johns Hopkins could have continued its dominant position in the field of southern history; his continuance at Columbia transferred the center of southern historical scholarship from Baltimore to New York.

Many years later Johns Hopkins would revive its interest in southern history, and able scholars of a new school would make enduring contributions in recording and interpreting the South's past. By that time the region's history and its place in the national picture would be fairly well established. Adams was a pioneer whose great service lay in starting an exploring expedition.

CHAPTER III

William P. Trent: The "Mountain Fastness" at Sewanee

William Peterfield Trent achieved merited recognition as professor of English literature following his appointment to Columbia University in 1900, but in the closing years of the nineteenth century, he was an enthusiastic devotee of southern history.[1] A native of the South, student in southern universities, and teacher of history and English in a Tennessee college, he pioneered as a promoter of historical activity and as a chronicler of the South's past. His *William Gilmore Simms,* berated by South Carolinians and commended by northern reviewers, has not been superseded during the sixty years that have passed since its publication. Trent's critical appraisals of southern statesmen have long since been forgotten, though some of his interpretive sketches of antebellum southerners have a distinctly modern flavor, and several viewpoints have been incorporated, perhaps unconsciously, in recent historical writings. Trent successfully weathered storms of protest from southern conservatives, but he welcomed the call to a northern university at the turn of the century.[2]

I

Trent was born in Richmond, Virginia, November 10, 1862. His paternal ancestors had been substantial citizens of the Old Dominion since colonial days. As landholders, tobacco planters, merchants, and doctors, they had prospered until the Civil War destroyed the family competence. Joseph Trent, William's grandfather, received the M.D. degree at the University of Pennsylvania; Peterfield Trent, his father, graduated in medicine at the University of Georgia, enjoyed a lucrative practice in the last antebellum decade, and sacrificed his fortune to the Confederate cause while serving as a surgeon. Trent's mother, nee Lucy Carter Burwell, counted prominent Virginians among her ancestors.

With adequate preparation at Thomas Norwood's University School in Richmond, Trent entered the University of Virginia in the fall of 1880. He studied ancient and modern languages, history and moral philosophy, chemistry and mathematics, natural history and geology, numbering among his teachers George F. Holmes, Charles S. Venable, and William M. Fontaine, and among fellow students Woodrow Wilson, Richard H. Dabney, and Oscar W. Underwood. Before graduating in 1883 with the bachelor of letters degree, he had served first as assistant editor and then as editor-in-chief of the *Virginia University Magazine* and had acquired considerable reputation as a literary critic. Another year at the university yielded further study of history, mathematics, and science—and the degree of master of arts. The years from 1884 to 1887 were devoted to teaching in Richmond schools and to reading law.

In the fall of 1887 Trent entered Johns Hopkins University for advanced graduate study, attracted there, as were so many scholars from the South, by the enviable reputation of Herbert B. Adams as an impartial teacher of history and politics and as a sympathetic and inspiring director of graduate study. Courses in finance with Richard T. Ely, historical jurisprudence with George H. Emmott, administration with Woodrow Wilson, and American history with J. Franklin Jameson supplemented Trent's work in ancient politics and Russian history with Adams. He was also a member of the seminary of historical and political science, directed by Adams but embracing other members of the departmental faculty. Trent performed before the seminary on at least three occasions. His report on "The Influence of the University of Virginia on Southern Life & Thought" received Adams' commendation, especially for its statistical tables indicating fields of activity entered by more than nine thousand graduates and former students in the half century from 1825 to 1874.[3] This study was honored by inclusion as a chapter in Adams' *Thomas Jefferson and the University of Virginia* (1888), to which Trent also contributed a bibliography of publications by the University of Virginia faculty, 1825–87.[4]

A second report considered "Jefferson and the Gilmer Correspondence," a by-product of Trent's association with Adams in the preparation of *Thomas Jefferson and the University of Virginia.*[5] From John Gilmer of Chatham, Virginia, Adams received a parcel of Francis Walker Gilmer letters which were turned over to Trent for recommendation as to their value in connection with Adams' study. The letters seemed largely irrelevant to the central theme, but Trent was encouraged to edit them for separate publication. Correspondence with his mother relative to the assignment led to the discovery of another group of letters. Selections from the two parcels, with copious editorial material—running comment, biographical sketches, and footnotes—were published under the title, *English Culture in Virginia* (1889). Trent performed his editorial tasks creditably as he set forth the career of the brilliant young lawyer and writer who was sent to England in 1824 to choose half a dozen men to fill chairs at the new University of Virginia.[6]

It was unusual for a student to make two reports to the seminary in an academic year; yet in the spring Trent read a third paper. His subject this time was "The Attitude of the Roman Catholic Church toward Education, Exhibited in the Acts & Decrees of the Third Plenary Council of Baltimore." [7] Industry was a characteristic trait.

Before leaving Johns Hopkins to accept a position at the University of the South in the fall of 1888, Trent had become a devoted admirer of Adams and an enthusiastic promoter of the Baltimore school. He hoped to return to complete requirements for the doctorate, but a combination of circumstances prevented further formal education.

II

At the University of the South, Trent became professor of English and acting professor of history. The appointment to a professorship in English seemed anomalous, for he had taken no work in that field either at the University of Virginia or at the Johns Hopkins. But his knowledge of ancient and modern foreign languages served him well, and independent reading partially compensated for lack of classroom instruction. It is therefore possible that, even at the beginning of his tenure, his courses in English language and literature, rhetoric, and American literature did not suffer greatly because of inadequate preparation. In the other department which he headed, Trent gave courses in political economy, politics, and general history.[8] Eventually he came to look upon literature as his primary interest, but in his early years at the University of the South, history was clearly his major objective. He identified himself on the title pages of *English Culture in Virginia* and *William Gilmore Simms* (1892) as "Professor of History in the University of the South." Writing to Adams in 1890, he complained that "it is impossible to concentrate my work on history when I have to teach English and Literature."[9] Soon thereafter he became mildly interested in a professorship of history and political science at the University of Georgia. Comparing his present position with the new opportunity, he wrote Adams: "I am worked very hard here on two very different branches—there I would only have to work in my specialty. . . . As I have often told you my ambition is to do good historical work & to make whatever mark I can in that way."[10] He did not confine his research and writing to history, however; in 1893 he explained to his Johns Hopkins mentor why he was working on a text in literature and an article on the teaching of the subject. "You mustn't think . . . that I am deserting history. I am still meditating deep schemes in that direction."[11]

Southern historical scholarship was in its infancy when Trent began his labors at Sewanee. Adams had produced two notable monographs on higher education in Virginia; the Johns Hopkins-trained Edward Ingle had been writing newspaper and magazine articles on the South since the early 1880's, albeit his first significant work, *Southern Sidelights* (1896), was still several years in the future; and a few other Johns Hopkins men, as Colyer Meriwether, Burr J. Ramage, Daniel R. Randall, Stephen B. Weeks, and Lewis W. Wilhelm, became productive scholars contemporaneously with Trent. At Columbia University William A. Dunning had begun his researches on the Civil War and Reconstruction, but it was more than a decade before he began turning out doctoral candidates with dissertations in that period of American history. Philip A. Bruce published *The Plantation Negro as a Freeman* (1889) the year after Trent went to the University of the South; the first of his trilogy on seventeenth-century Virginia—his *Economic History*—did not materialize until 1895. *The Genesis of the United States* (1890), by Alexander Brown, antedated Trent's own major work, the biography of William Gilmore Simms, by only two years; and a few other meritorious works by self-made historians supplemented an incipient scientific historiography.[12]

The student of historical activity in the South is indebted to Trent for inventories taken in 1889 and 1891. He realized that the southern states were apathetic toward their past, but he wished to determine whether "the cause of history [was] practically dead at the South." Consequently he made inquiry of competent people in the region, including the secretaries of the several historical associations. He discovered that there were no societies in Arkansas, Florida, Mississippi, and Texas, and that those in other southern states were handicapped by small memberships, inadequate support, and limited personnel. A few of the societies had small holdings, supplemented by the independent collections of the Virginia State Library, the Charleston Library, and the Howard Memorial Library in New Orleans. Three paragraphs were sufficient to list books and monographs in preparation. "It is obvious," Trent concluded, "that there is no overwhelming zeal for historical studies at the South"; but he was hopeful that the next decade would witness an awakening of interest. Meanwhile, there was "no reason why historians from other sections should neglect so promising a field." Awaiting the appearance of "the future historian of the South," materials should be assembled for his use. "For my own part," Trent wrote, "I care not from what State or section he comes, provided he come quickly. I know more than one scholar, born without the Southern pale, into whose hands I would trust our history without a fear; and I cannot help smiling, to think how thoroughly the tables would be turned, if it were a Northern historian who should first give to the world a true and complete history of the Southern people." [13]

On December 21, 1891, Trent read a paper, "Notes on Recent Work in Southern History," before the Virginia Historical Society. The data assembled from correspondence with key persons in the South indicated "that the Southern people are beginning to see the necessity for encouraging their historical students, and that the work these students are doing is being done on right lines." [14] Although he found some encouraging evidence from most of the southern states, he emphasized historical activity in Maryland, Virginia, the Carolinas, and Tennessee, though more often it was the work of a few individuals than of a state historical society. He could point enthusiastically to "the fact that the Johns Hopkins University of Baltimore is the centre of historical investigation in this country. It is no exaggeration to say, that the work Professor Herbert B. Adams is doing with his graduate classes is likely to be *the* most important factor in the future development of historical studies in the South. Every year Dr. Adams sends out one or more young Southerners trained for historical pursuits, ready to teach history in our colleges, and eager to prosecute historical researches in the history of their respective States. I know of three such students sent to Southern colleges within the past year." He called attention to the assembling of materials in the Johns Hopkins library, particularly the J. Thomas Scharf and William Birney collections, and to the monographs on southern subjects written by Adams and his students.[15]

In the Old Dominion the publications of two members of the Virginia Historical Society were noteworthy: William Wirt Henry's *Patrick Henry* (1891) and Alexander Brown's *Genesis of the United States.* In the Old North State William L. Saunders' *Colonial Records of North Carolina* (1886–90), the constructive influence of Kemp P. Battle, and the monographs of Stephen B. Weeks and others had probably incited her southern neighbor to activity. A state historical society committee, headed by William A. Courtenay, had aroused public opinion in South Carolina and influenced its legislature to pass a bill providing funds to copy additional colonial records in the London Public Record Office. The establishment of a chair of history and political science at the University of Georgia was an encouraging sign; and the publication of *The Origin and Growth of the English Constitution* (1889) by a Mobile lawyer, Hannis Taylor, was tangible evidence that "no one need despair of the future of historical scholarship in the South." [16]

Trent detailed one of his own activities, the founding of the Sewanee Historical Society at the University of the South. It was "organized like a German seminary" with a council that "meets frequently, hears papers read, and is responsible for the proper use of the materials gathered by the Society." The immediate objective was a compilation of a history of the college. The founder hoped to interest students, alumni, and friends, and thereby procure southern imprints, correspondence, magazines, and newspapers,[17] but by 1895 the society had become defunct. Like many other evidences of historical development that Trent thought he saw, progress was more apparent than real.

Four years later Trent addressed a newly formed Vanderbilt Southern History Society at Nashville. As he had made no new inventory of historical activity, he talked about the assembling of records and the writing of history that was literary as well as scientific. Despite the failure of his own society at Sewanee, he encouraged the Nashville group to believe that it could succeed.[18]

As a promoter of organized historical activity, Trent was more successful than in translating his own preachments into tangible results.

Two of Trent's early monographs deserve mention. In 1889 Jameson edited *Essays in the Constitutional History of the United States in the Formative Period, 1775–1789,* written by graduates, students, and faculty members at Johns Hopkins. To this volume Trent contributed a study of "The Period of Constitution-Making in the American Churches." [19] And in the first volume of the *American Historical Review* he published perhaps his most scholarly monographic article, "The Case of Josiah Philips," a study of a bill of attainder levied against the insurrectionary leader of a band of robbers in Princess Anne and Norfolk counties, Virginia, "who for three years (1775–1778) gave the authorities of his state more trouble than any one citizen had done since the death of Nathaniel Bacon." [20]

III

At the invitation of Charles D. Warner, editor of the "American Men of Letters Series," Trent contracted in 1890 to write a biography of William Gilmore Simms, and much of his time during the next two years was devoted to that task. Student of both literature and history, he was a happy choice to appraise the work of Simms as poet, novelist, and historian. His research was fairly exhaustive; he consulted sundry manuscripts as well as printed materials, visiting Charleston, Richmond, Washington, and Baltimore to assemble evidence. From his subject's friends and relatives in South Carolina and elsewhere, he sought letters and reminiscences.[21] Unpublished sources included several pages of autobiographical memoranda; over a thousand letters from Simms's correspondents in various parts of the country during the quarter century preceding 1870; and 175 of Simms's own letters to such men as Beverley Tucker, W. Porcher Miles, and Paul Hamilton Hayne.[22] Trent was especially elated at finding a parcel of letters to Tucker. "Some of the quotations I shall make from these letters will, I think, be very interesting—especially one in which Simms practically confesses that the Secessionists must use the arts of *conspirators.* He uses the word conspiracy right out & if I mistake not, the letter will be *nuts* to some historians. My own comments shall be brief as I don't care to get into hot water." [23]

An appendix catalogued an extensive bibliography of Simms's

works, mainly "the result of individual investigation," though previous lists had been examined. Poetry, romances, novelettes, collected stories, histories, and biographies, together with a few miscellaneous items, totaled eighty titles; his significant magazine articles numbered twenty-nine, and five others were "unhesitatingly assigned to Simms." Nine periodicals and newspapers which Simms served in an editorial capacity were listed in chronological order, and sundry translations and English reprints were also included. Trent had consulted the original issues of most of these titles; only two had been unattainable in any edition.[24]

It seemed to Trent that his task was interminable, but considering his heavy teaching load and the necessity for research in eastern libraries, his progress should not have been discouraging. He complained of having so few books in his "mountain fastness," and of procrastination on the part of South Carolinians who promised material aid. He delved into the historical background, he read "dreary" American novels, and he studied magazines of Simms's generation.[25] Research completed, he speeded his pen to meet the publisher's deadline. The first draft of 850 manuscript pages was composed in less than two months despite fifteen hours a week in the classroom; a revision which deleted 150 pages required a fortnight. This accelerated program left him "nearly dead," and he reflected over his experience "with a kind of shuddering wonder." [26]

From Trent's letters to Adams it is evident that he did not intend to treat his subject in a vacuum; and in his preface he explained why he had put so much history in a biography. As "Simms was a typical Southerner," his character could be completely revealed only through repeated allusion to southern history, which, according to Trent, had "been little studied and still less understood." His extended treatment "of Simms's political career was introduced with no desire to rake up dead issues or to say unpleasant things. I saw no way by which a conscientious biographer of Simms could avoid the mire of ante-bellum politics, so I waded in with very little hope that I should get through undraggled." [27]

Trent did not anticipate the full extent of the caustic criticism in store for him. But before the ebullient tirade is reviewed, it is expedient to analyze his account of Simms and his background. Beginning with the overemphasized premise that the South with its plantations and slaves and chivalry was a replica of feudal

England, he argued that southerners "were leading a primitive life,—a life behind the age." It afforded "few opportunities to talents that did not lie in certain beaten grooves," it "choked all thought and investigation that did not tend to conserve existing institutions and opinions," and it "rendered originality scarcely possible except under the guise of eccentricity." Slavery and feudalism, each dependent upon the other, were the twin evils that repressed talent and prevented a wholesome intellectual activity. The southerner's "imagination was dwarfed because his mind was never really free, [and] also because his love of ease rarely permitted him to exercise the faculty." [28]

It was Trent's belief that slavery shackled the master more than the slave, a view shared by some latter-day historians. Recent investigations have disproved his assertion—a traditional concept emanating from antebellum travelers—that the plantation system excluded yeoman farmers, artisans, and tradespeople from the South. The "mental and moral" evils "of overlordship—arrogance, contempt for inferiors, inertia of mind and body"—precluded state and individual virility.[29] He declared that slavery hindered the development of southern literature. The *Southern Review,* "conducted by brilliant men" and "backed by public sentiment," could not contribute toward the creation of southern letters in thralldom's shadow, and the *Southern Literary Messenger* illustrated "the thin quality" of the Old South's literature. In its early years the contrast with northern periodicals was less than after mid-century, "which is precisely what we should expect when we remember that freedom elevates, while slavery either keeps at one level, or lowers." [30]

Trent's philosophy was a doctrine of progress. In discussing the presence of a nationalistic feeling in the North and an absence of it in the South, he placed another charge against slavery. The only tie that united the southern states was their peculiar institution, but it "could not develop a true national feeling; for there must be a consciousness of progress, a desire to share in and further a common civilization. But progress and slavery are natural enemies, and the South had no great desire to progress except in her own way, which was really retrogression." [31] The present South was different; it was progressive. Trent, a pioneer of the New South who helped to usher it into existence, closed the chapter on the war period by writing: "For out of the ashes of the old South, a new and better South has arisen. A disintegrated and primitive people have become united among themselves and with their former foes, and are moving forward upon the path of progress. Instead of the past, they have the future to look upon; instead of a mere State, they have a nation to trust in and to maintain. They have retained all that was good in the old South, and to their inherited virtues and powers they will add, as the years go by, virtues and powers that must come to any people that move forward with civilization." [32]

Against this background of a primitive and unprogressive Old South, lacking in imagination and originality, depreciating the efforts of its own writers, Trent appraised Simms's poetry and prose. He thought the South Carolinian's memory could be served properly by depicting "him as the most conspicuous representative of letters the old South can boast of," [33] not "as an unjustly treated poet, which he was not, or as a partially successful romancer, which he was." His poetry could be so-called "only by courtesy." But it was hardly "his fault that, like nearly all Southern poets down to Sidney Lanier, he failed to exercise proper control upon his imagination. Self-control is essential to an artist, but there was little in Southern life at that time that could teach a man how to control himself. In fact, a self-controlled man would have been looked upon with distrust in the South." Trent agreed with Paul Hamilton Hayne that Simms was a talented but not a great prose writer. But he disagreed with Hayne's belief that Simms's work would not endure, for Trent concluded that the colonial and Revolutionary romances were ennobling and that they would live. Yet all of them were "marred by a slipshod style, by a repetition of incidents, and by the introduction of an unnecessary amount of the horrible and the revolting." Quality was sacrificed for quantity. Under the necessity of writing for a living to support a large family, he "must finish thirty pages of manuscript in the morning, or else make it up at night." Simms " 'would write page after page without stopping a moment for reflection or revision, and, without altering a word or reading what he had written,' " he would send it to the publisher.[34]

It was little wonder that Charlestonians in particular and southerners in general should lose their tempers as they read Trent's critical and penetrating study of their poet and romancer and the conditions that affected literary activity in the Old South. He had not hesitated to criticize the social system of the old regime by calling attention to inconsistencies and backwardness, and he had charged that South Carolinians, "while professing to hold culture and literary attainments in high repute," had "consistently snubbed or disregarded all efforts that looked toward the creation of a home literature." * The principles of objective detachment which Trent had learned at the Johns Hopkins infuriated conservatives who still believed that biographers should be personally and sympathetically acquainted with their subjects. "In the days of our fathers," said a contributor to the Charleston *News and Courier,* "if a man was thought to merit a memoir, his life was written either by an admiring friend and companion . . . or by an appreciative relative, . . . and we used to get some very good biographies under that system and usage." But the present "rage for realism—to get the plain, historic truth, free from prejudice"—seemed to demand new qualifications: either entire ignorance of the subject or an attitude of disbelief. Biographers therefore portrayed shadows rather than realities. Trent exhibited industry in assembling materials, but he pooh-poohed Simms and his southern contemporaries, scoffed at literary productivity in the South, and spoke disparagingly, even scornfully, of southern periodicals.[35]

A much fairer estimate by F. Peyre Porcher appeared in the same paper soon thereafter. He did not object to Trent's critical appraisal of Simms, for the biographer appreciated his fine qualities, made allowances for his deficiences, and explained his imperfections in terms of an atmosphere that did not promote a professional literary career. But Porcher defended South Carolinians against the charge of unappreciation; he insisted that Simms had a large and devoted group of admirers at home. Trent's "youth and inexperience" made it possible for him to answer all the questions that perplexed their ancestors—including secession and slavery. It was unthinkable that a professor in a southern university, with Virginia nativity, should utilize northern publishers to disparage southerners' political sagacity and to speak contemptuously of their accomplishments.[36]

W. Porcher Miles, former South Carolinian but now a Louisiana sugar planter, had provided Trent with some Simms letters, and he was indignant at the use the biographer had made of them. In a

* William P. Trent, *William Gilmore Simms* (Boston, 1892), 30. It troubled Simms that his work went unrecognized in the South Carolina city. He wrote in 1858: "'All that I have done has been poured to waste in Charleston, which has never smiled on any of my labors, which has steadily ignored my claims, which has disparaged me to the last.'" *Ibid.,* 239.

private letter for public consumption, he asserted that Trent's "New England ideas and prejudices" unfitted him for writing about a South Carolinian. Although the reputation of Simms and the South could hardly be damaged by the disparagement "of this feeble partisan and uninformed critic," it was only natural that South Carolinians "should resent such glaring and outrageous misrepresentations." [37] Fearing that the book might attract readers because the author was a history professor, J. J. Pringle Smith also called attention to its "calumnious misrepresentations" in "A Defence of the South," an article over three columns long in the Charleston *News and Courier*. Smith was especially incensed at Trent's attitude toward slavery, and he characterized the biography as a book that "abounds in jeers at the habits, modes of life and ways of thought of Southern but especially Carolina people." [38]

But if the southern press berated Trent's biography of Simms, northern reviewers received it generously. Well-known critics, among them Theodore Roosevelt and Brander Matthews, evaluated it for northern monthlies. Their favorable estimates did not go unrewarded. To Roosevelt, Trent dedicated his next book, *Southern Statesmen of the Old Régime* (1897), "in Friendship and Admiration"; he inscribed his *Robert E. Lee* (1899) to Matthews, "Who makes gratitude a pleasure and friendship an inspiration."

Roosevelt, writing in the *Atlantic Monthly,* praised *William Gilmore Simms* for its historical and literary virtues. The author of the biography was "a man of originality and of historic insight, capable of seeing the facts as they are, and fearless enough to state his conclusions as he sees them. His book is a credit to the scholarship of the South." Trent commanded several advantages in the performance of his task: an unbiased attitude, competence in American literature, a keen understanding of life in the Old South, and an esteem for Simms which would be shared by his readers. Disagreeing with southern critics, Roosevelt thought that Trent was at his best in treating the political background of the Civil War and Simms's relationship to it. He was endowed with that "rare quality of 'seeing veracity,' as Carlyle phrased it; he knows things as they really are, and recognizes their true significance." [39]

Professor Matthews of Columbia University, Trent's future colleague, reviewed the biography for the *Cosmopolitan.* The volume exhibited "a new spirit—a spirit not frequent even now in works of southern authorship. His book is solid in research, worthy in workmanship, dignified in manner and brave in tone; it is not only a good book, it is a good deed." The study was tangible evidence that a New South had been born. It possessed amplitude and interest impossible in pure biography, for Trent had described "the environment which made Simms what he was—which, indeed, kept him from being more than he was." As an analysis of southern "literary conditions," it was an accomplishment no other writer had undertaken. Matthews agreed that slavery was responsible for the literary backwardness of the South.[40]

Trent lost no time in writing the Columbia University professor a letter of thanks for his "delightfully kind and sympathetic criticism. . . . Such a notice from such a critic goes far to take the sting out of the attacks on the part of the Southern press." He anticipated some unfavorable reviews, but he was not prepared for "the virulence and the *density* of some of the gentlemen who have honoured me with a notice." He reiterated his justification for the discussion of political issues, and he thanked Matthews for his awareness of the book's major objective, "to make a thorough study of the conditions that controlled the production of literature in the ante-bellum South—with the further end, of course, of making a modest contribution to what I may call the general theory of literary development." Matthews' constructive criticism was encouraging "after one has been baited for several months without the privilege a bear always has of giving a good hearty roar and occasionally mangling a hound." [41]

Writing to Stephen B. Weeks before the controversy got under way, Trent observed that the North Carolina historian agreed in part "as to the effects of slavery." Research had, indeed, modified his own view of the institution, and he hoped that eventually the two would find themselves in substantial agreement. As Trent saw it, slavery might promote, rather than impede, literary development when it harmonized with other social factors. Athens, for example, produced "a great literature but then there was nothing to disturb the Athenian mind or to make it *self conscious* on the subject of slavery. How different was the case in the South! . . . Self consciousness either in an individual, a class, or a people is fatal to literary production of the highest order. It may produce a literature of apologetics . . . or of florid oratory &c but it will not give us a drama or a poem of the highest order." There were other reasons for southern failure, but they were all related to slavery.*

IV

At the invitation of two former Johns Hopkins men, Richard T. Ely and Frederick J. Turner, Trent delivered a series of lectures on prominent antebellum southerners at the University of Wisconsin in 1896. "If I may judge from the kindness of my own reception," Trent wrote, "Madison is a very paradise for lecturers; it is also one of the least sectional and biassed places that I have ever known." [42] It was his purpose to depict the old regime in the South through some of the able men of the middle period. He chose George Washington, a "Sophocles in his perfect balance and nobility" and "the greatest of all Americans"; Thomas Jefferson, "the Shelley of our politics" and "the most influential of all our statesmen"; John Randolph of Roanoke, that ill-balanced and eccentric "Heine of Virginia politics"; John C. Calhoun and Jefferson Davis, representatives of states that dominated the secession movement; and Alexander H. Stephens and Robert Toombs, Georgians who typified southern unionists and secessionists. He could not include William L. Yancey because his fire-eating qualities precluded statesmanship; he regretted exclusion of John Marshall from his portrait gallery, for in Trent's opinion the Chief Justice ranked behind only Washington and Jefferson. A dozen other names were discarded for one reason or another.[43]

Henry Cabot Lodge had already exploded the Washington myths emanating from Jared Sparks, Edward Everett, and the "farcical compilation of the notorious Parson Weems"; the current distorted and derogatory appraisals Trent traced to the Anglo-Saxon "incapacity for discriminating appreciation of greatness and genius." Exhibiting his usual nationalistic concept, the lecturer paraded the first President as one of the few Revolutionary statesmen "who recognized our national character." In the realm of politics, he was master of both Jefferson and Alexander Hamilton; notwithstanding the estimable writings of Hamilton and

* "When I began working on my book," Trent wrote in the same letter, "I had much your view of the matter but the more I read the more I was convinced that some previous utterances of mine (see my chapter in Adams' Thomas Jefferson &c) on the subject were wrong. One of these days some body will root out the passage and try the parallel column trick on me but I shall be ready for him." Trent to Stephen B. Weeks, March 12, 1892, Stephen B. Weeks Papers (University of North Carolina library, Chapel Hill, N.C.).

James Madison in the framing and adopting of the Constitution, Washington's "pen, his voice, his example,—his mere name,—were of more weight than all they wrote or said or did." Nor was he "commonplace" as a military leader. Trent ranked him with such warriors as Alexander the Great, Hannibal, Caesar, Cromwell, Napoleon, and Marlborough. Not that Trent knew anything about military science, but this deficiency did not unfit him "for forming an opinion on a matter in which imagination necessarily plays the most important *role*. . . . Imaginations, and the judgment that looks to wholes rather than to parts, are, it seems to me, essential in any such estimate." [44] One can agree with Trent when he emphasized "a judgment that looks to wholes rather than to parts," but the critical historian must restrain imagination after it has performed its proper function. Was Trent becoming artist rather than historian? Imagination is an essential qualification of a true historian; it is also an attribute of creative writing.

Trent's appraisal of Washington was uncritical—almost eulogistic. In treating Jefferson's career, he regained his historical composure and discovered some very human weaknesses as well as many praiseworthy qualities. He recognized Jefferson's versatility and discovered that he, like Washington, was more than a Virginian and a southerner; he was an American, and he was also a cosmopolite. His democracy stemmed from contact with the Virginia frontier. Despite his "skill as a drafter," Jefferson's reports as a cabinet member were inferior to those penned by Hamilton, but he surpassed his rival in wisdom and generosity, and in "breadth of culture, flexibility of genius, and positive service to humanity." On the other hand, he "was visionary and suspicious, sensitive and easy-going, ambitious and careless; like some whist-players, he knew the theory of the game, but was a very bad player." Yet the principles he advocated—majority rule, individual freedom, broad suffrage, promotion of the arts and sciences, and amicable relations with other countries—still guided Americans in the 1890's.[45]

Randolph gave Trent plenty of opportunity to exercise critical ingenuity. Yet he was not incorrect in classifying him as the ablest strict constructionist the South developed between Jefferson and Calhoun.[46] As for the South Carolinian, he was not a great man, for Trent evaluated men by the same criterion as "poetry,—both must appeal powerfully to my imagination in a noble and elevating way, nor will the possession of merely pathetic qualities suffice. Calhoun is a pathetic figure, but he is not inspiring, at least to me; and true genius, while it may be pathetic, is always inspiring." He disagreed with Hermann von Holst that Calhoun "was a born leader of men, and therefore a born politician. Calhoun led thought rather than men, and lacking imagination, he led thought badly." His doctrine of nullification was ridiculous; believing that slavery would not survive nationalization, he "unconsciously started with the conclusions he wanted" and "reasoned back to his premises." Then, admitting his premises, "he leads you willy-nilly to his conclusions." One should not read his treatises on government until he rejected the idea of divisible sovereignty and the compact theory, for "the sure grip of Calhoun's logic will end by making one a nullifier or a lunatic, it matters little which." At the same time, Calhoun deserved "to rank as our most original political theorist" because of his penetrating review of minority rights and the proper means of acquiring them.[47]

The portrayal of Stephens and Toombs is meritorious only in that it succeeds admirably in tracing their careers in parallel fashion and in indicating comparisons and contrasts.[48] In writing of Jefferson Davis, he found himself in a veritable dilemma, for the President of the Confederacy was the most controversial character of the old regime. Perhaps in a hundred and fifty years prejudice would be dissipated and Madisonians might be addressed on that subject "with a confidence and assurance that the present lecturer is far from feeling." Trent was conscious of the fact that "certain conclusions" were necessary if he expected acquiescence by a majority of southerners. Nevertheless, Davis was not "a thoroughly great man" in his opinion, though he credited him with ability, versatility, honest purpose, gallantry as a soldier, and gentlemanly qualities. His stewardship was imperfect, but he failed primarily because he espoused a house of cards.[49]

Trent's study of three Virginians, a South Carolinian, two Georgians, and a Mississippian reveals him as a revisionist who was attempting a liberal interpretation of his section's past. He could not accept the traditional view of slavery and other determinants that led to secession and civil war. The historical pendulum swung too far to the left in *Southern Statesmen of the Old Régime* as well as in *William Gilmore Simms;* yet it was courageous for a southerner of fifty or sixty years ago to question accepted history or to propose new interpretation. He blamed southern political leaders for not teaching the planter that slavery was an economic liability: "it was slavery that kept his roads bad, that gave him wretched 'Old-field' schools, that prevented his cities from growing, that kept immigrants from his public lands, that, in short, stamped its evil mark on everything he wrote or said or did." [50] While most of the charges laid at the door of slavery were overstated, no serious objection can be raised to the following observation, which might easily be attributed to Avery Craven rather than to Trent: "The more fiercely the abolitionist leaders inveighed against slavery, the more vehemently the proslavery advocates asserted their own virtue and the baseness of their enemies. The Northerner began to think all Southerners slave-drivers; the Southerner began to think all Northerners either fanatics or cowardly shop-keepers." *

Trent's *Robert E. Lee,* published in 1899, did not add much to his reputation as a historian. A tiny volume of less than twenty thousand words, it was written "to add a small tribute to the ever-increasing fame of one of the world's noblest sons." It was not an original piece of work, for he drew heavily upon previous biographies of the Confederate general and his contemporaries, though occasionally he "consulted the records." [51] The only useful purpose the book served was to provide in small compass a readable narrative of the highlights of Lee's career, based upon the undefinitive works of others. It was perhaps impossible for Trent not to become enamored of his hero, or to omit many parallels and analogies in the careers of Washington and Lee. The work does serve the historian, however, in indicating Trent's appraisal of sectional controversies. As causes of secession and civil war, he cited the compact theory, northern attitude toward slavery, abolitionist preachments of the 1830's, the territorial problem that followed acquisition from Mexico, and the fugitive slave law. But he emphasized the "logic of passion" as a determinant much as Craven did in his *The Coming of the Civil War,* except that Trent did not speak of "symbols." Unlike "the political theorist [who] must use a different sort of logic, the impartial historian must give the logic of passion its full weight in his endeavor to judge men and nations who have been actuated by it." The nature of abstract causes should not affect "the character of the passionate flesh-and-blood actors therein." Trent called for a revision of "judgments" that "touch[ed] the moral character" of participants in

* William P. Trent, *Southern Statesmen of the Old Régime* (New York, 1897), 184. Trent was at least prophetic when he wrote: "Until it is possible for one and the same person to render justice both to William Lloyd Garrison and to Jefferson Davis within the covers of one volume, we shall not have an impartial historian or an impartial history." *Ibid.,* 274.

"the drama of secession." As a case in point, Jefferson Davis would go down in history as "a thoroughly upright, honorable man, who did what he conceived to be his duty, and showed on the whole, remarkable powers in the performance thereof." If character be disassociated from the cause represented, "we shall find no purer life ever lived than that of Robert Lee, no matter whether or not we believe secession to have been justifiable from the point of view of history, or deny the right of a man to let his sentiments get the better of his reason." [52]

Of the men who were recording the South's past at the turn of the century, Trent and William Garrott Brown wrote history that contemporaries read. Neither attained an eminence that approached the stature of the distinguished group of an earlier generation—George Bancroft, William H. Prescott, John L. Motley, Washington Irving, and Francis Parkman—partly because of the brief period each devoted to the field, for Trent abandoned history for literature before his reputation was hardly established, and tuberculosis forced Brown into other activity during the closing years of his brief life-span. Both protested against the current dry-as-dust monography, though in this premise each was overshadowed by Colyer Meriwether.

Believing "that it was a man's duty to his readers not to be dull," Trent achieved a modicum of success in literary craftsmanship. Occasionally he resorted to dramatic episode, as the colorful debate between the venerable Patrick Henry, radical of a past generation, and Randolph of Roanoke, rising sun of a new era. The debate sent the younger Virginian to a seat in Congress. Trent had no difficulty in finding an ancient prototype for an antebellum southerner. Literary allusions punctuated his pages. His pen portraits were a medley of historic fact and tralatitious figure, of aptly selected illustration and strained comparison, all expressed with an artistry that stemmed from an extensive vocabulary, facile phrasing, and extensive learning. He was as effective in interpretive portraiture as William E. Dodd, whose *Statesmen of the Old South* (1911) and *Lincoln or Lee* (1928) remind one of the style and method of *Southern Statesmen of the Old Régime* and *Robert E. Lee.*

V

One of Trent's most permanent legacies was the *Sewanee Review,* which has had an unbroken existence from its founding in

1892. Two factors prompted him in this endeavor: first, the zeal of Johns Hopkins students to publish and to establish mediums of publication; and second, Trent's study of antebellum southern magazines which indicated a present need for a critical quarterly in the South. He had, it will be recalled, run the files of many of them in preparing his biography of Simms; and "the unformed nature of much of the comment upon the Simms volume . . . impressed upon him the need of a Review more specifically devoted to literary criticism and encouraging directly literary study and culture." [53]

Associated with Trent in founding the review were B. Lawton Wiggins, Thomas Gailor, and Benjamin B. Wells. Especially important was Wiggins, a South Carolinian who graduated at Sewanee, studied classics at the Johns Hopkins with Basil Gildersleeve, and became professor of Greek and eventually vice-chancellor at the University of the South.[54] Telfair Hodgson helped to finance the first volume, and his name appeared as managing editor. Trent, however, actually served as editor from the beginning, and he continued in that capacity until he left the university in 1900. The longevity of the review is due in part to the excellent foundations laid by Trent.

According to an announcement in the first issue, the magazine would follow the pattern of the English rather than the typical American review; the subjects treated therein would be accorded "fuller treatment than they usually receive in the popular magazines and less technical treatment than they receive in specialist publications." [55] The review emphasized literature and literary criticism more than the *South Atlantic Quarterly*,[56] established at Trinity College a decade later, but it also devoted attention to education, philosophy, the Bible, fine arts, contemporary questions, history, and biography. There was "nothing sectional and partisan" about it, and it sought "to extend its influence by representing, in the highest and widest sense, the best and most recent life and thought and culture of the South and of our country." [57]

A recent compilation reveals that the *Sewanee Review* published 130 articles on history by 1930, and of these 56 were on southern subjects. Sundry biographical articles treated southerners, and several of the contemporary problems discussed in its pages analyzed racial, industrial, and political issues in the South. Many of the contributors' names will be readily recognized by historians.

Trent himself contributed twenty-seven articles and reviews over a period of seventeen years, but most of them were in the field of literature.[58] A notable exception was "A New South View of Reconstruction," which contrasted the southern region of 1867, when Radicals with unlimited power forced Negro suffrage on unwilling whites, with the South of 1900, when, despite Republican control of the federal government, Negroes retained only such civil, political, and social rights as southern whites willingly permitted.[59]

Primacy as a southern liberal brought recognition in the East. When Walter H. Page determined to "report civilization" of the sections in the *Atlantic Monthly,* he turned as naturally to Trent for a portrayal of the South as he did to Turner for an analysis of the West.[60] Trent's articles on "Dominant Forces in Southern Life" and "Tendencies of Higher Life in the South" embraced a single theme: the cultural pattern of the region in the last decade of the nineteenth century, mirrored against a portrait gallery of southern states dressed in trappings of the old regime. His chief concern was the quality and capacity of the generation responsible for material advancement. If the metamorphosis of recent years involved only an increase in wealth and factories and urban population, the new epoch could not contribute to cultural development. What was the status of politics, religion, education, manners, and morals?

Recent tendencies pointed to an amelioration if not a disappearance of political and religious intolerance. In the field of literature, Joel Chandler Harris and Sidney Lanier merited enthusiastic praise, but the South should ponder whether they typified a literary awakening or illustrated the parable of the good seed that fell upon barren soil. An enduring literature could evolve only on a basis of self-criticism; southern writers were too sensitive to searching critiques. It was encouraging to find an increasing number of young liberals, educated in the North and in Germany, teaching in southern colleges; among them, the critical spirit had advanced most in the field of history. Improvement in public education, for both whites and blacks, was a clear indication of progress. Lynchings continued, for writers, editors, teachers, clergymen, and lawyers were "afraid to speak out"; apparently they had no clear understanding of the interrelation of society and law. "There is now less hospitality than of old, but there is more thrift; there is less refined and leisurely contentment, but there is more successful energy; there is less courtliness, but there is more individual freedom and originality; there is less pensive sentiment, but there is more radiant hope." [61]

VI

The 1890's witnessed a transformation in Trent's major interest. He began the decade with an ambition to gain recognition as a historian; before its close he had largely abandoned his enthusiasm for the subject and had acquired sufficient reputation in the field of literature to merit a call to Columbia University. He had continued to write history, especially biography, but never after 1892 did he delve into the sources with that thoroughness that characterized his life of Simms. He was content thereafter to write mainly from secondary works, supplemented by casual examination of original materials.

There seems to be no valid reason for believing that Trent was insincere in his critical presentation of antebellum southerners and their background, or that objectivity was compromised by a desire to startle northern scholars into a recognition of his merit and thereby pave the way for a call to a reputable university. On the subject of leaving the South, he poured out his heart to Adams early in 1898. Apparently he had received a feeler from Adelbert College in Cleveland, and was weighing the pros and cons of changing positions with the pros having the better of the argument. It was not inadequate library facilities that distressed him, he said, for he could write even at Sewanee. It was a question of whether he should forever "walk & sleep on briars," and "by this prickly figure of speech" he alluded to opposition at the University of the South, a minority of whose trustees regarded him "as a dangerous religious & political heretic." He disliked a role which made him "the object of prayer & other pietistic propaganda" looking toward his "spiritual regeneration." He had friends at Sewanee and elsewhere in the South, but their timidity placed the burden of the battle upon his shoulders. "Shallow thinking on political matters, provincialism of taste & sentiments—ignorance & vanity are the dominant characteristics of our people"—and a decade at a southern college had convinced him that it would require another generation before southerners became enlightened. Meanwhile, he had ambition—and ability, too, he admitted—as a lecturer and administrator, but Sewanee offered opportunity in neither direction.[62]

Certainly the lapse of time gave Trent greater balance. Writing in 1913 to Yates Snowden, professor of history at the University of South Carolina, he confessed: "I've abandoned a good many of the youthful notions I imbibed twenty years ago when the Americanism of Roosevelt seemed a great thing to me. . . . I am inclined to think I'm a better Southerner & Virginian than I ever was." [63] And two years later he wrote Snowden: "South Carolina makes me think of you and I wish I could have a good talk with you about books and the long ago. I'd apologize for all my shortcomings in 'Simms' and elsewhere." [64]

In the spring of 1900 John S. Bassett learned that Trent had been called to Columbia University, and a letter to the Sewanee professor brought in response a statement of reasons for accepting the invitation. The explanation seems plausible, though it is possible the letter did not tell the whole story:

> Many thanks for your kind letter. I fully understand the feeling that prompted it, and am only too glad that you think I have gotten some hold on the New South. My leaving here is due to two reasons: First, my work has been steadily tending in the direction of literature, and to make it more effective I need a larger library and the stimulus of graduate classes. Second, I feel confident that in the last few years a number of young men have come up in the South who are not going to let the good work die, that I shall never lose my own interest in the work, and that in my graduate work at Columbia I shall still have a chance to work upon Southern men. I cannot but believe that with its advantages sooner or later Columbia will become the largest center for post-graduate work in the country. Post-graduate work is national not sectional and I do not see why a Southern man should not do good work for his section in such a place. Please do not think that I leave the South and Sewanee without regret.[65]

Trent was correct in thinking that a group of young southerners would carry on the work his own pioneer efforts had inaugurated and that he could still have contact with southern students at Columbia University. His interest in southern historical activity continued to wane; he wrote history on occasion, but it was seldom the story of his native section.[66] But in the 1890's his vigorous enthusiasm for the subject had influenced young southerners of liberal principles; his preachments of that decade had been a substantial factor in the beginnings of southern historical scholarship.

CHAPTER IV

John Spencer Bassett: Trinity College Liberal

Among the pioneers who sought to promote historical scholarship in the South as the nineteenth century faded into the twentieth was John Spencer Bassett.[1] A native of North Carolina, he attended Trinity College, attained the doctorate at the Johns Hopkins University, and returned to his undergraduate alma mater as professor of history. His interests were varied and his ability was exceptional. A penchant for research and writing yielded monographs on North Carolina history, and as a corollary he assembled printed and manuscript records in the Trinity College library. He inspired in his students a Jeffersonian passion "to follow truth wherever it may lead," even though it undermined southern tradition. Southern liberal in a generation dominated by conservative thinking, his provocative preachments stirred reactionaries to protestations. A dozen years at Trinity College brought local and then national recognition and an invitation to a northern professorship. Thereafter his interest in southern history waned.

I

Bassett's father and paternal grandfather were democratic Virginians, devout Methodists, successful carpenters and contractors, slaveholders on a small scale, and critics of slavery but not antislavery agitators. His grandfather, Richard Bassett, a resident of Williamsburg, apprenticed his son Richard Baxter to a Richmond firm of contractors. After mastering the trade the younger Richard became a builder, first in Williamsburg, then in Norfolk, and finally at various places in North Carolina. In 1861 he joined the Edgecombe Guards, a company of the First North Carolina Regiment, but after the battle of Big Bethel he was assigned by the Secretary of War to the commissary department, where he manufactured army supplies until the close of the war. A turn at planting in the Reconstruction era provided temporary occupation, but after a few years he returned to his original vocation. Meanwhile, in 1863, a second marriage united the southern family with New England stock. Mary Jane Wilson was the daughter of a Maine millwright who had moved to North Carolina a generation earlier. The Bassett's second child, John Spencer, was born at Tarboro on September 10, 1867.

Early education at Richlands, Goldsboro, and the Jefferson Davis Military Academy at LaGrange prepared Bassett for Trinity College, then located in Randolph County. When he enrolled as a junior in 1886, the college was an ordinary backwoods institution with an antiquated curriculum, inadequate financial resources, and a temporary administration. The election of John F. Crowell, graduate of Yale University, to the presidency the year after Bassett entered resulted in liberalization of the course of study and introduction of the system of election. Bassett graduated in 1888, and after teaching for a couple of years in the Durham public schools, he returned to Trinity College as instructor in English and principal of the preparatory department.*

* Sketches of John Spencer Bassett are available in a brief transcript memoir, John Spencer Bassett Papers (Manuscript Division, Library of Congress, Washington, D.C.); *American Historical Review,* XXXIII (April, 1928), 713–14; *American Historical Review,* XXXIV (April, 1929), 483–84; *South Atlantic Quarterly,* XXVII (April, 1928), 113–16; William K. Boyd, "John Spencer Bassett," *Dictionary of American Biography* (20 vols.; N.Y., 1928–36), 38–39; Wendell H. Stephenson, "A Half Century of Southern Historical Scholarship," *Journal of Southern History,* XI (February, 1945), 8–12.

Bassett entered upon his career as a student and teacher at Trinity College in an era that witnessed profound developments in North Carolina education. Economic discontent that gave rise to the Populist revolt was accompanied by widespread demand for improved educational opportunities. Charles D. McIver and Edwin A. Alderman made constructive contributions in promoting popular education and a training program for teachers. At the higher education level, new schools were founded and old ones invigorated. The agricultural and mechanical college was established at Raleigh in 1889. Soon thereafter higher education for women received impetus with the founding of the North Carolina State Normal and Industrial College at Greensboro by the state, and Meredith College, a private school for girls, at Raleigh. The Slater Industrial and State Normal School for Negroes came into existence at Salem. The University of North Carolina, approaching its hundredth anniversary, sought to increase its revenues from the state, modernize its curriculum, and expand its patronage. This program brought it into conflict with such denominational colleges as Trinity, Wake Forest, and Davidson, which professed to believe that the university and other state-supported schools would have a "monopoly in higher education." First Wake Forest and then Trinity College led the fight against the university in the latter half of the 1890's. In the rivalry between the Chapel Hill and Durham schools, Bassett was an interested participant, and this brought him into conflict with Josephus Daniels. Long before the Bassett affair of 1903, the two had clashed in their private correspondence. For the educational

He was not long content to remain inadequately prepared. Inspired by Crowell and recommended by Stephen B. Weeks, Bassett entered the Johns Hopkins University. By the last decade of the nineteenth century, this Baltimore institution of higher learning had become an academic focus for graduates of southern colleges and universities. Its location south of the Mason and Dixon line prompted a feeling that it was a southern university; a generous supply of scholarships for residents of Maryland, Virginia, and North Carolina provided financial aid; and the liberal attitude of Herbert B. Adams, director of the department of history, political science, and economics, assured sympathetic treatment of southern scholars and southern subjects.[2] Bassett studied at the Johns Hopkins for three years, 1891–94, emphasizing history but delving also into economics and sociology. For the first two years he was a Hopkins Scholar; in his third he held a five-hundred-dollar fellowship.[3] His dissertation, a study of *The Constitutional Beginnings of North Carolina (1663–1729)*, was published in the university *Studies in Historical and Political Science*. Armed with a degree and a zest for historical scholarship in all of its ramifications, he returned to Trinity College as professor of history, a position to which he had been elected the year before. Ere long he acquired a reputation as the South's foremost scholar in the field of history.

Trinity College was already a Johns Hopkins colony before Bassett was appointed to the chair of history. His predecessor Weeks received the doctor's degree in 1891 under Adams' tutelage, and then served for two years as professor of history and political science until a faculty quarrel with the president caused his resignation. A prolific writer in the field of North Carolina history prior to his appointment, he continued to produce creditable monographs during his incumbency. Weeks immediately turned his attention to library acquisitions and sought to interest alumni and other friends of the college in assembling historical sources on the South. He founded the Trinity College Historical Society,

---

struggle in the 1890's, see Luther L. Gobbel, *Church-State Relationships in Education in North Carolina since 1776* (Durham, 1938), chap. iv. Popular education in the state received great impetus during the administration of Governor Charles B. Aycock, 1901–1905. He campaigned for office "on a platform of white supremacy and education" and "led the movement which took the ballot from the illiterate negro until he could be prepared by education and training for its proper use, thus committing the state to a program of universal education." See Edgar W. Knight, "Charles Brantley Aycock," *Dictionary of American Biography*, I, 447–48.

which was to play a vital part in stimulating historical activity under the leadership of Bassett and William K. Boyd.

The intimate relations between Adams and Bassett did not end when Bassett left Johns Hopkins, for they corresponded frequently, and the former student did not miss an opportunity to stop over in Baltimore when he made periodic migrations to work in eastern libraries. The Durham colony and the mother institution maintained a close relationship: Bassett explained his problems, whether academic or personal, recounted his successes, and reported upon the political and educational backwardness of North Carolina and the South; his mentor offered words of encouragement and counsel.[4] On sundry occasions Bassett expressed appreciation for tangible aid. Upon learning in 1901 that Adams had resigned because of ill health, Bassett wrote that "you have been to me more than an instructor. You have given me sparks of yourself, and you have made me hope that I might be a useful man in some not unimportant way." He alluded to those "touches of new inspiration in my work" which his contacts with Adams had incited.[5]

Most of Bassett's letters reveal a spirit of hopefulness for the advancement of the college, albeit an undercurrent of discouragement is discernible. His salary was only $1,200, and North Carolina was a "narrow & uninspiring" place in which to work.[6] Meager compensation did not permit research in the East every summer. Adams pointed to the overstocked condition of "the academic market" and encouraged Bassett to believe that he was doing constructive work under adverse circumstances. "You are very fortunate in having a field of work and influence all your own. You are transforming the historic consciousness of your people and your State. You are making constant contributions to North Carolina literature. You are dispelling illusions and bringing the truth to light." [7] Another expression of dissatisfaction with conditions under which he labored brought further praise for his work in the South. Bassett's ambition was justifiable, and Adams would keep an ear to the ground for a better location.[8] Learning from Bassett that "matters have taken a more favorable turn" at Trinity College, Adams wished him "increased usefulness." He pointed to accomplishments that came from "continuous residence and activity in one institution." That had been Adams' experience at the Johns Hopkins, where he had remained despite attractive offers elsewhere.[9]

Early in 1898 Bassett was "jogging on rather monotonously" because routine work prevented concentration on research. A "troublesome" French class that he had taught for the past three years clung in leechlike fashion.[10] He still complained of an inadequate salary and longed for a change of location. "Do you have a good salaried place waiting for a man?" he inquired of Adams in 1900. "I would like this place perfectly if salaries were larger." [11]

The attitude of churchmen toward the college was none too reassuring. A "holy element in the church howled," he wrote Adams in 1898, when an untrue report was circulated that Trinity College owned some stock in the tobacco trust. "There is an element in favor of withdrawing from the support of the college on account of this affair. I wish they would go. They are soreheads in general & will always be a source of annoyance to us. . . . There are a lot of fools in N.C. and it takes some time to lick them into shape. We are doing it gradually. Trinity is about the only place in the state that is trying to do it. I used to be aweary of the place; but as long as the fool-killing is to go on I want to be here to see the fun." [12] Several months earlier he had written Adams, after reading Andrew D. White's *A History of the Warfare of Science with Theology in Christendom* (1896), "a book containing many hard facts—and important ones too"—that he anticipated a time when he would "clash with the authorities here on the question of orthodoxy." [13]

Despite a meager salary, heavy teaching load, unsympathetic politicians, and bigoted clerics, Bassett found appreciation for his scholarly efforts. Donations for books and for a library building prompted faith in the future; he engaged in considerable research and writing; several of his colleagues were liberals; and he took genuine delight in promoting the interests of his students. Roughly processed products were shipped away to the educational homeland in Baltimore that they might partake of the same scholarly blessings that he had received from Adams. And he felt the same solicitude for their welfare that Adams had manifested in his own career. Charles C. Weaver was his first student to work for the doctorate at the Johns Hopkins and Bassett followed his progress with avid interest. Writing of his esteem for Adams, Weaver recalled his obligations to Bassett: "Your good name here has proved a wonderful aid to me as your pupil. . . . The inspiration of your example has gone far in aiding me to work." [14] When a tragedy occurred in the household of Mrs. N. B. McDowell of Weaverville, she requested that Bassett "comfort" her nephew William Kenneth Boyd. "He has spoken of you to me and I know he has a strong attachment for you, and I hope he has won your confidence and affection." [15] Boyd was Bassett's outstanding student, and he sought in vain to steer him to the Johns Hopkins. "He is a delightful student," Bassett wrote Adams. "He is a prize, I think." Boyd's paper on William W. Holden impressed Bassett as "the best thing ever done in N.C. Reconstruction times," and its excellence led William A. Dunning to encourage Boyd to enter Columbia University.[16]

Bassett served other students, less well known, in a multitude of ways. Nat C. Newbold inquired whether he and his brother should borrow money to continue their education at Trinity College, and if so, could Bassett persuade Washington Duke to lend them some money? [17] High school teachers called upon him for materials to aid students preparing for debates.[18] A Burlington man requested "a few points" on a subject he was to present at an Epworth League reception, and "also refer me to books where I shall be able to find some for myself." Bassett endorsed the letter "One of many." [19]

If Bassett had done nothing more than teach, he would have earned his salary. In 1904 he wrote to William E. Dodd that his weekly load had been fifteen hours for many years, the past year he had taught eighteen, and he had constantly engaged in library activity.[20] He did not mention the fact that he was then editor of the *South Atlantic Quarterly,* had sundry research products under way, devoted considerable time to his students outside the classroom, and was interested in civic affairs.

Bassett taught a wide variety of courses, some of them far afield from history, but here it is enough to present only those that were related to the history of the South. He did not introduce a course in that field; not until after Boyd succeeded Bassett in 1906 was a course in southern history inaugurated. North Carolina history entered the curriculum as early as 1896, and Bassett expressed the hope that students would be "able to understand the methods of original research from an examination of the materials at first hand. It is believed that this course will give students an impetus to historical writing and induce them to be more active in the collection of historical material." The graduate course in North Carolina's political and social development sent students to the sources: "Continual opportunity will be offered for preparing original papers."[21]

It was not state pride that prompted Bassett to introduce North Carolina history into the curriculum. Indeed, he told members of the Trinity College Historical Society, he would not delude them into thinking that North Carolinians were "the greatest people in the union, or in the world," for others "have had a greater influence on the development of our common country than we." If the necessity of choosing either national or state history arose, he felt the former should be elected. Fortunately, the course of study would admit both.[22]

The department's offerings were never static. In the spring semester of the 1899–1900 session Bassett taught as a junior-senior subject "Secession in North America." Its purpose: "to make a close study of the development of the political life of the South, both before and after the war, as well as to examine in an impartial way the military history of the great struggles between the North and South." Graduate students who had not taken the course during the senior year were eligible for a similar course with only a slight change in description. "Secession and Reconstruction" appeared for the first time in the 1901–1902 catalogue. It was designed to give students "an opportunity to study that correlative process by which that older idea of separateness rebelled against the newer idea of nationality and the effects which proceeded therefrom." These were not systematic courses in the history of the South, but apparently they embraced much material ordinarily included in the content of southern history.[23]

The Trinity College Historical Society had functioned for over two years before Bassett joined the faculty. "The object of the Society," according to its constitution, should "be to collect, arrange and preserve a library of books, pamphlets, maps, charts, manuscripts, papers, paintings, statuary and other materials illustrative of the history of North Carolina and of the South; rescue as far as possible from forgetfulness the names and deeds of our first settlers; to encourage original work in the field of Southern history and to promote the study of the same by means of lectures and publications."[24] There is reason to believe that no local historical association ever succeeded better in effecting its program than the society at Trinity College.

Both faculty and students participated in the meetings of the society, and officers were chosen from both groups with students predominating. Papers were read not only by students and faculty but also by visiting lecturers. Bassett vitalized the organization and gave it widespread influence. According to the society's historian, his contributions may be summarized as follows: "The establishment of a historical museum, the institution of a civic celebration held annually on February 22, the introduction of outside speakers, and the publication of *Historical Papers*. . . . But these external evidences of activity were merely a part of more fundamental aims for building a valuable collection of source materials and for promoting freedom of thought in the South." [25]

To stimulate interest in the society, Bassett resorted first to the assembling of a museum and second to the inauguration of a publication program. Both of these objects succeeded admirably. "From the day the museum was founded," Bassett wrote, "the interest in the Society sprang into new life. I am satisfied that it was the turning point in the life of the organization." The museum had its origin in the fall of 1894. Students, faculty, and friends of the college donated or collected relics, manuscripts, and books. In the spring of 1898 Bassett appealed "to the friends of North Carolina history," through the medium of the *Christian Educator*, for information that would lead to the acquisition of letters and other documents, books and pamphlets, addresses and sketches, or to the discovery of "abandoned" libraries.[26]

When Bassett began his labors at Trinity College, he wrote Adams in 1898, that no collection of documents existed. Now there were over two thousand, and he had been promised a fireproof vault in which to house them. He noted with satisfaction the Dukes's contributions for a library endowment and also funds for the erection of a building which Bassett hoped would be spacious enough to house a hundred thousand volumes. By 1900 the trustees had appointed him "manager of the library," and soon thereafter he noted a gift of $10,000 available for the purchase of books when the building was completed. He expected "to do something with Southern history on the strength of it." [27]

II

It was Bassett's ambition to provide a medium of publication for the society. Here again he was following in Adams' footsteps, for he was aware that the *Studies in Historical and Political Science* constituted a cornerstone of the Johns Hopkins program. Bassett's plan, a very modest affair at its inception, was launched in 1895. He arranged with the editor of a student publication, *The Archive,* to run off two hundred reprints of each historical article published therein, and at the end of the year they were bound into a booklet of eighty-five pages. The first issue cost only twenty-five dollars, and the administration was so impressed that it promised to contribute that amount annually. "So far as I know," Bassett wrote Adams, "this is but one of three historical publications (not including patriotic publications) in the South. It is the only one in N.C." [28]

The society now possessed an inexpensive but useful organ in which papers by students, faculty members, and others reached the printed page. It was Bassett's ingenuity that inaugurated the *Historical Papers;* Boyd's leadership that gave them permanency and substantial merit. Helpful as the papers were, they did not serve every purpose that Bassett had in mind. Dissatisfaction with the political situation in North Carolina, the necessity for a better solution of the race problem in the South, and in general the need for critical and independent thought as a basis for action prompted a desire for a medium with catholic scope and wider circulation. He therefore launched the *South Atlantic Quarterly* in 1902, and the *Historical Papers* were temporarily abandoned. Further inquiry into his teaching is necessary if one would understand the motive behind the quarterly.

At the beginning of the academic year 1897–98 Bassett had reason to feel optimistic. "Our college year has opened well," he wrote Adams. "I am doing more satisfactory work, to myself, than I have done since I have been here. . . . I am trying to put a new spirit into the historical work of the South—so far as my influence extends." The night before, he addressed the society "on our historical ideal," and the subject aroused interest. When he urged liberty to think, a renaissance in ideas, and "a respectful hearing" for divergent opinions, members applauded.[29]

The speech itself indicates that Bassett understood the status of history writing in the South and the need for improvement. Three factors circumscribed southern historiography: "a lack of proper historical ideals, a dearth of trained investigators, and a failure to collect sources of information." As to the first, southerners had written memoirs and newspaper anecdotes, magnified ancestral accomplishments, used "flimsy evidences" to establish the impossible, "and all of this we have called, and allowed others to call, history." This was wrong and should be stopped. A proper concept of history demanded a faithful, systematic, and comprehensive record of man's heritage; and, so far as biography was concerned, "a portrayal of all the forces of life" that influenced the subject.

In the second place, Bassett believed that the past should be recorded by trained historians. He paid his respects to the "Confederate-Brigadier-General type." In "public office of comfortable emolument" veterans of the war who "fought bravely with the sword are thus tempted to make asses of themselves with the pen." The historian of the future must have other qualifications than Confederate experience: "He must know how to weigh evidence; he must have the scientific spirit for facts; he must have the clear light of truth; he must have a knowledge of the habits of men in other places and in other times; he must know the bearings of other sciences and of literatures on history; more than all this, he must have facility in coming to historical judgments before he can so view the things that come before him that his view shall be valuable to us."

One thing was yet lacking. The scientifically trained historian could not record and interpret the past without original materials. Southerners had "pride of ancestry and . . . loyalty to our institutions," but they made few documents available to the historian. The society could stimulate North Carolinians with ancient lineage to provide the chronicler with records from chests and garrets.

Closely related to these difficulties was an absence of accuracy of thought. There was no substitute for "a devotion to truth!" As an illustration, southerners who had written about the Civil War and its issues had depended upon feeling rather than fact. "No man with instincts for accuracy can be satisfied with our statement of our own case. We have first of all to put beyond question the correctness of our position in the controversy." Southern people insisted upon "immunity from criticism," and when any one of their number advocated an untraditional view he was "denounced as a traitor and a mercenary defiler of his birthplace." Accuracy demanded that evidence on both sides of controversial issues should be heard. "Let us conduct ourselves," Bassett urged, "that the world may know that there is in the South at least one spot in which our history may be presented in all of its claims, and where it may receive a respectful and unimpassioned hearing. If we cannot do this we are no historians, we are but partisans." [30]

The views of the thirty-year-old Bassett disclosed to Trinity College students in 1897 were drawn in part from lessons learned at the Johns Hopkins with practical application to the needs of North Carolina and the South. His statements of the scientific concept of history, the need for trained historians, and the obligation to preserve historical materials are still valid after the lapse of half a century; the conservatism of southern society in the generation in which he expressed them made his doctrines little less than revolutionary.

Preliminary to launching the *South Atlantic Quarterly,* Bassett engaged in voluminous correspondence with friends, mainly in the South and chiefly in the historical guild. His letter files supplement the magazine itself in yielding evidence of the editor's efforts to build up a forum of liberal thought and of contemporary approval of his accomplishments. Sponsored originally by the "9019" society of Trinity College, it was soon taken over by a publishing company formed by a local group.[31] Bassett hoped eventually to pay contributors, but remuneration was impossible at its inception. During the first year certain contributors were given five subscriptions to the quarterly, one for the author and four for nonsubscribers designated by him.[32] The first year closed "with out loss or profit," a result that was indeed gratifying.[33]

The quarterly was in part modelled after the *Sewanee Review,* brainchild of William P. Trent, which began publication a decade earlier. The new venture would "be devoted to the literary, historical, and social development of the South"; the "sober and instructive articles" would be designed to appeal "to the smaller audience of serious minded" southerners. With friends in southern colleges and universities pledging an enthusiastic cooperation, Bassett brought out the first issue in January, 1902. The quarterly would be "a medium of encouraging every honest literary effort," he announced. To accomplish this end "there must be liberty to think," and the editor would therefore accept contributions even though the opinions expressed differed from his own. If he could stimulate among southerners a search for truth, the existence of the journal would be justified.[34]

For nearly two years southern conservatives ignored the quarterly and its liberal spirit. Friends of liberalism commended its policy, although some of them pointed to a preponderance of historical articles in early numbers and to a prominence of Trinity College professors among its contributors.[35] As the editor's acquaintance widened and the magazine acquired a creditable reputation, these imbalances were partially adjusted. In other premises commendation was unrestrained. Edwin A. Alderman, president of Tulane University, wrote Bassett "what a wonderfully good magazine you are making. It is the best thing that has ever appeared in my day in the South. Its dignity, its freedom of speech, its calmness, its evident determination to speak the truth, commend it most highly to me."[36] Acknowledging a copy of the quarterly, Charles M. Andrews of Bryn Mawr College asserted that "you have certainly undertaken a magnificent work in attempting to develop what you call a more vital literary activity in the South and the result of your experiment will be watched with the greatest interest and sympathy by every one who is concerned for the educational and literary future of this country. . . . I look with increasing admiration upon you men of the South, from North Carolina to Texas, for the enthusiasm and energy that you are all displaying in the endeavor, to show your historical colleagues of the Middle, North, and West that there is a great world south of Mason and Dixon's line, full of latent power and force, that only needs cultivation to show what it can accomplish."[37] Other appraisals, similarly phrased, came in letters from many scholars or appeared in newspapers and literary magazines.[38]

Bassett contributed frequently to the quarterly during his forty months as editor; less often after he retired from that position. He got to "The Bottom of the Matter" in the second number with a discussion of the South's literary backwardness. Literature, he said, would not emanate from the southern region until southerners desired it. He found "no strong love of books" in the South. The situation could not be explained by saying that no good books were written by southerners or that they were too indigent to purchase them. Four forces, Bassett thought, provided a foundation for future achievement: the development of southern urban life, an educational renaissance, a regional pride that demanded creative literary effort, and a sufficient esthetic sense for the appreciation of "at least the lighter and entertaining forms of literature."[39]

In presenting "The Problems of the Author in the South," Bassett named first the southern provincialism that fostered antiquated "matter of thought" and annihilated "that literary atmosphere which writers find essential to creative work." Some authors had left the South temporarily, some permanently, to breathe "the fresh air of cosmopolitanism." Southern institutions of higher learning were responsible for "poverty of scholarship," for education was "too shallow to give the culture which must underlie literary production." Poverty of the author was another factor. But perhaps the greatest impediment to creative and productive work was a resentful attitude toward criticism, notably among newspaper editors. Bassett cited the attack by a North Carolinian on Trent's biography of William Gilmore Simms. The editor might disagree with the author, but why should he characterize him as a miscreant and assail his personal rectitude? "The future of authorship in the South," Bassett concluded, "will be in the hands of the new man"—one "not descended from what are supposed to be the leading classes." [40]

Political intolerance in the South greatly disturbed him. In an article on "The Reign of Passion," he alluded to an unidentified convention in North Carolina (undoubtedly an assemblage of Republicans) —"a representative gathering of American citizens" who "were performing not only an innocent and a legal, but a beneficial act of citizenship." A Democratic paper in a nearby town reported the proceedings in "a spirit of contemptuous vituperation. Not content with attacking the views of its adversaries," the editor proceeded "to ridicule them personally and individually." Southerners had "long ceased to battle for ideas"; real statesmanship of the past was supplanted by "appeals to feeling." Bassett traced historically the growing dominance of passion in southern politics and urged tolerant differences of opinion as a desideratum.[41]

Bassett's most provocative article, "Stirring Up the Fires of Race Antipathy," appeared in the October, 1903, issue.[42] It is analyzed in some detail elsewhere; [43] here, it is sufficient to indicate that the piece caused a storm of protest from North Carolina conservatives and a demand that he resign. He successfully weathered the storm, and academic freedom gained a notable victory.

Soon thereafter William E. Dodd contributed an article on "Some Difficulties of the History Teacher in the South," and dissentients expressed themselves in strong language.[44] Bassett replied in "The Task of the Critic." According to the editor, Dodd "was pronounced a traitor to the South and a flatterer of those who were not in sympathy with the section in which he lives." Bassett did not attempt to "defend" Dodd nor to "controvert" his enemies. He spoke of the eternal war of the critic on conservatism: "It is not to be denied that both conservatism and criticism abuse their functions at times. Conservatism summons prejudice to its aid all too frequently. . . . the defenders of conservatism turn on the critic in furious personal attacks. They denounce his motives; they pronounce him a traitor to his people." But the critic also had his faults. He overstated, often deliberately, "the extent of the evils which he seeks to remedy." [45]

The *South Atlantic Quarterly* under Bassett's editorship contained more than literary criticism and analyses of present-day southern problems, for he published a generous proportion of historical articles. The editor himself made such contributions as the "Character of the Early Virginia Trade," "The Industrial Decay of the Southern Planter," "The Negro's Inheritance from Africa," and "A Revival of Interest in North Carolina History." [46] Among other articles written by southern men on southern subjects were: "The Anti-Slavery Sentiment in Virginia," by James C. Ballagh; [47] "North Carolina in the Revolution," by William E. Dodd; [48] "The Peace Movement in Alabama During the Civil War," by Walter L. Fleming; [49] "The Economics of the Plantation" and "Conservatism and Progress in the Cotton Belt," by Ulrich B. Phillips; [50] "The Removal of Legal and Political Disabilities, 1868–1898," by J. G. de Roulhac Hamilton; [51] and "Some Effects of Industrialism in an Agricultural State," by Holland Thompson.[52]

Bassett's valedictory as editor of the quarterly appeared in the first issue of 1905. He retired "reluctantly," he said, "because of an accumulation of other labors which cannot be declined." He expressed his obligation to "the intelligent men—most of them Southerners—who have been chiefly responsible for the success of the enterprise," and he was pleased "that the literary life of the South was being advanced. The difficulties of the undertaking, which at first were many, have continually decreased. The fact that every article in the present number is by a native Southerner is a matter of gratification to the editor." [53]

III

During Bassett's first half dozen years at Trinity College he established himself as a North Carolina historian. As a graduate student at the Johns Hopkins and as professor at Trinity College, he wisely exploited local sources; with few exceptions his publications before the turn of the century treated aspects of his own state's history. In concentrating upon local materials in his formative years, he was following sound principle, but perhaps a major factor in determining his interest was the publication, between 1886 and 1890, of that ten-volume storehouse of primary evidence, *The Colonial Records of North Carolina*. He began his monograph on "The Regulators of North Carolina" (1895) by suggesting that the printing of these documents would require a revision of the colonial epoch.[54] Nearly eighty per cent of the citations in this study were to that monumental work; his doctor's dissertation, *The Constitutional Beginnings of North Carolina* (1894),[55] depended upon it in equal amount; and more than half of the material in his *Slavery and Servitude in the Colony of North Carolina* (1896)[56] was drawn from it. Next in importance for his colonial and state studies were the North Carolina laws and codes. Court reports were used to good advantage and so were newspapers on occasion, particularly in *Anti-Slavery Leaders of North Carolina* (1898)[57] and in *Slavery in the State of North Carolina* (1899).[58] There was a sprinkling of citations to manuscripts, mainly to unpublished laws and to records of religious groups. Two colonial accounts—John Lawson's *A New Voyage To Carolina; Containing the Exact Description and Natural History of that Country* (1709) and John Brickell's *The Natural History of North-Carolina* (1737)—provided substantial contemporary evidence, and four or five early histories of the commonwealth were used with discrimination. John A. Doyle's *English Colonies in America* (1882–1907) and Justin Winsor's *Narrative and Critical History of America* (1884–89) were employed for background; and monographs by other Johns Hopkins students promoted comparisons with other states.

Bassett's study of the Regulators is easily the best of his North Carolina brochures. Most of the pertinent sources were utilized, the evidence was handled judiciously, and "The Regulation Proper" was prefaced by consideration of the country's topography, the colony's social and institutional patterns, the Regulators' grievances, the leaders of the movement, and the previous conflicts between authority and settlers. Although Bassett was fair to royal agents in the colony, he regarded the movement as "a worthy struggle for liberty," and he concluded that "justness" was "chiefly on the side of the Regulators." He insisted that the Regulation was "a peasants' rising, a popular upheaval," rather than a revolution, and that it was political and economic rather than religious.[59]

Beyond his North Carolina studies, Bassett's Trinity College tenure yielded two significant works, an edition of *The Writings of "Colonel William Byrd of Westover in Virginia, Esqr."* (1901), and a volume in the "American Nation Series," *The Federalist System, 1789–1801* (1906). Brief articles appeared from time to time not only in the *South Atlantic Quarterly* but also in historical periodicals and elsewhere.

The Byrd volume was published in an attractive format in a limited edition. An eighty-page introduction, "The Byrd Family in Virginia," was a creditable essay on social, economic, and political life in the Old Dominion during the latter half of the seventeenth century and the first half of the eighteenth, as reflected in the careers of the first two William Byrds. Material for the biographical sketches and their background was drawn mainly from the letters of the Byrds, father and son; the Noel W. Sainsbury transcripts of Virginia papers in the British Public Record Office; and the minutes of the Virginia council. Among miscellaneous sources were the "Byrd Title-book," the Alexander Spotswood letters, William W. Hening's *Statutes at Large,* and the *Virginia Magazine of History and Biography.* Bassett concluded that the elder Byrd "had a great deal of business capacity and somewhat less of social capacity, while the younger had a great deal of social capacity and somewhat less of business capacity." * Some errors in the essay were corrected by the later researches of Philip A. Bruce, Thomas J. Wertenbaker, and Louis B. Wright, and the last in particular greatly expanded our knowledge of the Byrd family and its background.

Encouraged by J. Franklin Jameson,[60] Bassett intended to publish many of the extant Byrd letters, but when he discovered that the Virginia Historical Society was assembling them for publication in its magazine, he decided to reprint only a few for illustrative purposes. He included in his edition of the *Writings* the "History of the Dividing Line," "A Journey to the Land of Eden," "A Progress to the Mines," and some "Miscellaneous Letters." As appendixes he printed "A Catalogue of Books in the

* John S. Bassett (ed.), *The Writings of "Colonel William Byrd of Westover in Virginia Esqr."* (Garden City, N.Y., 1901), xlii. The volume was not a money-making proposition for Bassett. He received $100 for editorial work and $40 to pay the cost of typing. Doubleday, Page and Company to Bassett, April 22, 1901, Bassett Papers. For correspondence relating to the $10 price of the volume, see Dodd to Bassett, October 6, 1901, Bassett Papers; Bassett to Dodd, October 11, 1901, William E. Dodd Papers (Manuscript Division, Library of Congress, Washington, D.C.).

Library at Westover Belonging to William Byrd Esqr." and a genealogy of the Byrd family prepared originally by William G. Stanard, secretary of the Virginia Historical Society.

It has been noted that Bassett resigned as editor of the *South Atlantic Quarterly* because "other labors" had been accumulating. The important task he had accepted was a volume in the "American Nation Series," with a deadline that required concentrated effort. Not until October 22, 1904, did Albert B. Hart, editor of the cooperative work, invite him to contribute the *Federalist System* to the series, and the invitation designated August 1 of the following year as the date when the completed manuscript must be in his hands. As Bassett had but nine months to do the research and write 70,000 words, it is understandable why he relinquished editorship of the quarterly.

Hart explained that Andrew C. McLaughlin had agreed to write volume XI as well as volume X (*The Confederation and the Constitution*), but that it would be impossible for him to finish the second on schedule. As Edward Channing, a New Englander, would write the *Jeffersonian System,* "there would be an obvious fitness in committing the previous volume to a Southern man whose reputation for fairness of view is so well established as yours." [61] Apparently the manuscript was finished on schedule, for Hart wrote on August 29, 1905, that he was returning it for slight revision. "The volume is an excellent one," he commented, "and will take an honorable place in the series. I am amazed that you have been able, under such pressure, to write so smoothly, incisively, and so much to the point. You have seized better than some of the other authors, on the fundamental idea that the series deals with large subjects in a large way." Hart was pleased with the "tone" as well as the organization, and as to composition, "the style has been polished to such a point of completion that the book might almost go to press as it reached me." The several pages of editorial comment and criticism that Hart enclosed concerned, for the most part, matters of minor import.

The manuscript was back in the editor's hands by October 10,[62] and it was published in January, 1906. Bassett's accomplishment in so short a time was almost incredible; few historians could have delivered the study so promptly. The task could hardly have been completed on time if the author had been required to examine manuscript materials. A letter of inquiry on this premise brought a statement of editorial policy: a plethora of printed sources would provide sufficient evidence, and a paucity of time would preclude research in manuscripts.[63] Footnotes as well as the "Critical Essay on Authorities" indicate that Bassett used the pertinent printed sources and that he also examined monographs and biographies.

Hart was too eulogistic in his appraisal of the work. Nevertheless, the organization of the volume was clear and logical; illustrative material was well selected and woven into the narrative unobtrusively; and the text was written in simple but forceful English. It emphasized political and diplomatic history, though an effort was made to round out and balance the dozen years under review by chapters on "The Republican Court," "The State of Society," and the "Economic Conditions." The warring political factions of the period were presented with less bias than in many treatises written thirty or forty years later, though the author was slightly prejudiced in favor of the Federalists and the system they established.

The Life of Andrew Jackson did not appear until 1911, but the project was under way as early as 1902. In that year Bassett received permission from the Blair family to use Jackson manuscripts in their possession.* The quarterly and the *Federalist System* occupied so much of his time that serious work was postponed until 1906. The two-volume biography of the seventh president of the United States was essentially the product of his early years at Smith College.

The work was based largely upon the Jackson papers, though the manuscripts of some of his contemporaries, notably Martin Van Buren, were utilized with advantage, as were also printed sources, monographs, and earlier biographies. Bassett's reliance upon unpublished sources as "the best portrayers of Jackson" is indicated in his preface. "They reveal faithfully a man who was great, spite of many limitations. He was badly educated, he was provincial, his passions frequently overcast judgment, he had a poor concept of a proper adjustment of the administrative machine, and he clung tenaciously to some of the worst political ideals of the past; yet he was so well endowed by nature that he broke over these impediments and became a man of distinction." Bassett depicted Jackson as a product of the American frontier and

* Edward G. Bourne to Bassett, November 19, 1902, Bassett Papers. Bassett was invited in 1903 to contribute a life of Jackson to the "American Crisis Biographies," edited by Ellis P. Oberholtzer, but he was already committed to Doubleday, Page and Company. Oberholtzer to Bassett, November 9, 1903, Bassett Papers.

emphasized its influence upon his thought and action.* Despite his southern birth and residence, his planting experience and the ownership of slaves, it was the West rather than the South that conditioned his genius for military and political leadership. The influence of the South was too largely ignored, for only incidental mention was made of Jackson the planter and slaveholder. The biography was, as a contemporary reviewer pointed out, "a *Life* of Jackson, not a *Life and Times.*" [64] The revolution in democracy, the great constitutional struggles, the development of a party machine, the social revolution, humanitarian trends, the agrarian-industrial cleavage—all these were touched upon but not emphasized. Later writers modified his treatment, offered new interpretation, and succeeded far better in making Jackson live again; but no later treatise entirely superseded Bassett's ponderous volumes. They were, in 1911 and after, important as a work of reference.

To Dunning, who commended him on the production of "a sound, substantial, solid and interesting biography in a spirit of scientific history," Bassett replied that he had endeavored to write a "dignified and clear" account that "would interest intelligent and serious minded people. I did not wish to make it sparkling or highly frivolous," for such a presentation "would not allow me to handle properly the new material." [65] Craftsmanship was acceptable, but the author's heavy style was devoid of literary artistry.

Bassett's understanding of Jackson matured but experienced no fundamental change in editing the six-volume *Correspondence of Andrew Jackson* (1926–35). To each of the volumes he contributed a useful introduction, although three of them appeared after his demise. Research on Jackson and his period led him to an interesting bypath, *Major Howell Tatum's Journal While Acting Topographical Engineer (1841) to General Jackson,* which appeared in the Smith College *Studies in History* (volume VII, numbers 1–3, October–April, 1921–22).

* John S. Bassett, *The Life of Andrew Jackson* (2 vols.; Garden City, N.Y., 1911), I, xi. The necessity of publishing the work in two volumes gave Doubleday, Page and Company considerable misgivings, and to appease the publishers Bassett agreed to forego royalties on the first six hundred sets. Two years after the work appeared, the company still lacked $600 of breaking even, and Arthur H. Page agreed to sell the plates for that amount despite the fact that they had cost $1,400. Negotiations continued until 1915 when Page agreed to sell them to the Macmillan Company for $200. Macmillan contracted to bring out a new edition and to pay the author 10 per cent royalty on the first five hundred copies sold and 15 per cent thereafter. Arthur H. Page to Bassett, October 13, November 7, 1913; August 20, 1915, Bassett Papers; Doubleday, Page and Company to Bassett, July 31, 1915, Bassett Papers; Macmillan Company to Bassett, October 29, 1913; August 10, 1915, Bassett Papers.

That Bassett did not abandon all interest in the history of the South after leaving Trinity College is evidenced by two pieces of editorial work. To the Smith College *Studies in History,* which he inaugurated in 1915, he contributed *The Westover Journal of John A. Selden, Esqr., 1858–1862* (volume VI, number 4, July, 1921), proprietor of a plantation once owned by the Byrds. His most important contribution to southern history after moving north was *The Southern Plantation Overseer as Revealed in His Letters* (1925). The volume embraced letters from overseers on James K. Polk's Mississippi plantation. Neglected by historians and romancers in favor of planters and slaves, the overseer was here revealed objectively through his periodic reports to his employer. The documents were reproduced in all their unlettered crudities, and they illustrated this most important plantation functionary's duties and responsibilities, his problems and his place in southern society. He was presented as a human personality, uneducated but intelligent, a liaison between the planter and his labor supply. Despite his illiteracy and his low station in society, he was entrusted with the care and management of property worth many thousands of dollars. The institution of slavery was also revealed in the letters, for there was much about abscondings and punishments, births and deaths, life and labor. The volume was more than a mere reproduction of letters, for Bassett wrote introductory chapters on the overseer's place in the plantation regime, the terms of his contract, and Polk's planting experience; and he concluded the volume with essays on the services of New Orleans factors to upriver planters and "The Lesson of the Letters."

Of Bassett's other works emanating from his Smith College period, two were textbooks for college classes in American history: *A Short History of the United States* (1913), which went through sundry editions and reprintings; and *Expansion and Reform, 1889–1926* (1926), a volume in the "Epochs of American History." *Makers of a New Nation* (1928) comprised volume IX of *The Pageant of America, A Pictorial History of the United States.* A hastily prepared historiographical study, *The Middle Group of American Historians* (1917), contained essays on Jared Sparks, George Bancroft, William H. Prescott, John L. Motley, and Peter Force; introductory and closing chapters dealt with the historians who antedated the middle group and the relations of historians to their publishers. Closely related to this work were two collections of documents contributed to the Smith College *Studies in History:* the *Correspondence of George Bancroft and Jared Sparks, 1823–1832* (volume II, number 2, January, 1917), and *Letters of Francis Parkman to Pierre Margry* (volume VIII, numbers 3–4, April–July, 1923). Bassett also edited, in the same field, *The Writing of History* (1926), and contributed to it a penetrating essay on "The Present State of History Writing." Three works concerned current American problems and international affairs: *The Lost Fruits of Waterloo* (1918); *Our War With Germany: A History* (1919); and *The League of Nations; A Chapter in World Politics* (1928).

By the turn of the century both Bassett and the cause of history in the South were recognized by the American Historical Association. The society's council appointed him a member of the general committee in 1902,[66] a position he retained for several years. Bassett and other southern historians, with Dunning as an ally, promoted a meeting on southern soil, and sessions on southern history became a regular part of the association's programs.

Late in 1900 an effort was made to fix upon Nashville as the place of meeting in 1902. Bassett urged Adams to use his influence with the council to provide a "missionary journey into the South" where there was "an appreciable revival of interest in the teaching of history." [67] A year later he encouraged Charles H. Haskins to sponsor Nashville's claims: "I believe it would do the cause of History in the South a vast deal of good if the meeting should be at Nashville. It would awaken interest on the part of Southerners. It would serve to strengthen the teaching of History in our colleges. It would, perhaps, give something of a thrust at the Confederate-Brigadier-General kind of an historian—and that is a snake which ought to be hit whenever it is possible." A meeting at Nashville did not materialize, largely because the South had very few members and the program as well as attendance might suffer.[68]

Meanwhile, in the spring of 1901, Bassett suggested to Jameson the expediency of establishing a permanent committee of the American Historical Association on southern history. Jameson thought it inadvisable to form a permanent organization for that field, but he was certain that the history of the South would be "adequately represented" at the next annual meeting.[69] A southern history section was arranged, and Bassett was invited to present a paper on "The Relations of the Virginia Planter and the London

Merchant." Other papers were read by Dodd, Lyon G. Tyler of William and Mary College, George P. Garrison of the University of Texas, and Bernard C. Steiner of the Enoch Pratt Free Library of Baltimore.[70]

Some southern historians were determined that the session allotted to them should accomplish more than the presentation of papers on the South. Dodd suggested to Bassett an "interchange of ideas and plans" among "the really industrious, active Southern men." David Y. Thomas, recalling a recent discussion with Bassett, proposed a federation of historical societies in the South "with an official organ—say the Southern Historical Review." He believed that the new organization should absorb the Southern Historical Society and the Southern History Association, though perhaps the former was too "exclusive" to federate.[71]

A journal of southern history did not materialize, but the southern section of the association adopted resolutions presented by Bassett proposing an investigation of the status of historical instruction in the South. He was appointed a member of a committee, headed by Frederick W. Moore of Vanderbilt University, to make the investigation. The committee's report appeared in the *Vanderbilt University Quarterly*,[72] and Moore also contributed to the *South Atlantic Quarterly* a brief article under the caption, "The Status of History in Southern Colleges." [73]

The association decided to hold its 1903 meeting in New Orleans, and Dunning was appointed to arrange a conference on "the study and teaching of history in the South." Bassett accepted a place on the program and proposed to talk on "the relation of history teaching and southern political ideals." Dodd was scheduled for "some difficulties in the way of the teacher of history," and Moore, Thomas M. Owen, and Franklin L. Riley completed the roster of participants. Severe illness prevented Bassett from attending the meeting. A score of southerners registered, less than the number that came from faraway Massachusetts. But the reports of the meeting which reached Bassett gave enthusiastic accounts of the southern section.[74]

Bassett continued to play an active role in the affairs of the association, though his interest in promoting the South waned after he transferred to Smith College. When "reformers," several of them southerners, undertook to reorganize the association in 1914–15, Bassett took a liberal but by no means extreme view. Soon thereafter, in 1919, he was elected secretary of the association, a position he held until his death in 1928. In that capacity he was one of the prime movers in a project to endow the association.

IV

That Bassett welcomed a call from a northern school cannot be doubted. The thing he desired most was leisure time to write, an ambition that antedated graduate work at the Johns Hopkins. A heavy teaching load at Trinity College, multifarious duties expected of a professor in a small school, inadequate library materials, and incipient faculty dissensions placed him in a receptive mood when an opportunity offered to move north.

Charles D. Hazen, head of the department at Smith College, approached Bassett in the spring of 1906 regarding a vacancy at the Northampton school. The position carried the rank of associate professor, a salary of $1,500, and a teaching load of ten or twelve hours. A library of 160,000 volumes and the proximity of several research centers were added inducements. As Bassett's salary at Trinity College was then $2,100, plus the use of a house, he could not consider the offer seriously; if the stipend were adequate he would "not hesitate to ask for the position." Hazen presented the matter to President Julius Seelye, with the result that an offer equivalent to Bassett's Durham salary was proposed and an invitation to an interview at Northampton extended. The negotiations materialized in an offer of a full professorship at a stipend of $2,500.[75] Meanwhile, Bassett sought Dunning's advice on the expediency of moving to Smith College, and the Columbia University professor offered to investigate conditions at the New England school. He would regret to see the South lose Bassett, but if he were determined to leave Dunning thought the Smith College offer was a great opportunity, and it might be a step toward something even better.[76] Before Dunning could write again, Yale University became interested in Bassett, and Dunning's next letter contrasted the two opportunities:

"It is beautiful to think that New England has at last discovered N.C., & especially that Yale has discovered anything outside of Yale. The distinction of an offer from Y. is greater than the other; *but* the general reputation of Y. for grinding the faces of its staff with class work is a bad one. You are in a position to make terms. Be sure to do it in that matter. They have a vast horde of students at Yale & no aspirations for higher than college work. Hence the necessity of grinding the profs. Smith is a *comfortable* place; Y. is apt to be the contrary. If from motives of Kudos you prefer discomfort, see that you are paid for it in good substantial coin of the realm." [77]

Bassett hoped to see Walter H. Page on his way to the Northampton interview, but having failed in that, he penned his reasons for deciding to transfer. He reiterated his aspiration to write, which would be promoted by "the quiet and stimulus of the New England town," and he pointed to the disadvantage of remaining in the South. He recalled Page's own pioneering efforts as a newspaper editor in North Carolina a score of years earlier, the state's failure to appreciate his preachments there, and his determination to leave the South. "No doubt twenty years from now young men will be doing glibly down here just what I should like to be doing today, writing freely without the drudgery of high school work and the impediment of scant library facilities; but twenty years from now I shall be nearly sixty years old. Can I do the world any good by sitting down waiting for the procession to come? And haven't I done about all I can do to hasten the arrival of the procession?" [78]

What were Bassett's reactions to his new environment? To William G. Brown, then nursing tuberculosis at Asheville, he wrote after a few months residence in Northampton: "I like the place very much, the people are pleasant, the work is not bad, the girls are studious, and I am satisfied. The New England ideals are not like those of the South, but they are not so different that I cannot like them. I know well what you felt in this country, the lack of the Southern touch, and the longing that the people of our part of [the] country had with their own virtues [for] some of the good things that the Northern people have shown so well how to establish. If to our warmth of spirit we could add the New England libraries, the New England Ideals of scholarship, and the New [England] wealth, how much could we not distance these people in the production of both literature and men! But you know better than I." [79]

William K. Boyd, Bassett's successor at Trinity College, spent the preceding year as instructor at Dartmouth and acquired an unfavorable view of New England life and students. He regretted that Bassett transferred to the Northeast, and a year after removal he took inventory of his reaction, to which Bassett replied: "You ask if I do not really want to be back in the South. Candidly, No." He then reviewed his labors at Trinity College and contrasted his new environment with the old. If he could retire after a decade on a Carnegie pension, he would spend his winters in the South, but the New England atmosphere, mental and physical, was too stimulating to think of returning permanently.[80]

Departing from formal historiography, it should be recorded that Bassett was a prodigious worker, a successful businessman, and a friendly colleague. He budgeted his time systematically, reserving a large portion of it for research and writing. Periodically he resorted to a diary, particularly with the view of recording the number of words he wrote each day. Frequently he became discouraged with progress and noted a determination to do better. Lapses in entries, when other activities interfered for weeks with his daily stints, were followed by periods of sustained accomplishment, with a thousand words an average performance and three thousand a peak attainment.[81] If there were dinner guests who tarried too long, he might drowse until they departed, and then resume animated work at his typewriter. Some of his books, particularly *A Short History of the United States,* yielded substantial royalties, and good investments increased his income.[82] Among his closest professional friends were Dunning, Dodd, Boyd, and Frederic Bancroft. Cordial relations with Bancroft ended when Bassett refused to follow extremists in efforts to reform the American Historical Association; friendship with Dodd persisted despite critical reviews of some of Dodd's books; correspondence with Dunning revealed that Bassett as well as the "Old Chief" possessed a keen sense of humor; epistolarian congeniality with Boyd continued unbroken for more than thirty years.

It is difficult to estimate Bassett's place in American historiography, for he did not concentrate upon a theme with single-minded devotion, nor did he have the opportunity as a graduate professor to train a body of students in historical methodology. His interests were so diversified that his productive work defies classification. The North Carolina monographs were the product of immaturity, however much they may have contributed to his own development as a historian. An abiding interest in southern history found expression in *William Byrd* and the *Southern Plantation Overseer,* but these and other studies of the South cannot justify listing him among the leading authorities in the field of southern history. He reached historical maturity in the *Federalist System,* which marked a transition from local to national history and brought recognition beyond the limits of the South.

Recent and contemporary history—an interest dating from the 1890's—occupied much of his attention during the last decade of his career, but creditable productivity in this field yielded no permanent monument to his memory. Historiographical studies, especially *The Middle Group of American Historians,* will have more lasting value. As a biographer of Andrew Jackson and as an editor of his correspondence, Bassett attained authoritative stature. Despite lack of concentration, however, the total picture of published miscellanea is large and significant. These, together with his pioneering efforts in behalf of southern history and his contributions to the American Historical Association, make his career worthy of chronicling for posterity.

CHAPTER V

John Spencer Bassett: Transitional Concept of the Negro

John Spencer Bassett, pioneer in the origins of southern historical scholarship, was also an advocate of liberal thought on the race problem in the South.[1] As the nineteenth century drew to a close, he expressed himself frankly on the political and social questions of the day and urged fellow southerners to break with tradition and face practical realities. From the vantage point of a professorship in history at Trinity College, he preached a doctrine of liberalism to students who came under his tutelage, and he aroused the ire of conservative politicians, editors, and churchmen. The Negro was not a central theme in Bassett's varied activities as teacher, researcher, editor, and lecturer, but the subject was of sufficient importance to merit careful examination.

I

His paternal ancestors, Bassett asserted in a brief memoir, were antislavery in their views despite the fact that they were slaveholders on a small scale in Virginia and North Carolina. His grandfather, Richard Bassett, carpenter and contractor at Williamsburg, was faced with the dilemma of purchasing a cook who had served him faithfully as a hired slave for many years or of seeing her sold to an unacceptable master. He chose the former alternative. Richard's son, Richard Baxter Bassett, followed his father's trade and purchased skilled laborers to promote his business. According to the memoir, neither father nor son was an agitator in the antislavery cause. Richard Baxter served the Confederacy, first as a soldier and then as a manufacturer of army supplies, and emerged from the war slaveless and "practically empty-handed."

How relevant these statements are in explaining Bassett's own attitudes is problematical, but at least one point is clear: he believed that he was emulating the example of his forebears. He emphasized the democratic spirit which made them "unwilling to ignore the rights of inferior people." Of his father he said, "He was an ideal democrat." [2] It is possible, too, that the influence of a piedmont environment in his formative years accentuated his faith in the common man, whether black or white.

It should be noted also that graduate work at the Johns Hopkins University prepared Bassett's mind to challenge conservative thought and traditional belief. His greatest teacher there, Herbert B. Adams, inspired an openmindedness that was determinative, and the atmosphere of the whole history, political science, and economics department gave him a critical and impartial approach in the treatment of past and present.

It was not unusual in the 1890's for Johns Hopkins graduates in history to return to Baltimore to address the Seminary of History and Politics or to deliver formal lectures before larger groups. Adams inspired his students by example as well as by precept, and the appearance of former scholars in the role of lecturer had a stimulating effect upon his current group of doctoral candidates. Bassett was perhaps his most outstanding product from the South, and an assignment was not difficult to arrange. In 1899 the Trinity College professor wrote Adams that he was contemplating preparation of some studies on the Negro which would consider "his past, his present, and his future," and that he would welcome the opportunity to deliver them as lectures at the Johns Hopkins. "I want to show," he said, "that the nature of the negro is such that he is destined—when he shall have been civilized and greatly developed—to be a great and valuable force in American society." He would probably prepare the studies anyway, but the prospect of presenting them in Baltimore would serve as further motivation.[3]

Bassett received the invitation, but the lectures were postponed from time to time as a result of Adams' absence from the university on account of illness and of Bassett's delay in completing them. Meanwhile, he kept Adams informed of progress, revealed his thinking on the Negro problem, and modified his organization. The series would use as a point of departure slavery's disintegration in the later period of the Roman Empire, and by analogy and contrast show how the South should develop "reliable freedom" among the former slaves. Even "the most blinded 'Bourbon' " could hardly disapprove an objective consideration of the Negro's accomplishments and potentialities.[4] Further maturity of thought eventually yielded lectures on "the Negro in Africa," "the Negro in American slavery," and "the Negro in American freedom," all with a "historical rather than sociological approach," though present-day problems were not ignored.[5]

One of the lectures, perhaps in greatly modified form, was published a few years later in the *South Atlantic Quarterly* under the title, "The Negro's Inheritance from Africa." It is not apparent what sources of information Bassett used in its preparation except that he referred approvingly a few times to Friedrick Ratzel's three-volume *History of Mankind,* published in 1896. Bassett's brief article was a description of the Negro's physical environment and its conditioning factors, a statement of his dependence upon simple argicultural processes, and an analysis of such institutions as the village community, the family, and the religious organization. He did not indicate how the Negro's traits and habits of life were modified by two centuries of residence in the South.[6]

Soon after delivering the lectures early in 1901, Bassett conceived the idea of expanding them into a book and inquired whether Richard T. Ely might be interested in publishing it in the "Citizen Series." The chapters into which the proposed study would be organized indicate a rather comprehensive view of the subject:

The Negro in Africa
Conditions of the Slave Trade
The Negro in Contact with the White Man in Africa
The Negro in American Slavery
The Iron Law of Slavery
Free Negroes in the South
The Negro in the Old Free States
The First Lessons in Freedom
The Debauching of Citizenship
The Negro in Modern Industrial Life
The Religious Progress of the Negro
The Educational Progress of the Negro
The Negro's Social Life
The Rise of a Negro Upper Class[7]

The volume did not materialize, either through failure to find a publisher or inability to carry out his resolution.

Bassett's writing before the turn of the century was concerned primarily with the history of North Carolina. Three of his monographs dealt with the institution of slavery and antislavery leaders: *Slavery and Servitude in the Colony of North Carolina* (1896), *Anti-Slavery Leaders of North Carolina* (1898), and *Slavery in the State of North Carolina* (1899). Like most of Bassett's other early works, these were neither comprehensive nor exhaustive. Material was drawn from a limited number of sources, partly because there were few great collections available but also because historians of that day had not thought of rich mines of information that later scholars exploited. Despite inadequacy in this premise, the studies serve a useful purpose in revealing Bassett's thought in an important field of knowledge. Slavery in colony and state was presented in an orthodox arrangement, with a revisionist point of view tempered by an appreciation of complex factors that collectively formed the warp and woof of the old regime. Interpretations and conclusions are illustrated by a sampling of his statements.

Despite disadvantages of slavery to both blacks and whites, "it is difficult to see how the aimless, good-natured, and improvident African could ever have been brought as a race to plow, to sow, to reap, to study, and at length to create thought, except for the tutelage of his slaveholding master." On the other hand, Bassett insisted that "the negro went side by side with the white man in the van of the civilizing forces of the country." [8] The harshness of slavery legislation in the 1830's and afterward did not emanate from "deliberate cruelty on the part of the slave-owners. There are throughout the period of greatest restriction enough humane laws and more than enough humane custom to show the contrary." Again, "the central idea of slavery in North Carolina was a determination to perpetuate the institution, whatever the price, and at the same time a disposition to make it as gentle as possible for the slave, provided that doing so did not tend to loosen his bonds." And, if Bassett "were defending a side of the never ended controversy about the treatment of slaves by their masters, it would only be necessary to point out here that the essence of the misery of slavery in the South and elsewhere was not physical suffering, however frequently or infrequently that may have occurred, but the mental and spiritual wretchedness that follow a loss of liberty." He concluded that "it was slavery itself that defeated the humaner forces of civilization." [9]

The second of Bassett's trilogy of studies on the Negro in North Carolina sketched the careers of five antislavery leaders: Hinton R. Helper, Daniel R. Goodloe, Eli W. Caruthers, Lunsford Lane, and Benjamin S. Hedrick. It is the least satisfactory of the three, for it represents only a modicum of research and the author did not always sense the true import of abolitionist literature. He correctly evaluated the political significance of Helper's *Impending Crisis of the South* (1857) and the *Compendium* (1860), but apparently he accepted at face value much of the economic fallacy that found its way into these publications. The fact that Helper was still living and that Bassett carried on considerable correspondence with him may account for the mantle of charity which covers the extremist and his works.*

The fate that befell Hedrick is of special interest because it paralleled in part Bassett's own experience at Trinity College a few years later. Native of North Carolina, student of Louis Agassiz at Harvard, and professor of analytical and agricultural chemistry at the University of North Carolina, Hedrick admitted in 1856 that he would vote for John C. Frémont if Republican electors were presented in the state. His boyhood among antislavery farmers in the western part of North Carolina and his sojourn in the North had made him an abolitionist, albeit an inoffensive one. William W. Holden, editor of the North Carolina *Standard,* demanded that Hedrick be removed from his professorship. Feeling ran high, and eventually Hedrick replied in a statement published in the paper. In it he said that he preferred Frémont because his views on the slavery issue were correct, and in his defense cited the antislavery opinions of western North Carolinians and also the attitude of such Virginians as Washington and Jefferson. But the president, faculty, and students favored removal, and the board of trustees in effect dismissed him.

Of Hedrick's first communication to the *Standard,* Bassett wrote feelingly: "In the light of present knowledge, the South knows that he spoke the truth, and one ought not to criticise a man for speaking the truth, especially if he be an instructor in an institution of learning, which ought at all times to be a leader of truth."

* Hinton R. Helper to Bassett, May 16, October 21, November 2, 4, December 26, 1896, January 14, 1897, Bassett Papers. Helper supplied Bassett with considerable information about his efforts to find a publisher for the *Impending Crisis* and its reception in the South; and he also forwarded some papers relating to Benjamin S. Hedrick, the property of his son, Charles J. Hedrick, a lawyer of Washington, D.C.

Of a later exchange between Hedrick and Holden, Bassett said: "On the one side we have a clear, strong argument, unanswerable, a sense of outrage, a protest against passion; on the other we have an avoidance of argument in the beginning, a ruthless unwillingness to concede a desire for truth to the other side, an appeal to passion, and a supercilious tone of superiority." [10] Five years later Bassett found himself confronted with a similar situation, but the effort to remove him from his professorship was counterbalanced by support from students, faculty, and trustees.

II

Just before the opening of the twentieth century there was a revival of the Negro issue in North Carolina politics. The Old North State had recovered "white supremacy" in the 1870's, but a fusion of Republicans and Populists in the 1890's brought the Negro into politics again—and into public office. The Democrats won the election of 1898 and set about to eliminate the Negro permanently. A constitutional amendment to that end was proposed and adopted. Soon after the Democratic victory, Bassett wrote Adams that North Carolinians were exulting because the issue had been solved. He was of the opinion that it had been temporarily shelved. Admitting that he did not concur with the majority of white people in the state, he suggested three alternatives with regard to the political future of the Negro: permit him to vote and hold office, "nauseating as the dose is"; administer impartially a literacy qualification; or use fraudulent and violent means of denying him office. Personally he preferred the second method, but a campaign of passion had produced the third solution and had inaugurated policies which sensible government could not correct in a score of years. The recent Wilmington riot, Bassett asserted, resulted from the attacks of the Democratic press against Negro misrule which did not exist. There were only a few Negroes in local offices, and they were "guided in their action by the advice of white men." He believed that the Negro had behaved admirably in the face of the newspaper onslaught. "Vilified, abused, denounced as the unclean thing he has kept his peace; he has been patient." [11]

While Bassett spoke as plainly as a college professor could on a political issue, he feared his efforts would not promote reform. Apparently Adams gave acceptable advice when Bassett asked what remedy he would prescribe if he "were the physician," for Bassett wrote that his duty was now clear: "If I can set a limit to this wildfire of prejudice that is in the South I will do it. It is a difficult task, and a delicate one: the point is to come at the people—not through blows & kicks; but through kindness. Tell the northern philanthropists that *the way to help the Negro in the South is to educate the white man.*" If a "broad churchman" were available, reform could be promoted by the church, for the southerner could be reached "through his religion." Returning to the subject of the Wilmington riot, he expressed the opinion that the difficulty would not "set us back any more than the social & intellectual conditions behind it—which we have had all along. I cannot believe that any outside capital will ever develop the South: it must come from the Southern people themselves, if it comes at all." [12]

On May 3, 1900, Bassett delivered the commencement address at the Slater Industrial School, an institution for Negroes at Winston-Salem, North Carolina. The invitation may have come as a result of his liberal attitude on the race issue. Promising Adams a copy of the address, he alluded again to the "commotion" that arose over the suffrage amendment. "On all hands the negroes are frightened—they know not what lies in the future for them. Out of it all the politician reaps fatness." [13]

Two of Bassett's *South Atlantic Quarterly* articles merit analysis, one because of its intrinsic value, the other because of the furor it aroused. "Two Negro Leaders," a contrast of Booker T. Washington and William E. Burghardt Du Bois, was inspired by the appearance of the latter's book, *The Souls of Black Folk, Essays and Sketches* (1903). The president of Tuskegee Institute, in *The Future of the American Negro* (1899) and *Up From Slavery* (1900), had revealed his emphasis upon an industrial education for the Negro, peaceful relations with white neighbors, abandonment of politics, and economic advancement to the point where it would be an honor to belong to the black race. Du Bois, a New Englander, graduate of Fiske and Harvard universities, and author of scholarly books, repudiated economic self-sufficiency as the chief desideratum in favor of cultural development. The door of learning had opened Shakespeare, Balzac, and Dumas to him, and he drank at the fountain of Aurelius and Aristotle; yet race prejudice closed to him, from the days of his youth even in New England, participation in many aspects of life reserved for members of the white race.

Bassett saw no eternal conflict between the concepts of these leaders. The great majority of Negroes—perhaps nine-tenths of them—needed just what Washington sought to give them, "industrial training and business competency." His policy of peace, despite caustic criticism of whites, was destined to make the Negro "more patient and self-controlled," and it would eventually win adherents among southern liberals. On the other hand, the Negro needed leadership from his own race, and higher education should therefore not be discouraged. As Bassett saw it, there should be vocational education for the many, cultural education for the few; and a sympathetic attitude on the part of white people toward Negro advancement in both directions.[14] He was one of the first scholars to appreciate the significance of the two schools of thought that emanated from the teachings of Washington and Du Bois, and one of the first to rationalize the variation.

In founding the *South Atlantic Quarterly*, promoting the "liberty to think" was a fundamental purpose; discussion of the race problem an incidental theme. Yet one will find in the issues during Bassett's brief tenure as editor from 1902 until 1905 considerable space devoted to slavery and the Negro. James C. Ballagh discussed "The Anti-Slavery Sentiment in Virginia"; [15] Robert W. Winston, "An Unconsidered Aspect of the Negro Question"; [16] Carl Holliday, "National Supervision of Negro Education"; [17] and John C. Kilgo, "Our Duty to the Negro." [18] Bassett himself contributed, besides "The Negro's Inheritance from Africa" and "Two Negro Leaders," an editorial article on "Stirring Up the Fires of Race Antipathy." [19] Because of a provocative sentence that incited protest, the nature and content of the article require some discussion.

Published in the October, 1903, number of the quarterly, "Stirring Up the Fires of Race Antipathy" was for the most part a dispassionate discussion of the race problem in the South. Bassett indicated how "present antipathy" emanated from the political issue, and he traced that vexed question from colonial days to the past decade. The disfranchisement of the Negro eliminated him as a political issue, but "sensational appeals to the race feeling of the white man" supplanted it as a disturbing divisive factor. Bassett pointed to the progress some Negroes had made since the war, and to the supposed retrogression of others into idleness, viciousness, and criminality. The optimist "was apt to point to Booker T. Washington as a product of the negro race." Then followed the fateful sentence which aroused a storm of passion over North Carolina: "Now Washington is a great and good man, a Christian statesman, and take him all in all the greatest man, save General Lee, born in the South in a hundred years; but he is not a typical negro." [20]

Soon after the article appeared, the Raleigh *News and Observer* reprinted it, and through news stories, editorials, and headlines distorted the meaning and inflamed the public mind: "Professor Bassett says Negro will win equality"; "Southern leaders slandered"; "Dire predictions of coming conflict between the races"; "The people feel that Professor Bassett's utterances are an outrage." The author's name appeared as "bASSett," and the editor of the *News and Observer,* Josephus Daniels, alluded to him as a freak. Other newspapers published ebullient tirades, and many of them were reprinted in Daniels' paper. A few presses, such as the *Progressive Farmer,* the Charlotte *Observer,* the *Caucasian,* the *Biblical Recorder,* and the Durham *Herald,* defended Bassett and his article. He received hundreds of letters, some denunciatory and others commendatory. Friends in the historical guild offered sympathy and counsel. On November 10 Bassett published an explanation in the Durham paper. "Between the races," he said, "is a wide gulf and I should be the last man to try to bridge it. I had no thought of social equality in mind. I was thinking only of the industrial and civic outlook of the negro race." He explained the word *greatest* as the "capacity to break over fearful impediments and achieve success."

The attack spread to President Kilgo and the entire college; a boycott was proposed, and parents were urged to remove their children from Trinity College. Under the circumstances Bassett submitted his resignation, and the trustees met in special session December 2 to consider it. President, faculty, and students appealed to the board, emphasizing the principle of academic freedom. Few of them could endorse Bassett's appraisal of Washington, but they could plead for a spirit of liberty and toleration. The trustees voted eighteen to eleven not to accept Bassett's resignation. Trinity College had a larger enrollment the next year, and the college continued to grow in prestige and influence.

Much of this was well known to contemporaries, for it appeared in print many times.[21] Some men who knew Bassett well professed to believe that he was trimming his sails for a call to a northern university, following the example of William P. Trent, another southern liberal who had moved in 1900 from the University of the South to Columbia University. It would be useless to speculate upon motive, for the historian is upon dangerous ground in attempting to read another's mind except as it is revealed in documentary evidence. Some recently discovered material in the Bassett Papers may offer a clue, though whether it tells the whole story is a matter of conjecture.

Despite abuse from the North Carolina press, Bassett declined then or later to defend his course in public, except for the brief explanation that appeared contemporaneously in a Durham newspaper. William K. Boyd urged him in 1908 to write up the "Bassett Affair," but the central figure of the controversy replied that he did not have all of the documents at hand. "I did not write in the first instance," he said, "with the idea of raising a controversy, but to do a certain good in a certain situation; and in spite of the insane ravings of those whom I had hit, I think some good was accomplished. I always felt that the affair cleared the atmosphere to some extent with regard to the negro question. I think it showed some people in North Carolina that they were likely to get into trouble by cultivating the anti-negro spirit. It awakened to a saner position a certain influential minority who have in certain crises since then been able to hold down the radicals to a milder attitude." [22]

In private correspondence Bassett revealed several years after the incident the origin of the sensational sentence in "Stirring Up the Fires of Race Antipathy." Writing in 1909 to Edwin Mims, then coeditor of the *South Atlantic Quarterly,* Bassett urged him not to resign his position and suggested that he should write more for the magazine. Recalling his own contributions to the quarterly, he came abruptly to the question, "Did I ever tell you why I put in the reference to Lee? . . . I had written several articl[es] which were calculated to make people think, but the papers would not notice them. I felt that they did not want a discussion. I put in the Lee reference to make them take notice. I remember well how, when it was written, I looked lovingly at it and remarked to myself, 'I guess that will wake them up.' As a waker it was eminently successful." [23]

In 1911 Bassett explained in a seven-page letter to Charles Francis Adams the origin of the Lee–Booker T. Washington allusion. "Your well known service to the cause of impartial history," Bassett wrote, "makes it pleasant to me to make this personal statement for your use." His object in establishing the quarterly, he explained, "was to have a medium of expression for the more critical younger men in the South, and in each number I would have an editorial of about 2,500 words on some topic which seemed to me most timely. I wished particularly to counteract the reactionary feeling in the Southern press in matters on which tradition had developed ideas provincial and intolerant." His articles, particularly "Two Negro Leaders," attracted attention in the North, but southern papers ignored them. "I came to feel that the only way to be heard by my own people was to say something very striking, and the opportunity soon came."

In the summer of 1903 delegates returning from a Negro businessmen's convention in Chattanooga stopped for breakfast, by prearrangement, at Hamlet, North Carolina. The Negroes on the train, who were traveling by pullman, were accommodated in the large dining room of an eating house, while the less numerous whites were crowded into a smaller room. Among the white passengers on the train was Senator Augustus O. Bacon, of Georgia, who created quite a stir. "State papers took it up in a most sensational way," whereas Bassett thought they "ought to seek to calm rather [than] raise the feeling that the incident aroused." He and some of his friends believed that the press was trying to make political capital out of the matter, and he felt obligated, "as an editor of a calm and enlightened journal, to raise my protest." The answer was "Stirring Up the Fires of Race Antipathy." It was written in haste and in an "exhausted state of mind and body" because of the death of his mother, heavy routine duties at the opening of school, and other pressing matters. Before sending it to the printer he concluded that, like preceding editorials, it would "fail to be noticed." So he added the fateful sentence. It "was not a sudden thought. Putting it into the article, however, was sudden."

It would be difficult to find a better statement of the case for Washington's greatness than the evidence cited by Bassett in his letter to Adams. He had long thought highly of the Negro's "constructive work." His "greatness consists in the success with which he has won the support of a mass of ignorant people, taught them to bear their burdens, and made them willing to labor hard and patiently while they lay in industrial and educational progress the foundations of their future progress. This seems to me statesmanlike. The fact that he has done this in the face of coolness from the Southern whites and for their indifference or contempt returned always words of gentleness, seems to me most Christian. Besides this, his oratorical and literary ability mark him for eminence in these two lines. I know not what recent Southern orator has been more influential than he through his oratory; I know not what Southern writer of recent years has been more widely read and appreciated; I know not what Southern minister has more fully exemplified the spirit of the patient and forgiving Christ; and finally I know not what leader of men in the South in all the recent school has shown a better grasp of the real secret of progress in the South. But Washington unites all these qualities in his own person. I remember talking these sentiments during the summer of 1903 to my friend, Frederic Bancroft, of Washington, and he agreed with me. His extensive research into the life of the Old South makes him worthy of all confidence on this subject."

And then Bassett came to the point about which he had written Mims nearly three years earlier: "I remember well how when I had written . . . [the sentence] I said to myself: 'I hope they will notice that!' I thought it might lead them to criticism from editors and other sensible people, calm and intelligent discussion, which I should have welcomed; and such would have been the result, could I have got a fair showing. There are in the South as many fair-minded men as elsewhere. I was and am as Southern in my feelings as any of them, even if I do not agree with them in the way to achieve the best interests of the section." [24]

III

In appraising Bassett's article and in evaluating his explanation of the provocative sentence, it should be remembered that in his earlier years, at least, his interests were varied and he used different methods of accomplishing his ends. In this instance he was writing not as a historian but as a crusader for independent thinking and for justice, as he understood it, for the Negro. A startling statement may provoke thought, arouse discussion, and thereby promote a discovery of truth. Certainly he was unhistorical in stating categorically who ranked first and who second among southerners born during the nineteenth century. That is a subjective matter, impossible of accurate testing according to the principles of scientific criticism which Bassett had learned so well at the Johns Hopkins.

Was Bassett an agitator for liberal thought because he loved the role of agitator? Few college professors leave their ivory towers of scholarly seclusion to mingle in the public forum of current issues. Of the scores of former students who corresponded with Herbert B. Adams, Bassett was one of the few who wrote on nonprofessional subjects. The North Carolina of his early years was a fruitful field for one who would convert the conservative and "Thinkless South," as Bassett's friend, William Garrott Brown, put it, into a region that contemplated its status and labored for improvement.[25] Yet Bassett, like Trent, eventually became discouraged with his dual role and welcomed an opportunity to move to the East.[26] To most of his correspondents he assigned as the chief reason for leaving the South the opportunity for research and writing that New England provided. To William E. Dodd he wrote: "It was the conviction that I could not write history and direct public sentiment too that made me willing to come North." [27] To William K. Boyd, who served as confidant on numerous occasions, he explained "that it is very well in the South to be an antiquarian but difficult to be a historian in a cosmopolitan sense. It is easy to do the work of popular 'arousement,' but not that of mature and scholarly thinking. All the impulse to stir up something leads to a stage of achievement which a cultured community ought to have passed a generation ago." [28] And to Boyd he also wrote very confidentially on another occasion that it was fear of dissension among the faculty at Trinity College that caused him to leave. It was not a bigger salary at Smith College, nor a lighter teaching load, nor residence in "the most advanced portion of the country intellectually" that were decisive. "I merely wanted a peaceful atmosphere." [29]

Whatever Bassett's reasons for leaving North Carolina, his removal to a northern college deprived the South of the services of an able southern liberal. He remained at Trinity College long enough to indicate that a man of unorthodox views on southern political and social conditions could express himself freely and continue in his professorship. His writings on slavery and the Negro did not add substantially to the literature in those fields, and the tangible results from his preachments were slight if measured by a contemporary yardstick. After the lapse of nearly half a century it is clear that his pioneering efforts were an important landmark in the development of southern liberalism.

CHAPTER VI

George Petrie and the Auburn Oasis

The organization of the new Alabama Historical Association provides a propitious moment for looking backward to the pioneers who labored in the vineyard a generation ago.[1] It is gratifying to observe that in an earlier age, when history as we know it today was in its infancy, Alabamians were contributing to the new departure in a significant way. Although this segment of the story is primarily concerned with George Petrie, he was only one of four notable men who began their work as the nineteenth century merged with the twentieth. They did not form a school of historical thought, nor were they closely associated in any joint enterprise. Each worked independently in accomplishing a task that he marked out for himself. In a limited measure their diverse interests harmonized into a mosaic that covered pretty thoroughly all the significant functions of the historical guild. Petrie was a master teacher who inspired in his students a genuine love for history. Walter L. Fleming delved into the records and produced monographs that were generally acceptable to contemporary critics. Thomas M. Owen was a gifted organizer who convinced the state that it should preserve and make accessible its historical archives. William G. Brown excelled as a skillful craftsman in an era when the new "scientific" approach stressed dry-as-dust facts at the expense of literary artistry. All of these men were born during the critical years of Reconstruction, Owen at Jonesboro, Petrie at Montgomery, Fleming at Brundidge, and Brown at Marion. Each of them embodied the essential characteristics which collectively came to be known as the "Spirit of a New South."

It should be pointed out at the beginning that they were not the only Alabamians who pioneered in historical activity at the turn of the century. Indeed, they were not the earliest who might be said to qualify as historians. Albert J. Pickett had published in 1851 a two-volume *History of Alabama, and Incidentally of Georgia and Mississippi,* and a year earlier Dr. Basil Manly had organized the Alabama Historical Society. An exhaustive study of Alabama historiography could hardly ignore the work of Peter J. Hamilton, author of *Colonial Mobile;* of Hannis Taylor, North Carolina-born Mobile lawyer, who wrote widely in constitutional and international law; of John W. Du Bose, who produced a *Life and Times of William Lowndes Yancey;* of Joel C. Du Bose, who was associated with Owen in founding the *Gulf States Historical Magazine* and who wrote some Alabama history; of Thomas C. McCorvey, who taught history at the University of Alabama and who wrote about the history and government of his native state; and of other Alabamians whose contributions, great and small, formed a part of the complete picture. Regrettably, the limits of the present essay must exclude an examination of their work.

I

In seeking a college education and in entering the teaching profession, George Petrie was emulating his father's example. George Laurens Petrie attended Davidson College, received the bachelor's and master's degrees from Oglethorpe University, and the bachelor of divinity degree from Columbia Presbyterian Theological Seminary. After two years' service as chaplain of an Alabama regiment during the Civil War, he taught in a Montgomery classical school and at Oakland College in Mississippi. He entered the Presbyterian ministry and held pastorates at Greenville, Mississippi, and at Petersburg and Charlottesville, Virginia.[2] It was while the elder Petrie was pastor of a church at Charlottesville that the future historian attended the University of Virginia, 1883–87.

Numbered among Petrie's professors were some of the outstanding scholars of that generation. Perhaps the ablest men with whom he studied at the University of Virginia, if inclusion of sketches in the *Dictionary of American Biography* may serve as a criterion, were Maximilian Schele de Vere, Noah K. Davis, and Charles S. Venable.[3] It was probably something else than a liking for philology that caused Petrie to enroll in Professor Schele de Vere's class in modern languages. This Swedish-born philologist, educated at Bonn, Berlin, Greifswald, and Harvard universities, taught at the University of Virginia from 1844–95. Author of books on comparative philology, English studies, and the American language, he was also a popular teacher whose enthusiastic presentation of his courses led many students to elect them. Davis, with whom Petrie studied moral philosophy for two years, "was an effective teacher, learned, diligent, and sincere." Before Petrie entered the university, Davis had published *Theory of Thought,* and he subsequently wrote widely used texts in psychology, inductive and deductive logic, and ethics. Petrie studied mathematics for two sessions with Venable, as "affectionate as a father with his students." He, too, wrote a series of textbooks.

Ancient languages and physical sciences rounded out Petrie's education at the University of Virginia. He studied Latin with William E. Peters, Greek with John H. Wheeler, chemistry with John W. Mallett, and natural philosophy with Francis H. English, all competent teachers. He could not have taken history had he so desired, for none was offered at the university until after Richard Heath Dabney joined the faculty in 1889. At the close of his fourth year, Petrie was awarded the master's degree. But courses and degrees did not have the same meaning then that they have today. "At that period of the University's history, one did not become a graduate of the institution by graduating from a course, and one might graduate from the University many times before he finally took the titled degree George Petrie received in 1887." [4]

If a southern scholar aspired to become a doctor of philosophy in the closing years of the nineteenth century, he was likely to consider seriously the opportunity presented by the Johns Hopkins University at Baltimore.[5] From its inception in 1876 it provided superior training, whether in the sciences, the humanities, or the social studies. The intellectual statesmanship of its president, Daniel C. Gilman, soon made the university a dynamic factor in graduate instruction. With such scholars as Ira Remsen in chemistry, Basil Gildersleeve in the classics, and Herbert B. Adams in history, the Johns Hopkins soon acquired an enviable reputation. The New England-born Adams, graduate of Amherst College and Heidelberg University, built up a strong department of history, political science, and economics, emphasized institutional life as a significant segment of knowledge, and made the Adams seminary the keystone of the arch in a well-rounded program of study and research. With such able colleagues as Richard T. Ely in economics, George H. Emmott in political science, and John M. Vincent in history, and with such special lecturers as Woodrow Wilson, J. Franklin Jameson, and James Schouler, graduate students in the department were assured of scholarly and stimulating experiences.

Armed with a master's degree from the University of Virginia and two years' service as adjunct professor of modern languages and history at Alabama Polytechnic Institute, Petrie cast his lot with the Johns Hopkins in 1889 as a candidate for the doctorate. He fully intended to take his degree in romance languages and, with the exception of the Adams seminary, he concentrated in that field during his first year. He enrolled in two classes taught by A. Marshall Elliott, "Italian Dialects & Philology" and "Old French Philology." With Henry A. Todd he took Italian and Spanish and also the "French-Major Course." Perhaps the member of the department who impressed him most favorably was Frederick M. Warren, with whom he studied French literature, 1550–1789, the first year, and Renaissance literature and Victor Hugo's works the second.[6]

More than half a century later Petrie recalled his purpose in going to the Johns Hopkins, his change in plans after arrival, and personal traits of some of his instructors. He was interested in literature, especially French literature, and he was disappointed to find an emphasis upon phonetics and philology. With the exception of one course, he abandoned the field during his second year. Two persons were responsible for "pulling" him in the direction of history: Adams, director of historical studies, and Amelia B. Edwards, Egyptologist, who gave a series of lectures in Baltimore which Johns Hopkins students could attend upon payment of a fee. She inspired him with the "charm of research." Adams, too, was an inspiring teacher: Petrie "often went to his classes tired and came away refreshed—and not because of taking a nap during the lecture." [7] In addition to his work in the seminary, Petrie studied "Early Institutions and Greek Politics" and "Church History" with Adams, "The Sources of History" with Vincent, "Advanced Political Economy" with Ely, and "Historical and Comparative Jurisprudence" and "English Constitutional Law and History" with Emmott.[8]

Among the special lecturers at the university with whom Petrie took courses were Jameson and Wilson. Jameson, who acquired the doctorate at the Johns Hopkins under Adams' tutelage but who soon moved on to Brown University as professor of history, returned annually to his alma mater to lecture on such themes as the "Constitutional and Political History of the Southern States."

The lecturer, Petrie recalled, was gifted with a penchant for exactness and often corrected Adams, so that his former mentor did both himself and Jameson a favor by finding his erstwhile student a permanent position elsewhere. Petrie attended Wilson's lectures in public administration for noncredit and retained vivid recollections of his instructor after the lapse of half a century. The future president was a dynamic teacher, punctuating his points by his right forefinger, which was "loaded," and by twitching the end of his nose with an up-and-down movement. Wilson's brother-in-law and Petrie roomed at the same house, and Wilson often called there when in Baltimore. On one occasion he laughed at Petrie when the Alabama student came in with an overcoat several sizes too large. He was "low on cash," and could hardly afford an overcoat; but finding one for $7.00 he bought it "even though it was too long and too big around. The latter defect was remedied by setting the buttons over, so that the coat buttoned under the right arm rather than in front." [9]

The distinguishing feature of the Johns Hopkins department was the seminary which assembled every Friday evening for a two-hour period. All graduate students—about fifty in number during Petrie's period—as well as all faculty members attended; and if a former student who had established a Johns Hopkins colony at some other college or university returned to Baltimore, he was sure to be invited to participate in the proceedings.* The secretaryship of the class rotated among the members, and Petrie served twice in this capacity.[10] In the spring of 1890 Stephen B. Weeks of North Carolina reported on a controversial subject, "The Settlements of Sir Walter Raleigh in Virginia and their Historic Survival in the Nineteenth Century." Adams commented that such a question ought to be treated cautiously, and before adjourning Petrie was appointed a member of a committee "to examine thoroughly the arguments brought out by Mr. Weeks in support of his view." On May 9 the committee reported that although Weeks's "conclusions were exceedingly plausible, yet it was a matter that could not with existing information be demonstrated." [11]

On April 3, 1891, Petrie "read the paper of the evening." It was

* In March, 1903, Petrie visited the Johns Hopkins and "exhibited his collection of the manuscripts of William L. Yancey to the students [in James C. Ballagh's course in 'Southern History'] and discussed their use." Petrie to Thomas M. Owen, March 15, 1903, Thomas M. Owen Papers (Alabama State Department of Archives and History, Montgomery, Ala.); *The Twenty-Eighth Annual Report of the President* [of Johns Hopkins University] *with Accompanying Reports* (Baltimore, [1904?]).

a digest of his dissertation, later published in the Johns Hopkins University *Studies in Historical and Political Science* under the title, *Church and State in Early Maryland* (1892). Gifted with keen wit, he explained "that his treatment had been from a constitutional standpoint and the drier it was found the more he would be complimented." In the discussion that followed the presentation of the paper, Adams said he "considered it a new departure and commended Mr. Petrie's treatment by sharply defined propositions, but thought he did not do himself quite full justice in his final summing up." Apparently some member of the class raised the question as "to what was new in his thesis," for Petrie took the floor again to insist that "his constitutional treatment was new"; that his discussion "of the attempt of 1676 to establish the Church of Eng. from a conl standpoint" was original; and that "he thought he had also reached some new conclusions in his treatment of the Charter & the comparisons instituted with contemporary documents." [12]

II

Soon thereafter Petrie received his degree and returned to Auburn as professor of history and Latin. He had native talent as a teacher and a modicum of experience before he went to the Johns Hopkins; he came back to his position well equipped in subject matter, possessed of an infectious enthusiasm for history, and indoctrinated with new concepts of education. One of the last is worth noting. Adams was a pioneer promoter of extension education in the United States, and his Alabama student decided to inaugurate that type of work in his native state. In the early 1890's he arranged to give a series of lectures in Montgomery. It was with considerable trepidation that he launched the project while still in his twenties, for the subjects upon which he spoke—Homer, Plato, and Aristophanes—were indeed formidable.[13]

When Petrie began his labors at Alabama Polytechnic Institute in the fall of 1887, history had been a subject of instruction for only a few years. It first appeared in the catalogue of 1884–85 as "general History, ancient and modern," a junior-senior subject taught by John T. Dunklin, who held the master's degree from La Grange College and an honorary LL.D. from the University of Alabama.[14] Dunklin was explicit in stating the purposes of the course: "To learn the facts of History" which would serve as "lessons of warning and instruction," and to train students' minds in "proper modes of thought and reflection in reference to human action." [15] W. S. Fleming, who held the bachelor's degree, replaced Dunklin the following year and taught history at the freshman and sophomore levels.[16] Then in 1887 Petrie began a period of fifty-five years of service at the Auburn institution, first as a teacher of French, German, and history, and, after his return from the Johns Hopkins, as professor of history and Latin. His philosophy of history and his methodology are worth transcribing, for they stood in sharp contrast with former announcements.

"In this department," he wrote, "the aim is not so much to memorize facts as to understand them . . . The students are taught to investigate the growth of ideas and institutions, the rise and progress of great historical movements, and the reciprocal influences of men and circumstances. Frequent use is made of diagrams, photographs, charts and maps . . . Instruction is given by textbooks, lectures and class discussion, but a constant effort is made to stimulate to wider reading and research in the library." [17]

College catalogues not only state the aims of education but also record some of the means of accomplishing them. In contrast with the great variety of courses, dozens of systematic texts, and hundreds of volumes on any period or aspect of history available to students of the mid-twentieth century, collegians of the 1890's had little choice of offerings, few manuals, and limited library resources. Despite a paucity of materials, a competent teacher could guide apt pupils to a mastery of considerable subject matter and promote critical, reflective thought. An examination of the history curriculum, available texts, and basic reading will serve to indicate the meager diet of half a century ago. The story is incomplete unless one remembers that at Auburn the master teacher was molding physical resources into human understanding of the historical heritage.

In the freshman class United States history and government were taught for two terms, followed by a spring quarter devoted to English history. Alexander Johnston's *A History of the United States,* Jesse Macy's *Our Government,* and David H. Montgomery's *Leading Facts of English History* served as texts. Two terms of general history were provided for sophomores, with Philip Van Ness Myers' *General History* used as a guide. Juniors and seniors in the "General Course" could elect history instead of laboratory if they desired. Woodrow Wilson's *The State* served as a text, but it was supplanted in the middle 1890's by John R. Green's

Short History of the English People. The feature of advanced work was research and class reports upon selected topics chosen from ancient, medieval, and modern European history. During the third term of this course, Petrie lectured upon European governments but invited "experts in some field of present or past history" for occasional talks.[18] The junior-senior course was changed in 1900 to American constitutional, political, and social history, with special lectures on such southerners as John Randolph, William L. Yancey, Jefferson Davis, Alexander H. Stephens, and Robert Toombs.[19]

It was not uncommon in the period under review for departments of history to speak of laboratory work in the subject. Advanced courses might be designated in catalogues as seminaries or seminars, but instructors pointed with pride to "laboratory" equipment in their classrooms: to books and magazines, manuscripts and maps, charts and diagrams, and to tables, cases, shelves, and walls utilized to display them. The word *seminar* had little to recommend it in an agricultural and mechanical college, and from the turn of the century forward history courses for juniors, seniors, and graduate students at Alabama Polytechnic Institute were "conducted by the laboratory method" to elevate the subject to the level of a science in a school that stressed technology. "Emphasis is laid," Petrie said, "on the importance of securing proper material for investigation and every incentive is given to the collection and use of new documents, papers and letters illustrative of Southern, and especially of Alabama history."[20] Graduate students were required to participate in the activities of the junior-senior class, to hold frequent conferences with their instructor, and "to devote a large part of their time to original research upon some topic on which they can consult the original sources of information." Woodrow Wilson's *Division and Reunion* was used as a text for graduates, and they were expected to study selections from Alexander H. Stephens' *A Constitutional View of the Late War Between the States,* James Ford Rhodes's *History of the United States from the Compromise of 1850,* John Fiske's *Critical Period,* Henry Cabot Lodge's *Alexander Hamilton* and *Daniel Webster,* John T. Morse's *Thomas Jefferson,* Carl Schurz's *Henry Clay,* and William G. Sumner's *Andrew Jackson.*[21]

Enrollment in history included a sizeable proportion of the student body at Alabama Polytechnic Institute. For the session of 1891–92, Petrie's first year after returning from the Johns Hopkins, 137 out of a total of 225 of college rank took history, and in addition

72 students were enrolled in his Latin classes. Two decades later there were 365 history students and 110 Latin pupils among a total enrollment of 737. Approximately 60 per cent of the student body throughout this period took history.[22] By 1911 two instructors and an assistant were aiding Petrie in teaching history and Latin.[23]

The Auburn professor acquired no great reputation as a productive historian. In appraising his first piece of research, it should be observed that the modern scholar is startled when he examines doctoral dissertations of Petrie's day. Many of them would hardly qualify as a master's thesis of a later generation, and not a few would be rejected as term reports by meticulous present-day directors of graduate work. Unless one understands the elementary level of much graduate research in the 1890's, he will discount *Church and State in Early Maryland* too severely. Of its fifty pages, nearly half were quoted. A score of works were consulted in its preparation, most of them primary sources. About half of its eighty-odd citations were to the *Archives of Maryland.* The organization is clear and logical, the style is simple and direct, and the conclusions, presented in divisional summaries, seem sound and restrained.

Aside from his dissertation, Petrie contributed articles to *Historic Towns of the Southern States,* the *Transactions of the Alabama Historical Society, The South in the Building of the Nation, The Library of Southern Literature,* and the *Sewanee Review.* He also wrote some school histories, and he assembled material for a biography of William L. Yancey that did not materialize. An article on the Alabama fire-eater appraised his place in history. Petrie concluded that Yancey would be chiefly remembered by posterity as the southern movement's "impassioned leader, who by his boldness, his earnestness and his eloquence did more perhaps than any one else to make . . . State rights doctrines a powerful force in practical politics." Like Trent and other Johns Hopkins men, the Auburn historian foresaw an end to sectional bias in the writing of American history. He demonstrated his own unprejudiced view in the opening paragraph of the Yancey article: "The time is rapidly coming when men can think and speak of our Civil War without passion and without prejudice. Indeed considerable progress has already been made in this direction. Southern writers have shown a ready appreciation of the many admirable qualities of Lincoln, who was once known to us chiefly as the leader of what we termed the 'Black Republican Party.' On the other hand, Calhoun, the most influential of Southern statesmen, a man whose views have long been an incomprehensible riddle to our Northern friends, has received no fairer treatment or more graceful recognition than in the recent life of Webster written by Mr. Lodge, a senator from Massachusetts. These two cases are typical of a growing tendency toward fairness and even generosity on both sides in dealing with men and events connected with that period." [24]

Emulating the example of Herbert B. Adams at the Johns Hopkins, Petrie inaugurated the Alabama Polytechnic Institute *Historical Papers,* of which four series were issued in the early 1900's. He encouraged his students to prepare papers for publication in scholarly reviews and popular magazines. In the early years of the century they contributed to the *Transactions of the Alabama Historical Society,* the *Gulf States Historical Magazine,* the *American Historical Review,* the *Cosmopolitan,* and the *Review of Reviews.*[25]

III

It has already been indicated that Petrie excelled as a teacher. Several prominent historians, as well as men in other fields, were attracted to the subject because he made it a living, fascinating, and meaningful matter. A compilation made in 1941 by a former student who was then a colleague lists twenty-two who "received their early training and the inspirational urge for further graduate work in history and political science from Dr. George Petrie." Several will be recognized by historians as men who became well established as teachers and productive scholars. Among them were John B. Clark, Charles S. Davis, William Watson Davis, Walter L. Fleming, Dallas T. Herndon, Sydney W. Johnson, Albert B. Moore, Herman C. Nixon, Frank L. Owsley, Alfred W. Reynolds, and William O. Scroggs.[26]

The accomplishments of these and many other students are in part a tangible tribute to a master teacher. In summarizing his attributes as an instructor, an unusual source provides the essential information. In 1911 Petrie addressed the Alabama Education Association on the subject, "The Necessary Qualifications for a Teacher of History." Modest man that he was, he disclaimed possession of the qualifications he emphasized, yet perhaps those who profited from his inspirational guidance would insist that Petrie himself approached the ideal he described.

He spoke of two sorts of qualifications, "natural and acquired." Of native gifts he listed that contagious and "abiding enthusiasm that comes from a deep interest in history and a strong belief in its importance, along with an unwavering faith that others can be led to the same view"; a resourcefulness that adjusted interpretations of a broad and inexact field of complex knowledge to the level of each individual student; "the imagination of a great actor" or of a Sherlock Holmes that provided charm of atmosphere and unlocked hidden mysteries or personalities; and judgment that eliminated partiality, maintained balance and proportion, and resulted in "glorified common sense." Acquired qualifications, Petrie thought, could be compressed into the one word *knowledge*—knowledge of the subject, knowledge of the pupil, and knowledge of teaching methods. History was more difficult to teach than mathematics or chemistry or physics, for it was not a systematic science. Its breadth and its unity demanded a mastery not only of standard authorities but also of the primary sources. The historian must be all things to all men; he must know where to fish and how to bait the hook. And as to pedagogical methods, many were good but there was no substitute for "perfect naturalness and simplicity." [27]

Who can doubt that Petrie's success as a teacher derived in part from the breadth of his knowledge? Few contemporaries in the South, or beyond its borders, came into the profession so well equipped to lead students toward a mastery and meaning of historical subject matter or to relate it to the vast periphery known as civilization. We know that he studied ancient institutions of the Western world, Egyptology, church history, English constitutional law and history, and the political and constitutional history of the southern region. In related fields he read political science, public administration, historical and comparative jurisprudence, and political economy. He was also a competent scholar in Greek and Latin and in modern foreign languages. Renaissance and French literature fascinated him; the works of Victor Hugo excited his keenest interest. He had more than a casual acquaintance with moral and natural philosophy and with comparative philology. To repeat a sentence from the introduction, George Petrie was an educated man; he was also a historian. The fact that he was an educated man and a dynamic and inspiring teacher led to other duties and responsibilities.

In his later years at Alabama Polytechnic Institute, Petrie was drawn more and more into administrative work. He served as dean of the academic faculty from 1908 to 1922, and from that year until his retirement in 1942 as dean of the graduate school. He taught summer sessions at Peabody College, the University of Virginia, and the University of Chicago. In 1915 he served as president of the Alabama History Teachers' Association and in 1932 as president of the Association of Deans of Southern Colleges. Significant as his services may have been in these capacities, his great work was as a teacher of history. Estimable performance at this task entitles him to a conspicuous place in southern education.

CHAPTER VII

William A. Dunning: Teacher, Humorist, and Scholar

"Not long after you were here last spring," Milledge L. Bonham of Louisiana State University informed J. G. de Roulhac Hamilton in 1916, "I wrote Dunning as follows: 'Hamilton delivered a lecture here recently, after which Fleming and I accompanied him to the hotel, where we sat talking until nearly midnight. At first we conversed about Dunning, then we discussed Dunning, after which we talked about Dunning.' " To Bonham's letter the major professor of the three admirers replied: " 'Judging from the topic of conversation, there were no ladies present at the recent meeting of Hamilton, Fleming and yourself.' " [1]

This bit of banter between William A. Dunning and a former student illustrates the Columbia University professor's propensity for wit and humor. He had rare gifts of whimsicality and repartee, whether in conversation or in correspondence. Several of his book reviews and even a few of his articles sparkled with clever phrases and facetious criticisms, and one time, upon the witness stand, he "made monkeys" of legal luminaries. Students and colleagues esteemed him for his charming personality as well as his scholarship and wise counsel. Imperfect "deportment" in his high school years and dismissal from Dartmouth College were tangible evidence of some very human qualities that endeared him to students who realized that the "Old Chief" bore little resemblance to the proverbial pedagogue. Matching wits with Dunning was an exciting experience, whether in the seminar, the hotel lobby, or epistolarian exchanges.

I

In a sense the title of this essay is misleading. The commas and the conjunction that separate three of Dunning's accomplishments imply a triplicity that did not exist. He was a dynamic, inspiring teacher who mastered the difficult art of penetrating the barrier between learning and learner through unaffected witticism. An amalgam of the attributes, rather than their dissociation, helps to explain the magister's success in the classroom.

If there was a lingering doubt that wholesome humor could contribute to the learning process, it was dissipated by Gilbert Highet in his mid-century classic, *The Art of Teaching,* an embodiment of more educational wisdom than a dozen formal textbooks on how to teach. Humor, Highet asserts, is a means by which a schoolmaster builds "a bridge between youth and maturity." Pupils are individuals whose individuality should not be violated, but a collective rapport that narrows the gulf between master and student without destroying mutual respect and esteem stimulates a desire to learn. "When a class and its teacher all laugh together, they cease for a time to be separated by individuality, authority, and age." The "shared experience" is only a means to an end: if it "can be prolonged or re-established, and applied to the job of thinking, the teacher will have succeeded."

Some of the qualities that made Dunning a superior teacher were apparent in his teen-age years. Report cards from the Plainfield, New Jersey, high school show grades consistently in the nineties, and his diary reveals conscientious preparation of assignments as well as leisurely reading. His development was not one-sided, for the diary frequently mentions afternoons devoted to baseball, archery, and kiteflying. Further indication that he was a normal boy is afforded by his deportment ratings which stood in sharp contrast with his academic marks. School authorities deducted one point for each instance of misconduct, and term records of 84–74–65 reveal a progressive inclination toward mischief. Such diary confessions as "Mr. Mervin gave me one mark for cutting up with James" and "cut up like every thing" are helpful in explaining lack of correlation between reports of studious William and capricious Billy.

Despite misdemeanors, Dunning applied himself seriously to academic achievement. One of his teachers recalled that the blue-eyed, auburn-haired pupil possessed "poise and balance, intelligence and reflection." At graduation exercises in 1874 he was awarded "three handsome volumes" for submitting the best essay on "The Elizabethan Age of English Literature." His valedictory address, "Ancient and Modern Civilization," revealed capacity for effective expression and an early interest in the development of moral and political philosophy, a subject on which he eventually published three volumes. A local paper called it "the finest written oration of the evening." The serious purpose of the prizewinning essay and the valedictory yielded to frivolity in his speech to the high school's alumni.

Dunning was fifteen when he temporarily abandoned high school to accept a position as elementary teacher at the nearby Jackson School, and he taught there three more years after graduation. In our present-day era, when college degrees and professional subjects ordinarily described as "education" are required of prospective teachers, it is difficult to comprehend that there was an age when literacy, intelligence, knowledge of subject matter, and a comprehensive examination were the only prerequisites for him who would instruct. This mistaken concept prevailed when Dunning began his career as a teacher, and it survived well into the twentieth century. Nowadays it seems preferable to encourage the teacher, and the pupil too, to ignore the great fundamental truths of learning while they unctiously elaborate the obvious to insure preparation for social living. Unaware that teachers are made and not born, patrons at Jackson School expressed appreciation for the youthful schoolmaster's efforts. "His peculiar fitness for the position of a Teacher," they wrote, "has been markedly shown in his general management of his pupils, as also in his excellent influence over them both intellectually and morally."

Disciplinary dismissal from college is not ordinarily regarded as a steppingstone to successful teaching, but an episode during Dunning's freshman year at Dartmouth College served that useful purpose. In the late seventies and early eighties an unpopular president, the Reverend Samuel Colcord Bartlett, incited friction and bitterness. Freshman-sophomore altercations occurred frequently, with "crimes" ranging from greasing chapel seats to more serious pranks involving violence. In March, 1878, a hat-snatching affair terminated in a nocturnal saturnalia that reached climactic proportions between two and three o'clock. Armed with a club and some bottles, presumably empty, several freshmen made "an organized attack" on the room of two brothers, one of them a sophomore. Meager records do not indicate the extent of Dunning's implication beyond the fact that he and some other freshmen were in an adjoining study hall. He must have been more than passively involved, for his original sentence of suspension for the remainder of the year was soon changed to dismissal. A few days later the president, formerly professor of biblical literature at Chicago Theological Seminary, posted a two-hundred-dollar reward for the capture of two instigators of the rumpus, and immediately there appeared on the campus a handbill offering two dollars for the apprehension of President "Samtel Discord Blartit" and requesting his return to the "Illinois State Lunatic Asylum." Whether Dunning tarried in Hanover to participate in printing and circulating the poster cannot be established, but copies of it and the president's notice were treasured for preservation in the Dunning Papers. The following fall he entered Columbia University and continued there, as undergraduate, graduate student, and teacher until his death in 1922.

Dunning's "peculiar fitness" for teaching, noted by the Jackson School patrons, became more evident at Columbia University, with professional criteria and classroom experience to supplement natural endowment and doctoral training. Some university teachers have special gifts as undergraduate instructors; others make their great contribution in the graduate seminar. Dunning excelled at both levels, and he continued to teach large classes of neophytes well beyond the period when many reputable scholars abandon the beginners for the less cumbrous task of directing the work of mature students. His concept of education was applicable to the novice; challenge and stimulus in teaching undergraduates made him genuinely reluctant to forego the privilege of contact with immature and pliable minds.

II

The clearest statement of Dunning's philosophy of education appeared in a 1914 convocation address on "The University as a Rationalizer." With subtle suggestion he observed that students returned to school "languid and weary with the laborious pursuit" of vacation's pleasures to "enter with becoming reverence into the realm of intellectual life." Whether the immediate interest be "in pastry or in skyscrapers, in locomotives or in cosmic philosophy, in etymological hypothesis or in a constitution for China," or in any of a thousand other purposes, he would focus attention on the "remote and ultimate end" rather than pass judgment upon present desire.

Dunning divided mankind into two categories, men of sentiment and men of reason, though action might derive from both emotion and rationality. Whether illustrations were drawn from the age of Aristotle or the summer of 1914, they proved "that feeling rules mankind," that man was not "essentially a rational being." Emotion rather than reason determined "the spectacular transformations of human affairs": rivalry for religious domination, quest for equality, liberty, nationality. These were noble ends which feeling and passion inspired, but reason should supply the means of attaining them; and a university's function was to qualify students to apply it in defining and advancing "social and individual ends." Rational man was not barred from pursuing ideals predicated upon imagination and feeling, but he must restrain and rescue "hapless possessors of hair-trigger emotions and untempored zeal."

Rationalists, small in number and scanty in reward, would "be denounced as reactionaries and . . . pilloried for the heinous crime of seeing two sides of a question, when the myopic vision of their fellows assures that there is but one." It was as idle to speculate on relative contributions of reason and emotion to ultimate welfare as to "debate whether the firebox or the steam chest does most for the progress of a locomotive. The combination is what makes the thing move." When passions raged, reason served to restore balance. "To reduce to the minimum the number and the evils of these relapses into the barbarism of unregulated emotion, is a prime function of the educated man."

The emotional factor supplemented rationalism in Dunning's teaching; that he applied both to the learning process appears in appraisals of former students. Among the undergraduates who recorded expressions of commendation was Frederic R. Coudert, who attended Dunning's class in ancient history as a sophomore in 1887. "I was constantly struck," he recalled, "by the objective lucidity of his every statement tinctured and made alluringly human by a note of humor." Describing Columbia University in the next decade, Dr. Frederick P. Keppel explained that the focus of interest was in the various graduate schools; the small undergraduate college received little attention from reputable faculty members. Among the exceptions was Dunning, who "paid us the compliment, which young people appreciate far more deeply than is always realized, of never talking down to us." Later Keppel learned to know him intimately as a colleague, yet he heard nothing from him "finer than he gave us in his undergraduate classes." The distressing Dartmouth College episode proved helpful in winning affection of the undergraduates. According to

Keppel, "the exciting rumor" that a New England school had dismissed him was a factor in Dunning's success; but the student was certain "that the main reason for the extraordinary influence he had upon us was our instinctive feeling that we were in the presence of a man of the first water who was giving us the best that he had."

Except in seminars Dunning used the lecture method. He did not quiz his students, and they seldom interrupted him. According to Charles E. Merriam, the "lectures were full of acute characterizations and of dry wit; they were well organized and were developed steadily and effectively, like the calm unrolling of a scroll." Of Dunning's technique, J. G. de Roulhac Hamilton wrote: "As a lecturer he was keen, lucid, always interesting. . . . He possessed to a high degree skill in making rapid and sweeping summaries of events, movements, and theories. . . . Never at all monotonous, his delightful wit frequently lightened his treatment of a subject." He was a master teacher, James W. Garner recalled, "who not only knew his subject, but had the rare gift of presenting it in an attractive and forceful manner."

A master in the lecture room, Dunning was equally competent in seminar direction. The unrestraint of informality all but shattered mechanical obstructions in the path of learning, yet no graduate student doubted who sat at the head of the table. Dunning taught by example as well as by precept. Holland Thompson wrote him in 1915 to express appreciation for the "Old Chief's" books: "You showed me that it was not necessary to be dull in order to be scholarly, that one could put the results of long research into good English instead of into jargon, and that it was not necessary to be colourless in order to be fair." But Dunning did not neglect precept: he was a most exacting director of research. He demanded thorough investigation and attention to style before he appraised his students' work. The better it was, observed Merriam, "the more searching his analysis of sources, ideas and style, and the poorer it was the less he heeded it." But "no amount of trouble was too great for him to take with an earnest seeker after truth." He would often challenge a student's conclusion and force him to restate the case, or set up a problem similar to the one under discussion to promote better understanding. In editing graduate productivity, he cut and slashed his way through bramble and brier, the blue pencil dulling its sharpness with constructive suggestion and ironic remark. "This is the worst sentence that was ever written," he penciled on the galley margin of Hamilton's dissertation. His annotations were so exciting and humorous, Dora Neill Raymond observed in the preface to *British Policy and Opinion During the Franco-Prussian War,* that she wished they might be retained in the text.

A perusal of the Columbia University *Studies in History, Economics and Public Law,* which served as a medium for many dissertations, indicates the range of fields in which Dunning advised students. Thirty Ph.D.'s in the period 1900–1923 acknowledged his assistance. Thirteen students worked in the Civil War and Reconstruction era, others in earlier and later periods of American history, still others in European history and political theory. Students whose research was unfinished when Dunning died felt the loss keenly. Roy F. Nichols, who was investigating the Democratic machine in the early 1850's, wrote that Dunning's death reinforced a "realization of the quality and value of his influence, an influence powerful because of the rare combination of human sympathy and natural dignity which made this teacher a great man." An inscribed volume, *Studies in Southern History and Politics,* and a book of memorial essays, *Political Theories, Recent Times,* commemorating Dunning's election to the presidencies of the leading historical and political science guilds, are tangible evidence of graduate students' esteem for his teaching, admiration of his scholarship, and appreciation of his personality.

III

It is a mistake to suppose that Dunning, or any other teacher, confined his teaching to the classroom. Highet directs attention to a broader concept of instruction: fathers and mothers, husbands and wives, doctors and executives, clergymen and publicists, authors and artists—all engage in the business of teaching. Dunning's books and articles and reviews, his correspondence with colleagues and students, his conversations with acquaintances—all involve the art of teaching and illustrate his humor as an ingredient. Most of his wit in the classroom escaped recording, but there is no reason to believe that it differed essentially from what he incorporated in letters and published history.

Aptness in this premise appeared in the youthful Dunning's "Alumni Address" delivered the year he graduated at Plainfield high school. The valedictorian opened his speech with amateurish humor that probably seemed wittier to his listeners than to present-day readers of the yellowed fifteen-page manuscript. He reminded former graduating classes that the high school had not always had an alumni association. "The time is not so many years beyond the recollection of the oldest, or even the youngest inhabitants," he continued, "when Plainfield was a small & correspondingly hopeful country village; when parents gave their sons a little 'schoolin' in the winter, but kept them home to 'hoe corn and taters' in the summer. . . . In those days there were no Alumni to speak of. True, there were those who might be called 'graduates.' For 'graduate' may be rendered etymologically, 'a stepper out.' And there were numerous 'steppers out'; only there [*sic*] steps had not been taken in the orthodox manner. All that was necessary for a Commencement in those 'good old times' was for the departing member to raise as much disturbance as possible, and then calmly inform the irate pedagogue that he might turn him out if he wanted to, 'cause he wasn't coming anymore anyhow.' A brief but emphatic valedictory, administered by the teacher, and that boy's school life was a thing of the past." Meanwhile, "Terra and Luna waltzed around Old Sol" five times since the first formal commencement was staged in 1870. Younger students regarded graduating seniors with "awe & admiration": "We looked upon the boys as demi-gods at least; and the girls—angels already—we knew not where to place them now. We could now discuss the valedictory and the salutatory with the indifference of Sophomores."

The mature Dunning must have winced at the fribbling frills of this boyhood indiscretion, if indeed he ever read the manuscript of his oratorical effort again. But the jests reveal an embryo talent for wholesome, good-natured humor that eventually made him the life of the party and a thrilling correspondent. A naturalness about his flow of wit relieved it of all taint of artificiality. Let us examine a few of his letters, reviews, and articles for illustration thereof.

Among Dunning's intimate personal and professional friends was John Spencer Bassett, who esteemed the Columbia University professor so highly that he sought to make him Herbert Baxter Adams' successor at the Johns Hopkins. Each of them contributed a volume to Albert Bushnell Hart's series "The American Nation: A History"—Bassett, *The Federalist System* and Dunning, *Reconstruction, Political and Economic;* and each of them appreciated the humorous side of his relations with the editor of the series. Bassett completed his volume first and, having suffered while Hart applied the editorial "axe," apprised the Reconstruction historian of the fate that awaited him. He would have particular difficulty with the "Critical Essay on Authorities." "Let me suggest some ways of saying that a book is good," Bassett wrote early in 1907. "You may say 'a creditable performance,' or 'a reliable source,' or 'well digested,' or 'an undoubted authority,' or 'a more modern book is,' or when you are tired of the affair say 'the following works will be found useful,' or 'the reader is referred to.' "

Dunning was grateful for the suggested phrases; he would paste them in his "hat for frequent reference." His "special job just at present," he wrote, "is erasing the suggestions of the editor of the series for modifications in my Ms. I have used up three rubbers already on as many chapters and I am good for the destruction of as many more." Bassett was "very sad to think of the large number of erasers" Dunning had wasted, but, he added, "just think of the number of 'hads' you will have left over after Hart has cut them out. I had enough to fill a paddock," for, as Hart had written him, an editor does not like the pluperfect.

Incidentally, someone had written Bassett that he had found over 175 mistakes in an earlier volume of the series. Dunning professed to believe that that number of errors had been discovered in Bassett's *Federalist System*. "Only 175 mistakes and you so young," Dunning chided in his next letter. "By the time you are a hundred you will be able to do better than that and make it an even 500 errors. All this, of course, is on the assumption that the mysterious volume of which you speak is yours. I am awfully glad mine is not yet published, because all suspicion is thus averted."

Early in June Dunning wrote that his book was finished. "I am sending today the revised proof of the Preface, together with some impudent comments on the editor's Preface." "I hasten to reply to your sassy letter," Bassett countered, "because I am glad to see you so completely yourself. I suppose it is the reaction from the arduous tasks of authorship and 'Hartship.' "

"Tell me," Bassett inquired of Dunning, "what are in your opinion the twenty best books on U.S. history in the last two years"?—leaving out of consideration of course the *Federalist System* and *Reconstruction* volumes. With this inquiry began a series of exchanges that both correspondents, especially Dunning, must have enjoyed tremendously. Bassett had agreed to write an article for *Putnam's Magazine* appraising twenty outstanding books in American history published during the past biennium. He solicited Dunning's judgment in selecting them.

"At half-past seven o'clock next year," Dunning replied, "I will send you that list of the 'twenty best books'; though, of course, you cannot understand, with your poor head for mathematics, that there cannot be 'twenty best books' if you leave out the two best which are duly left out in your letter. I refer, of course, to the two volumes with which we are most familiar in the *American Nation*."

A fortnight later Bassett inquired again about twenty best books. He wanted "to know what books beside the immortal two are most deserving of lying about for Putnam's. When a man has written a dozen book reviews he has no conscience left, or reputation either." This second appeal brought no suggestions from Dunning, and Bassett published the review article without benefit of his correspondent's judgment. But Dunning did not hesitate to poke fun at Bassett's selection and evaluation: "I unexpectedly stumbled upon your article in *Putbam's* recently, wherein you distribute so beautiful a collection of nosegays to your associates in the great work of history-writing; but do tell me, what was the matter with the end of the thing? From internal evidence, I should judge that it had been edited with an axe. Is my surmise correct? I was just getting interested in the subject, and was expecting a long and delightful continuance of the treat, when, on turning the page, I found that the incident was closed." "If you will let the Putnam's article be a closed incident," Bassett replied, "I will love you for it. I have not read it since publication."

Annual meetings of the American Historical Association provided opportunities for Dunning and his "boys" to enjoy reunions. A group of former students honored him at a dinner during the Charleston meeting, and apprised him that a volume of dedicatory essays was in progress. "I am living over again at frequent intervals that very delightful Tuesday evening with you and the rest of the boys at Charleston," he wrote one of them. "It is a memory of continuous and unfailing delight." Certainly no members of the association esteemed the presidential address, "Truth in History," more than his own students. Milledge L. Bonham recorded the reaction of two disciples: "The night of his presidential address . . . I sat with a former college mate. On the other side of him was Professor Hamilton of the U. of N.C., another Dunning disciple. Our delight at the scholarly and scintillating address was so great that we had to relieve ourselves by pounding someone on the back and knees. As we couldn't quite reach each other, Professor Moore had to bear the brunt. He swore that never again would he sit between two Dunningites when Dunning was speaking."

Students who attended the Cincinnati meeting in 1916 persuaded their teacher to have dinner with them. According to one of the group, "We shall treasure the memory of that evening until we die." It was at this dinner gathering that Ulrich B. Phillips asked: " 'Professor Dunning, did you know that Jefferson Davis was blind in the left eye?' 'No, was he really?' Phillips said: 'I have long felt that I could die happy if I could produce some point of Southern history that Dunning didn't know. Now I've done it.' 'Yes,' said Dunning, 'and if you do it again you *will* die, happy or unhappy.' "

The Columbia University professor could even jest about the physical ailments that soon led to his death. Unable to attend the Cleveland meeting of the American Historical Association in 1919, former students became solicitous about his health. A letter to one of them was reassuring. "Please don't give yourself any discomforting thoughts about my physical condition," he wrote early in 1920. "If my moral and intellectual status were only on a par with the physical there is no telling what grand results might be expected." A year later he explained why he had been unable to attend the Washington meeting in 1920: Appendicitis, of short duration, and "a most exasperating series of other things, for which it was responsible," kept him away from work for a month. Of the debilitating consequences, "the most lasting was a thrombosis in the left leg, which is just now getting straightened out. Thrombosis is a plug in the circulation; and I am told that if it had located in my head instead of my leg, it would have made a noise like Woodrow Wilson."

IV

The reader in search of "light" literature does not turn to the pages of a scholarly magazine with much hope of a rewarding experience. Its articles and book reviews are deadly serious, as they should be; though most of them overemphasize the dry-as-dust style for which scholars have a special aptitude. A few historians, such as Carl Becker, successfully combined critical evaluation with clever presentation. His review of Bassett's *Middle Group of American Historians,* and especially his caricature of George Bancroft's style of writing, are evidence of nimble-witted craftsmanship. Clever whimsy was even more apparent in Dunning's reviews and articles. Occasionally, trained historians fell afoul of facetious comment, but he reserved his most pungent paragraphs for politicians turned historian. With Mephistophelian delight he paraded their passions and prejudices, shortcomings and imperfections.

The reader can almost hear Dunning chuckle as he appraises George F. Hoar's two-volume *Autobiography of Seventy Years.* The senator's reminiscences were a "paragon of pellucidity," but he left "one distressing uncertainty in the reader's mind": Is it "the population of Eastern Massachusetts in general or the Boston Saturday Club or the Worcester bar that is to be regarded as the most perfect human embodiment of religious, moral, intellectual, and political virtue"? Even a "casual reader" would observe "that no other aggregation of human beings in this wide world, past, present or future, has any place in the competition." The autobiographer "places himself, with a genial frankness that disarms criticism, in the foremost rank of that band of ancestor-worshipping Massachusetts Puritans whose mission has been, and is, to imbue a skeptical world with some measure of their own unwavering conviction that the whole history of the United States, and probably that of mankind in general, has hinged principally upon their thoughts and deeds." The senator was grateful to his Creator for the privilege of birth and upbringing "among the Concord Puritans," for the opportunity to serve the state of Massachusetts, and for membership in the Republican party, or rather in its more important Bay State branch. If the reader survives such solemnity, the utmost pleasure awaits him, for Hoar's party service, his travels, and his law practice reveal a keen sense of humor and an appreciation "of those incongruities in things that make men merry." A notable exception was inability to reconcile Benjamin F. Butler's election to the governorship with his own philosophy. Finding "no element of humor" in the incident, his "unwonted gloom" was dissipated by "only two morsels of comfort: that the Democratic party was chiefly responsible for it, and that it did not happen again."

Theodore Roosevelt's biography of *Gouverneur Morris* provided Dunning with ample opportunity for critical ingenuity. He lamented the fact that Morris' dogmatism aroused a "corresponding chord in his biographer," for Roosevelt was dogmatic "even in denouncing dogmatism." Predicating suffrage upon a natural rights basis was "idle folly," the reviewer thought, but "Mr. Roosevelt prefers to express his convictions as absolute truth, without the authority of nature." Dunning discovered only one indication in the whole volume "of a faltering judgment on any point," and it occurred in the statement that the Constitution was " '*probably* the best that any nation has ever had.' " His "perfect acquaintance with the ultimate standard of 'right' and 'wrong' " permitted him to express judgments with "easy confidence." Despite imperfections among Americans of the Revolutionary generation, " 'we were a great people' " when compared with the English and especially with Continentals. The " 'wretched beings' " under frivolous " 'French noblesse' " and " 'Swinish German kinglets' " were in a pitiable plight " 'until the whirlwind of the French Revolution swept their carcasses from off the world they cumbered.' " "The force of this passage," Dunning commented, "is marred only by the uncertainty in which the reader is left as to whose carcasses are referred to."

Appraising the first volume of Ellis P. Oberholtzer's *History of the United States since the Civil War,* Dunning pointed to the way in which the author entered upon his task. There was no preface, introduction, or bibliographical note, "no brief synopsis of his interpretation of history in general and of American history in particular, no acknowledgments of valuable aid from assorted librarians and specialists, no deprecatory suggestions aimed at possible reviewers. He does, indeed, present a table of contents; but promptly at the conclusion of that the first chapter of the history opens bristly and precisely 'On Sunday morning, April 2, 1865.' Where the story is going to end is nowhere stated. Probably the author does not know and does not care to guess. All that he feels reasonably sure of is that it will be five volumes long."

Becker and Dunning had another common trait: both enjoyed playing with words as a cat toys with a mouse. The Cornell University professor's gift appeared to good advantage in his presidential address, "Everyman His Own Historian"; Dunning's in "A Generation of American Historiography," a paper read before the American Historical Association in 1916. Before launching into a critical and penetrating discussion of writings in American history since 1884, he circumnavigated the word "historiography" several times. Its meaning? "And in particular what does it mean for him who has to deal with thirty-odd years of it in one-third of an hour? From its etymology the term is almost ridiculously simple. 'History' means history, and 'graphe' means writing; *ergo,* historiography means either the writing of history or the writing about history or the writing about the writing of history—which does not solve our problem at all. If the first sense be taken . . . we are confronted with the question, what is the difference, if any, between a historian and a historiographer? And is there any distinction, in form or in substance, between historiography and plain history? Must we dismiss as unworthy our instinctive conviction that the longer word connotes the greater dignity—that a man may become a historian by a single duodecimo volume, but may never get a footing in the sacred precincts of historiography on less than five volumes octavo, with a special library edition in calf with gilt top and uncut edges? . . . And is a doctoral dissertation historiography? Even if it is 800 pages in bulk and covers as many as ten years in time?"

This medley of miscellany from Dunning's moments of mirth partially explains his reputation as a teacher. Sparkle survived the witticism; a gift of conveying ideas in humanizing context assured a plateau of continuous human interest; expectation of another flashing instant when merriment came consciously to the surface inspired attention. Dullness was dispelled. Listeners were alert. Apt description, appropriate illustration, deft characterization, sweeping summary—lifted lectures and essays above humdrum monotony; and a mind cognizant of the timelessness and universality of the classics stimulated thought among students capable of thinking. A blend of many factors, with ingredients inseparable and often indistinguishable, sped pen and voice over smooth terrain, gave grace and quality to what he wrote and said.

A sense of humor seldom inspires continuous attention if knowledge is superficial. College students, even sophisticated sophomores, recognize authoritative stature and differentiate between textbook teachers and genuine scholars. Dunning's success in the classroom, like his enviable position in the scholarly world of historians and political scientists, was based upon learning that ran in deep channels. Attention to his contributions to knowledge will provide the fundamental ingredient in the mixture that made him magister.

V

The most striking revelation afforded by a study of the publications that earned for Dunning his reputation as an authority on the Civil War and Reconstruction is the paucity of his writings. The meagerness is explained in part by the fact that he gave much attention to the work of the American Historical Association, to the editorship of the *Political Science Quarterly,* and to publication in other fields. In 1914 he issued *The British Empire and the United States,* a survey of diplomatic relations during the hundred years of peace following the War of 1812. The book appeared the same year that Dunning addressed Columbia University students on "The University as a Rationalizer"; the themes of the volume and the address were essentially the same. Men of sentiment, emotion, and passion, on both sides of the Atlantic, stirred feelings of distrust, misconception, and suspicion; yet through a century of time, English-speaking peoples "exhibited, on a steadily growing scale, that loftiest of human attributes—the will to adjust the frictions of social life by reason." It was a book for the year, not a product of diligent research; neither was it a "pot-boiler" in the usual sense of that term.

The most time-consuming undertaking that intruded to prevent constant attention to the era of the Civil War and its aftermath was a three-volume work in an entirely different field, *A History of Political Theories* from ancient times to Herbert Spencer. In substance the study was restricted to a consideration of European Aryan philosophy. Ever the historian, Dunning did not write of political theory in a vacuum, for it had meaning in relation to the development of institutions and to juristic and moral concepts. The volumes became standard reading during the first quarter of the twentieth century; and some students sought enlightenment from them after inevitable supersedure by later works. The author's self-questioning nature led him to discount his contribution; he often regretted that he had embarked upon the project. "The silly mass of political theory that I have been engaged in precipitating on a defenseless public," he wrote in 1920, "has now passed out of my hands into those of Macmillan . . . but my interest in it has dwindled to the vanishing point." No doubt Dunning derived some satisfaction from labor on the first and second volumes (1902, 1905), but the fifteen years that elapsed before the final installment appeared indicate that it was a product of reluctant effort.

A parallel between Dunning and Frederick Jackson Turner should not be pushed too far; yet in certain respects their publication records were similar. Neither man wrote extensively in his chosen field of history. Albert Bushnell Hart boasted that he was the only man who succeeded in getting a book out of the frontier historian, and he might have said the same thing about Dunning. The Columbia University professor proposed no great seminal idea, but contemporaries included his *Reconstruction, Political and Economic* and Turner's *Rise of the New West* among the abler volumes contributed to the first Harper series. Both men were better known for their articles than their books; and their essays, assembled for republication, were often quoted. Again, both historians greatly influenced the thought of young scholars who studied with them, though Turner seemed more embarrassed than Dunning by "discipleship" of intellectual offspring.

Dunning's bibliography on the critical years of the nineteenth century's third quarter consists of a dissertation on *The Constitution of the United States in Civil War and Reconstruction;* the volume on the period 1865–77 in "The American Nation" series; a dozen articles, seven of which were reprinted in *Essays on the Civil War and Reconstruction* and others in a posthumous publication, *Truth in History;* and some notable book reviews. A pioneer in the scientific and scholarly investigation of the era, Dunning's limited productivity was an important factor in explaining his eminence in the profession. As a second basis, he inspired a capable group of students to supplement his work by more specialized studies, and these have been characterized as a distinct "school" in the historiography of the period. Despite a professed predilection for "that fascinating war time" and for "the most dramatic period in our national history" that followed, Dunning seems never to have contemplated a comprehensive study of the era. He was convinced that "conditions in the South must be set forth by students qualified not only by scientific training but also by a personal contact or an inherent sympathy with southern society." Realizing that "the South bulks largest in the history of Reconstruction," Dunning seemed content to guide the work of southerners who were attracted to Columbia University by his contemporary reputation as an impartial authority.

Dunning's writings in the field of the Civil War and Reconstruction, which he began as a graduate student, display a marked concern with constitutional problems. Emphasis on this aspect, as well as his concentration on the national scene, was to be expected of a pupil of John W. Burgess, an eminent constitutional historian noted for his intense nationalism. The *Essays on the Civil War and Reconstruction* received enthusiastic praise from the critics. They agreed that the volume was a significant contribution to constitutional history and noted that Dunning seemed thoroughly familiar with the sources of the period. His "conspicuous self-restraint" and detachment aroused wide comment. "Everything is as remote as if he were speaking of Athens under the Solonian constitution," remarked the New York *Bookman* reviewer whose appraisal was captioned "A Dispassionate View."

Although the series to which *Reconstruction, Political and Economic* belonged required presentation of the era "as a step in the progress of the American nation," there is considerable evidence of a conscientious effort to understand the southern viewpoint in the chapters dealing with the process of restoration. "The Judgment of North and South on Reconstruction," "Radical Reconstruction in the South," "The Climax of Radical Reconstruction," "Political and Social Demoralization in the South," and "The Movement Towards White Supremacy" describe effectively if incompletely the position of the region's white people. Dunning's views struck a responsive chord in his generation, and recognition of the book's "extraordinary excellence" was immediate. "His mastery of the subject and of its literature is ideally thorough," wrote the appraiser for the *American Historical Review*. "His analysis of causes and situations is keen and correct." Years later a critic remarked: "The chorus of approval which greeted the book was almost unanimous. The reviewers were lavish and unrestrained in their praise." Other recent writers saw merit in the volume, but they also disapproved of Dunning's conservative interpretation and his "southern attitude" toward the Negro.

In the judgment of specialists more than half a century ago, the pioneer historian of the years 1860–77 made two significant contributions. In the first place, he examined the sources available to scholars of his generation and greatly augmented knowledge of the period. In the second place, he evaluated the writings of the Civil War epoch and corrected mistakes of contemporary chroniclers—with due regard for the influence of their misconceptions. Of these two contributions, the expansion of knowledge was more important than the correction of error, for the truth that he discovered was in itself a corrective device.

That Dunning was no ordinary scholar is indicated by his election to the presidencies of the major historical and political science associations and by volumes of essays inscribed to him by students in both areas who esteemed his superior qualities. Space permits attention to only one of these honors, the presidency of the American Historical Association. Members assembled in Charleston and Columbia, South Carolina in 1913 with Dunning's presidential address a feature of the program. It was appropriate that this meeting should be held in the South. A decade had passed since the New Orleans convention in which Dunning had played an important role. Nearly a third of those in attendance were southern members; and as in 1903 a special train from New York brought northeasterners to the South. Dunning's address, "Truth in History," was heard "with manifest appreciation and delight by a large audience of the Charleston public and members of the Association." It was described as "one of the most stimulating addresses ever delivered before the American Historical Association."

Departing from his favorite field of Reconstruction history, and referring only incidentally to political theory, Dunning summarized his understanding of history from a knowledge of the subject that spanned the centuries from ancient times to the present. History's province, he assumed, "is to ascertain and present in their causal sequence such phenomena of the past as exerted an unmistakable influence on the development of men in social and political life." Breaking with the concept of the preceding century's closing decades, he rejected "absorbing and relentless pursuit of the objective fact" as the primary function of the historian. That concept circumscribed history's scope, emphasized material rather than "spiritual or psychic forces and influences on human life," and dismissed "what men believed to be true" by enthroning absolute truth.

As illustrations of his theme, Dunning cited beliefs from earlier centuries that had in recent times been relegated to the realm of mythology. Yet who could deny the influence of "a divinely revealed record" of children of Israel on the development of Western institutions and ideas? And who could ignore the effect of legend and tradition from Rome's early history accepted by Machiavelli, Dante, and Montesquieu? Such misconceptions were warp and woof of acceptable fact through ten centuries of western Europe's advancement toward modern times. But the most pertinent example of Dunning's concept that men's thoughts and deeds "have been affected more by the beliefs in what was false than by the knowledge of what was true" came from English history. Magna Carta did not actually establish trial by jury, yet six centuries of Englishmen believed that it did; and Edward Coke and William Blackstone and other constitutionalists consumed "floods of ink and myriads of goose quills" in praising "the foresight and wisdom of the barons of Runnymede in providing for later generations this singularly beneficent safeguard of human rights." And on the American side of the Atlantic, Joseph Story and St. George Tucker associated the jury system with Magna Carta "as the foundation of our free institutions."

Twentieth-century historians, Dunning advised, "must recognize frankly that whatever a given age or people believes to be true *is* true for that age and that people." The importance of error in history should stimulate humility among historians who discover new truth.

In part Dunning's address was a reply to the New History which his colleagues James Harvey Robinson and Charles A. Beard had recently proposed to a believing social science world. Robinson's essays, *The New History,* appeared in 1912; Beard's *An Economic Interpretation of the Constitution* in 1913; Dunning read his presidential address in December of that year. His allusions to Robinson's discovery that Rome never fell and to the "most hardened devotee of economic interpretation of history" were not directed at new conceptions nor at expanding breadth of subject matter, for Dunning himself recognized the limitless bounds of mankind's records. Rather, he questioned the new use for the past that his reforming colleagues were parading. In battling against the forces of conservatism and reaction, they utilized history to promote social reform and human betterment: it should be studied to understand the present to improve the future. Dunning's "objectivity" required "retirement and observation," not participation in the hurly-burly public activities in which his associates engaged. Past-mindedness permitted a search for evidence that enlightened the present if new truth did not ignore the influence of former misconceptions.

Whether in writing or in speaking, Dunning attained precision, a goal he achieved in composition by painstaking polish applied through original construction rather than successive redrafts. Precision to Dunning meant more than grammatical sentences, structured paragraphs, and direct diction. The vehicle of expression involved conscious art in attaining balance and rhythm, in selecting interpretive adjectives, in contriving exact shades of meaning, and in forming alliterations. Charm and grace and imagination combined to provide "Truth in History" with literary quality. An effective use of the simile merits transcription:

"Many a fact of history is like the grain of sand that intrudes within the shell of the pearl oyster. Tiny and insignificant, it is quickly lost to sight and knowledge; but about it are deposited the ensphering layers of myth and legend till a glimmering treasure is produced that excites the mightiest passions of men. Under the charm of its beauty, art, religion, civilization, are developed; through the lust to possess it a dynasty is overthrown, an empire falls into ruin. The historian may crush the pearl and bring to light the grain of sand; but he cannot persuade us that the sand made all the intervening history." *

Students recognized and esteemed Dunning's breadth of knowledge and depth of learning, and these qualities were sufficient to

* The writer began assembling evidence on William A. Dunning in 1944. Some of the material used in this chapter came from Dunning's books, articles, and reviews, a larger portion from manuscript files. A small collection of Dunning Papers, particularly valuable for his early years, is preserved in the Low Memorial Library, Columbia University, New York. Other manuscript collections contain letters from Dunning and carbon copies of letters to him. Especially helpful for his interest in southern historical scholarship are the following: American Historical Association Papers (Manuscript Division, Library of Congress, Washington, D.C.) ; John Spencer Bassett Papers (Manuscript Division, Library of Congress) ; William E. Dodd Papers (Manuscript Division, Library of Congress) ; William K. Boyd Papers (Duke University Library, Durham, N.C.) ; J. G. de Roulhac Hamilton Papers (University of North Carolina library, Chapel Hill, N.C.) ; Thomas M. Owen Papers (Alabama Department of Archives and History, Montgomery, Ala.) ; Dunbar Rowland Papers (Mississippi Department of Archives and History, Jackson, Miss.) . Two previous studies of Dunning have considerable merit: Charles E. Merriam, "William Archibald Dunning," Howard W. Odum (ed.) , *American Masters of Social Science* (New York, 1927) , 131–45; and the introduction to a compilation of articles and reviews, J. G. de Roulhac Hamilton (ed.) . *Truth in History and Other Essays* (New York, 1937) , xi–xxviii. In 1953 the writer lent his assemblage of Dunning notes to a competent graduate student and assistant, (Mrs.) Virginia Orkney (Philbrick) , for use in her master's thesis, "William A. Dunning: Historian of Reconstruction" (1955) , to which the writer contributed a chapter on "A History Professor's Sense of Humor" and a few other segments. He is grateful to Mrs. Philbrick for permission to use material that she collected.

attract a loyal clientele. But erudition did not differentiate him from some of his colleagues at Columbia University; a few of them may have surpassed him in breadth or depth or both. Contemporaneous as well as posthumous tributes seldom failed to include in the portrait a genial and happy disposition and a suggestion of ready wit. These qualities animated his letters and discussions, and endeared him to enthusiastic devotees.

CHAPTER VIII

Ulrich B. Phillips: Georgia Historian

The eminence that Ulrich B. Phillips attained at northern universities as a historian of the South overshadowed his early interest in the University of Georgia and the Georgia Historical Society.[1] When he left his alma mater in 1900 for advanced graduate work at Columbia University, he may have dreamed of returning to his native state as professor of history, as director of the historical society, or as librarian at the state university. Soon after the turn of the century, Phillips became the foremost authority on the history of Georgia. But he was never invited back to the state in an official capacity, except for a summer term at the university, though he returned periodically to exploit its historical records in public depositories and in private possession.

I

Phillips prepared for university work in local schools in La-Grange and in Milledgeville, and also at Tulane University's preparatory school in New Orleans. Thither he journeyed as a lad of fourteen in the fall of 1891 for his junior and senior high school years. If he possessed a youthful ambition to become a historian, his record in that subject at Tulane produced a temporary cure. A grade of 73 for the 1891–92 session discouraged him from enrolling for another course in history his senior year. Other grades were uniformly good, but his best marks—95 and 96—were earned in Greek.[2]

When Phillips entered the University of Georgia in the fall of 1893, the faculty consisted of thirty-four members including the chancellor, William Ellison Boggs, who also served as professor of metaphysics and ethics. The aggregate number of students in all divisions of the university was 1,500, of whom only 212 attended school in Athens. Most of these were enrolled in Franklin College, the liberal arts division, which utilized the services of fourteen members of the staff. One of them, Dr. John H. T. McPherson, was assigned to the recently created history and political science department.[3]

The man with whom Phillips studied history and allied subjects was a native of Baltimore who earned both his undergraduate and graduate degrees at the Johns Hopkins University, and who also studied history at the University of Berlin and at the Sorbonne. Johns Hopkins was, in McPherson's period as a student, the outstanding graduate school on this side of the Atlantic. The superiority of the history, political science, and economics department was largely attributable to the organizing genius of Herbert Baxter Adams, who developed at Baltimore reputable scholars in the social studies, an adequate library, and an enthusiastic spirit of scholarship. After obtaining the doctorate in 1890, McPherson taught for a year as instructor in history at the University of Michigan and in the fall of 1891 began his labors at the University of Georgia where he continued for more than half a century.

Correspondence that brought McPherson to Athens was initiated by Henry Clay White, professor of chemistry. Establishment of the history chair, McPherson informed Adams, "has been delayed by some complication of their revenues with the Negro Question, involving tedious discussion with the authorities at Washington," but White anticipated an early solution of the problem and the election of a historian to the chair without great delay. The prospective appointee requested a "testimonial" from Adams—one that would promote his interest "with as effective a 'puff' as you can conscientiously give me." [4] Adams already had considerable experience as a "puffer"; his students were occupying responsible positions in so many institutions that he kept a map in his office on which he indicated the settlements in his vast colonial system. He wrote of his protégé:

> This is to certify that Dr. J. H. T. McPherson studied at the Johns Hopkins University for seven years, three years as an undergraduate and four years as a graduate. As a college student he took high honors in mathematics and classics and won a University Scholarship. As a graduate he took honors in history and politics and was awarded a Scholarship and Fellowship in this department. He did very satisfactory work throughout his entire course of collegiate and university study and is remarkably well prepared for advanced work in

his chosen fields of historical and political science. He is also well grounded in historical jurisprudence.[5]

Appointed to the position, McPherson set about at once to emulate the Johns Hopkins department as fully as possible, and to inform Adams of his accomplishments and problems. Assignment of quarters above the gymnasium "in a remote corner of the campus" proved unsatisfactory, but by "persuasion and insistence, with some tact and wire-pulling," he "succeeded in capturing the rooms . . . situated just over the Library," formerly occupied by geology. These quarters, with a floor space of 55 by 100 feet, reminded McPherson of the Johns Hopkins history location. Other Johns Hopkins arrangements were imitated, for McPherson obtained money to build "shelves like those in the Bluntschli [Library], dividing half the room into alcoves, which I'll fix up with tables and chairs. When this is done I'll make a raid on the General library and get all the books I can. I have $500 to order books for my Dept, and have hopes of $1,000 more at the next meeting of the trustees." The department's library would also serve as a lecture room; a large room behind it would house a "Museum of Southern and General History." He thought that the Athens, Atlanta, and Augusta vicinities would yield many museum pieces.[6]

McPherson's teaching load, fifteen hours at Michigan, would be eleven at Georgia. In his freshman course in ancient history he would use as texts Sir Charles Oman's *History of Greece from the Earliest Times to the Death of Alexander* and Theodor Mommsen's *History of the Roman Republic.* The sophomore course in English and French history would be based upon Samuel R. Gardiner's *Student's History of England* and Victor Duruy's *History of France.* United States history would be reserved for the junior year, with Alexander Johnston's *United States; Its History and Constitution* and his *History of American Politics* serving as guides. In the senior year political economy would be based on Francis Amasa Walker's *Political Economy,* with books by John Stuart Mill, Richard T. Ely, and Alfred Marshall for reference.[7]

McPherson was hardly settled in his chair before the Athens *Banner* raised a great hullabaloo about the use of Johnston's history of the United States. The historian thought it "above reproach," but the *Banner* editor "discovered what he is pleased to consider unsound doctrine." Hearing of what was brewing, Mc-

Pherson stopped "the appearance of a flaming sensational article." He thought "most people know me to be a good Southerner"; still there was "some danger of stirring up a regular hornet's nest. That editor wants to know 'whats the matter with Alexander Stephens?' What would you advise me to do? Use Stephens nominally as a parallel?" [8]

The tempest in a teapot subsided for three weeks; then the *Banner* editor, unable to restrain himself longer, "came out with a flaming, sensational, two-column attack on Johnston's History, and kept it up daily for over two weeks." McPherson ignored the attack, other faculty members maintained discreet silence, but students published resolutions in another newspaper. The Augusta *Chronicle* defended McPherson, the Atlanta *Constitution* remained quiet, but most local Georgia presses followed the *Banner*'s lead. The Athens paper's "effrontery" eventually disgusted readers, and stockholders became indignant. "The loyal support of the students was very gratifying to me, as were also the numerous expressions of good-will and sympathy I received on all sides during the attack. I've had a tremendous amount of free advertising, though!" [9]

McPherson had been at the university for a biennium when Phillips enrolled as a freshman. The four-year program in the department, slightly changed since 1891, was still quite standard for that period. The freshman course was now a study of "general history and historical geography," with Philip Van Ness Myers' *General History for Colleges and High Schools* as a text. French history was relegated to a secondary position in the sophomore program in order to concentrate on the political and constitutional history of England. The trouble-making Johnston had been superseded by the cooperative three-volume "Epoch Series," by Reuben Gold Thwaites, Albert B. Hart, and Woodrow Wilson, as a guide to junior United States history. Political economy, with principles applied to American economic history, served as a diet for seniors.[10] The university's library holdings increased from about twenty thousand volumes when Phillips enrolled as a freshman to thirty thousand when he left Athens in 1900.[11]

A perusal of Phillips' undergraduate record leaves the impression that the student was as good as he wanted to be—or at least as good as health permitted. His grades varied from 75 to 100, with eight of the former offset by seven of 95 or higher. Normal improvement is indicated by advancement in average from 81 in his first year to 93 in his fourth.[12] Twice he made the Blue List in history: as a freshman when he ranked ninth in a class of 45; and as a junior when he ranked sixth in history as against second in French and fourth in analytical chemistry.[13] No one would have guessed that a reputable historian was aborning. But registrar's records, then as now, represent performance rather than talent. The stimulus of research, so inspiring to Phillips, was a future experience. It came before he left the University of Georgia.

In 1897 Phillips enrolled as a candidate for the master's degree, encouraged by McPherson who recommended him for a fellowship in the department. The following year he became a tutor in history, and he continued in that capacity, and as assistant librarian, for the year following attainment of the M.A. degree in 1899. As a tutor he taught the sophomore course in English history, and he shared with McPherson responsibility for the freshman course in general history.[14] That he was already looking forward to the doctorate is indicated by courses in French and German to supplement graduate work in his major field.[15]

Among the surviving documents from Phillips' student days at the University of Georgia are graduate examinations in the history of Europe since 1815 and in universal history. The first bears the date May 14, 1897; the second June 4, 1898. The date of the first examination tablet provides a minor problem in historical criticism, for Phillips did not receive his bachelor's degree until June, 1897, and internal evidence in the examination creates further doubt. In discussing nineteenth-century European colonial expansion, Phillips wrote: "Probably the expulsion of Spain from the West and East Indies will fall within the 19*th* century, but, as it has not yet been fully accomplished, in spite of the fact that Dewey has gained the greatest naval victory in the history of the world!!! (??), that subject belongs more properly to the realm of conjecture and prophecy than to history." Since the battle of Manila did not take place until the last of April, 1898, he could not have written the examination in May, 1897. The exclamation points and question marks suggest that the student was attempting facetiousness, but he could hardly anticipate Dewey's victory. Perhaps anxiety attending tests may have produced a seven for an eight as he gave attention to import of the questions rather than to a correct heading.

In discussing the status of Spain in the western hemisphere, Phillips brought history down to the present. The perspective from which he wrote was the closing years of the nineteenth century. To students of the late 1890's, the unification of Italy and of Germany was as recent as the stock market crash of 1929 is to students of 1957.

Examinations have changed considerably in the last sixty years. The emphasis in Phillips' tests was decidedly on political history, with some attention to the diplomatic aspects. There was no discussion of classes and class conflicts, of social and economic history, of fundamental causes of wars. Phillips' "summary of the Peloponnesian War" simply begins with the "Rivalry of Athens and Sparta. . . ." The climate of opinion at the Johns Hopkins may account for McPherson's accent on political history, for in Adams' department, history was "past politics and politics present history." It may not be surprising that answers to the fifteen questions relating to universal history and the ten to Europe since 1815 were chiefly factual in nature and political in content. Many topics called for factual political data.

Discussions were for the most part accurate presentations of topics, though errors found their way into some answers. A question that began, "What can you tell of the following treaties," led to guessing: "Ryswick closed one of the wars of aggression of Louis XIV. (It was at the end of the war of the Spanish Succession—1715) (?) Utrecht 1763 closed Seven years war. Paris (first Peace of Paris) 1814 deposed Napoleon, and set up Louis XVIII." Perhaps a text printed before 1890 occasioned the statement that Bismarck "still holds the office" of German chancellor. Despite such slips the answers are essentially intelligent discussions, particularly in the test on Europe since 1815. After the lapse of more than half a century, it still appears that Phillips passed his examinations. Sentence structure is clear and concise, spelling is good, and the handwriting is legible. He used the English language much better than many master's candidates today.[16]

If anyone doubts that a historian was in the making during Phillips' postgraduate years at the University of Georgia, let him read "The Passing of a Crisis. A Study of the Early History of the University," contributed to the 1899 volume of *Pandora*. His interest in the history of the university dated from his first day on the campus in 1893. The "lonesome and forlorn Freshman walked sheepishly down College Avenue and through the campus gate," homesickness accentuated by the complacency of older students who were chatting in front of the chapel or lounging on lawn or terrace by the Ivy Building or the library. Chance brought him to the "old weather-beaten, mosscovered corner-stone" of New College; with absorbing interest he endeavored to decipher the inscription. In doing so he completely forgot embarrassing loneliness. Only a few words on the stone were legible, but his personal crisis disappeared while reading them, for two upperclassmen approached and invited him to their clubrooms. He promised himself that he would later solve the mystery of the cornerstone.

The solution came nearly six years later. While running the files of the Milledgeville *Georgia Journal,* he chanced upon an Athens item in the issue of July 9, 1822: "By the Liberality of the Legislature of 1821, this Edifice was erected. The cornerstone was laid on June 24, 1822, A.L. 5823, by the Mount Vernon Lodge, at the request of the Trustees of the University of Georgia."

The inscription was the key to the crisis that faced the university for many years. The discovery inspired Phillips to write a history of the school from the year 1784, when an institution of higher learning was a dream in the minds of such pioneers as Abraham Baldwin, a recent migrant from New Haven, Connecticut. To him rather than to John Milledge or James Jackson, Phillips gave "the credit of originating the plan of the University." So he traced the steps in the school's history from the founding through its vicissitudes until it reached maturity during the presidency of Moses Waddel, with an income of $12,000 and a student body of 120, "an enrollment which was not materially excelled for more than forty years."

Why did the university mark time during the next generation, Phillips asked in bringing his history to a close, and why was advancement so slow in another forty-year period just ended? The historian did not know the answers, but he was aware of the large service the university could render the state in the future: "Georgia is well able to devote three or four hundred thousand dollars annually to higher education, and the major part of this should be put at the disposal of the University. The impetus to education must extend from above downward; from the State University to the public schools of the State. In order to lessen the proportion of illiterates in her population, she must begin by increasing the proportion of those who have the higher learning. The material progress of the State depends upon the intelligence of its citizens, which of course is to be increased by education. Very evident then is the still magnificent opportunity of the University of Georgia, but quite as evident is the tremendous responsibility of its task."[17]

It was no great undertaking for Phillips, after writing the 4,500-word *Pandora* article, to prepare a "Report on the Local Archives of Georgia: The University of Georgia," an unpublished document dating from 1904 or after. His opening statement is a summary of problems and factors that affected the university during its first hundred years of existence. Its career, he said, "is largely typical of Southern educational history. The idealism and devotion shown in its founding, the indifference of a large mass of the people to its work and aspirations, the petty animosities arising from political and social antagonisms, the parsimony of the legislature, resulting in some degree from the philosophy of individualism prevalent in the commonwealth, the depressing effect of war times and economic crises, the long continued emphasis upon the classics in the curriculum, and the heroic struggles of the champions of progress and liberalism, are each in turn eloquent of the times, the men and the manners."

A brief introduction lists the manuscript minute and inspector's books, tuition account books, treasurer's records, register of students, records of student absences, and sundry printed documents and records housed in the university secretary's office; the letter books, treasurer's records, and minute books of the Demosthenian and Phi Kappa Literary societies, housed in the history department's library. Phillips then appended extracts of archival materials and newspaper items to illustrate the history of the university. His "Notes from the Minutes of the Senatus Academicus," 1799–1819, and "Notes from the Minutes of the Board of Trustees," 1786–1822, are a highly skeletonized picture of the university in its formative years. Supplementing formal archive materials, Phillips included notes and extracts from Georgia newspapers, 1800–1857. As a concluding segment to his "heterogeneous report," he transcribed half a dozen letters from private possession relating to the university in the period 1854 to 1871.[18]

II

Phillips could not foresee in 1902, upon completion of the doctorate at Columbia University and acceptance of an instructorship at the University of Wisconsin, that he would never labor again in his native Georgia except when historical records lured the researcher or his alma mater called him for a summer session. The course he would follow was largely uncharted as the nineteenth century faded into the twentieth. McPherson might need a permanent assistant or the university library might renew its offer in more attractive terms. A reorganized historical society might require the services of a secretary or editor to exploit its resources. Only the last came near to materializing.

A few months after Phillips began teaching in Wisconsin, a letter from Lucien H. Boggs of Savannah brought the welcome news that the Georgia Historical Society, moribund for many years, would likely experience a revival. Its "degeneration" had brought "grief" to Phillips, who confessed that he "had a dark design of agitating for a real Historical Society to be established at Athens or Atlanta, in the event of my returning to Georgia." He was especially interested in the historical society's publication plans. "There are stacks of valuable documents now being eaten by the rats in the state capitol," he observed, "and lots of others in private hands in every part of the state." He had been "nosing out" William H. Crawford letters, and although periodicals had expressed interest in printing them, Phillips preferred incorporation of the letters in a "Life and Times" if he could find a publisher. But as Georgians bought few books, publication presented a problem—unless the society sponsored the work. He would "roam through middle Georgia" in late summer, and upon arrival in Savannah he would talk to George J. Baldwin, who supposedly was sparking the "revolution" in the Georgia Historical Society.[19]

Boggs replied that determination of a publication program and employment of an active secretary would have to await formal reorganization, and that Baldwin would then give Phillips' "Life and Times of Crawford" careful consideration.[20] A few days later Phillips sent tangible suggestions: the society's publications should be printed in editions large enough to permit sale as well as distribution, and the quantity for sale should be available to university and public libraries, for state historical societies "tend to become fossilized." Using the State Historical Society of Wisconsin as a model, the Georgia society should seek state financial aid; and the society rather than the state should undertake the assembling and publication of colonial and war records. Former Governor Allen D. Candler, a political appointee as state historian, was incompetent for this significant task.[21]

In the spring of 1903 Boggs informed Phillips that the society had adopted a new constitution and bylaws and that Savannah would appropriate $3,000 a year to support the society's public library. He also reported that a state bibliography should be the first publication of the society. Would Phillips make suggestions as to how it should be compiled? [22] The historian cited as models Thomas M. Owen's Alabama and Mississippi bibliographies, published by the American Historical Association.[23] Phillips thought that Owen might be well advanced in compiling a Georgia bibliography, for he contemplated compilations for all the lower South states eventually. He would agree that the society should give its attention first to the state bibliography, but he did not believe it should be the first publication. The bibliographical project would require many years for completion. Meanwhile, a calendar of state papers in Atlanta might be an initial project, and the society might undertake publication of letters of prominent Georgians. The most important document awaiting publication was Governor Wilson Lumpkin's autobiography.[24] But good history was more important than bibliographies, correspondence, and other documents. "The Society should encourage historical writing in Georgia and about Georgia." [25]

Who was George J. Baldwin, with whom Phillips exchanged many letters on the problems of the society? He was trained as a mining engineer at Massachusetts Institute of Technology. For brief periods he worked as a chemist at the Woodstock Iron Company of Anniston, Alabama, and as superintendent of the Bradley Gold Mine at Nacoochee, Georgia. Service with Baldwin and Company, dealers in fertilizers and cotton factors of Savannah, led to the presidency of the Baldwin Fertilizer Company. Associated with Stone and Webster of Boston, he organized and became president of several southern public utility companies, including the Savannah Electric Company. Years later he became interested in a mail steamship company and also in shipbuilding. Meanwhile, toward the end of the century, he developed an avocational interest in history and became an active member of the Georgia Historical Society.[26] He was forty-seven in 1903 when he began writing to Phillips; the historian was twenty years younger.

Apparently Baldwin found Phillips' suggestions, communicated through Boggs, of practical value, and he invited further discussion of problems facing the society. In a long letter of April 17, Phillips was emphatic in declaring that "the most important policy is for your Society to keep the old fossils out of office, and prevent the Society from becoming antiquarian rather than historical. The antiquarian tendency is always the most dangerous foe to the usefulness and life of historical societies. Of course the genealogists and collectors of arrow-heads, who think they are historical students must be coddled sometimes; but for practical work men of true historical interest and training must be had." He was sure Candler would make no valuable contribution, though his office might be expanded into a state agency that, "in competent hands," could serve creditably. The Alabama and Wisconsin examples "should influence public opinion"; his own pen would be available to that end. Reuben Gold Thwaites secured annually "tens of thousands" for the State Historical Society of Wisconsin. Phillips cautioned "against too much modesty in outlining a policy" for the Georgia Historical Society. "A modest plan often fails in such cases, where a striking one will succeed." In addition to money for buying and printing books, an attractive salary must be budgeted for a competent secretary. Georgia should not embark upon a program of inventorying state records without the services of a trained historian who understood "the relative value of historical documents." Phillips advised a "preliminary report" on Atlanta documents; with it as a basis, the society should approach the legislature for funds to publish the text of important documents and synopses of others. North Carolina's admirable accomplishment might serve as an example for Georgia, a "backward [state] in the movement for attention to history." [27]

To this letter Baldwin penned an appreciative reply. Phillips' suggestions revealed many aspects of historical work of which he had been unaware. But he exhibited a trait that was to become increasingly apparent as correspondence continued: he had little initiative, and he moved slowly. "I fear that we shall be compelled to get along in a very poor way for a while until I can give the time necessary to work out the Society on the lines you have laid down." [28]

One of the motives behind Phillips' encouraging counsel was a desire for a call to head the work he outlined to Boggs and Baldwin. He wrote on May 2 that he was "even tempted a little to undertake the work at Savannah, so much interested am I in what is to be accomplished." But Phillips could not relinquish his attractive task at the University of Wisconsin "without commensurate advantages elsewhere." The work about which he was so enthusiastic was the virgin field of southern history. He wrote some two or three hundred words on the errors that had been committed by Bostonians, on the necessity for trained historical scholars from the South seeking the truth, and on his own inspiring lectures on the Old South in Wisconsin.

Phillips could think of no available person who had all the qualifications of an able secretary. The society might "select some young fellow now at college in Georgia and direct him to equip himself, at Wisconsin perhaps, for the work which you wish done. . . . He should have a faculty for getting votes in the Legislature for desired appropriations." Robert Preston Brooks, University of Georgia student and the chancellor's secretary, might be developed; and Lucien Boggs would make a competent secretary if he had the necessary training. If a permanent appointment could not be made, Phillips might arrange to function "as editor and corresponding secretary in a non-resident capacity with occasional trips to Savannah." Under that arrangement Crawford's life and letters and some of the documents about which they had corresponded might be published; and the legislature might be approached for funds to survey Georgia's archives. Phillips admitted the theoretical quality of the plan, but he thought it had potentiality. His contract left him considerable time for research and editing. "My problem is how to employ that part of my time and energy to the best effect. My field is so broad and fertile that it is hard to decide where to work or what crop to raise, or whom to engage as allies in the task." [29]

Encouraged by Thomas M. Owen, who had recently visited Governor Joseph M. Terrell and Candler in Atlanta, and who reported that the legislature was in the mood to follow the Alabama pattern in establishing a department of archives and history,* Phillips wrote another urgent letter to Baldwin, enclosing Owen's communication. It indicated, Phillips thought, "that now is the psychological moment for your Society to apply for state aid." He strongly urged the Wisconsin over the Alabama and Mississippi models. A nonpolitical historical society, with its excellent collec-

* Owen reported the appointment of Allen D. Candler as compiler of records to publish Georgia colonial, Revolutionary, and Confederate records. See his short-lived magazine, *Gulf States Historical Magazine,* I (March, 1903), 378–79. A department of archives and history was established by legislative act in 1918, and on January 1, 1919, Lucian Lamar Knight became director and state historian. See Lucian Lamar Knight, "Georgia's Most Vital Need: A Department of Archives," *Proceedings of the First Annual Session of the Georgia Historical Association* (Atlanta, 1917), 36–44; Knight to Owen, August 20, 1918; January 16, May 18, 1919, Lucian Lamar Knight Collection (Georgia Department of Archives and History, Atlanta, Ga.); Knight to George H. Carswell, April 29, 1919, Knight Collection; "Sketch" of Knight's career, Knight Collection.

tion of Georgia materials and its opportunity to procure trained personnel, could "do the work desired by the state in the most efficient way. The plan should not be restricted to war records; for the records of peace are more important in themselves, and more valuable in studying the history of the past" or in the application of its lessons to the future. A campaign for state aid "would find enthusiastic acceptance in many quarters, and would meet opposition only where personal hopes and political prospects may be interferred with." [30] On the same day that Phillips penned this letter, he received a telegram from Baldwin: "For the benefit of your State and the Georgia Historical Society would you be willing to undertake joint duties of librarian public library and historian of the society provided I could arrange to have this position offered you. My ultimate object would be to secure your entire time solely as executive officer and historian of the society, but present economy demands consolidation of offices. If you could accept, wire salary you would expect and earliest date you could arrive writing fully concerning library experience. We must have a moderately expert librarian." [31]

Phillips eagerly proposed a plan that he thought would meet the telegram's spirit. The University of Wisconsin would approve second-semester teaching each year, which would leave more than seven months for work in Georgia. Moreover, he could devote much time during the spring months to research, editorial work, and correspondence for the society. Phillips rationalized the arrangement. "It would give me better facilities and a broader view than could be had either at Savannah or in Wisconsin. It would improve my lectures here, since it would put me in constant touch with the South. And it would keep the administration of your Society in touch with the historical and university circles of the country. It would, furthermore, be probably a saving for the Society, for I could accept a salary of $1400 from it, and give it by far the greater part of my energy during each year." After indicating that an assistant librarian, as well as clerical help, would be necessary, for the secretary would have to absent himself a part of the time from Savannah in the society's interest, he returned to the advantages of the plan. Despite eagerness to return to Georgia, he could not abandon his university position. "The two kinds of work are really supplementary in character, and not at all antagonistic." As to his fitness for the librarianship, his biennium as the University of Georgia's assistant librarian was supplemented by later attention to administration. "I have reason to consider myself a capable librarian," he wrote. "Please consult the Chancellor of the University of Georgia upon this point." Phillips would lecture at the University of Tennessee during the summer; he would be available at Savannah after August 1.[32]

Baldwin was not favorably impressed with Phillips' proposal. The executive officer of the Georgia Historical Society, he thought, should be on the job the whole year rather than just seven months. This was especially true while the reorganization of the society and the expansion of its work were getting under way. He would, however, present Phillips' proposal to the board.[33] Three days later, perhaps before the historian received Baldwin's discouraging letter, he wrote again, certainly with plenty of enthusiasm:

> The more I consider the plan I have proposed, for combined work in Georgia and Wisconsin, the more feasible it seems in my judgment. It would mean very hard work for me; but hard work is what I am always seeking. I have discussed the plan with several gentlemen in historical work here, and they all consider the plan quite good. . . . You cannot afford to have your Secretary out of touch with historical interests elsewhere in the country; and you should not employ a Secretary, or 'historian' whose work, lectures, and opinions are valuable only to the people of Savannah. The late stagnation of the Society was probably due in large part to its isolation from the general movements in the country.

If the society were to be a state rather than a Savannah organization, its secretary must travel to all parts of Georgia in search of historical records; he could not "always be present at the loan desk." Traveling expenses could be met in part by lectures. "But all this means heavy work upon the secretary, if he is to write history and edit documents as well, and the Society must provide him with adequate help in his work." [34]

Baldwin's reaction to Phillips' eagerness revealed the reason why little came of all the talk about a "revival." The historian "must realize that there are a number of important elements to be considered in laying the plans for the work of the Society, and the importance of beginning right will make it necessary for us to go very slowly in coming to a conclusion about so important a matter." Phillips' proposal would receive careful attention, and he would learn "promptly as soon as there is anything more definite to communicate." [35] Phillips inquired again on June 8 as to progress in arriving at a decision. Baldwin replied: "The work of the Historical Society has been going very slowly and I see now that it will be impossible for us to make any definite arrangements before Fall. . . . It will take time for me to carry through my ideas."[36] Convinced that Baldwin and his associates would not accept his proposition to give part-time service to the society, Phillips offered his editorial talent whenever it could be used and recommended his young protégé at the University of Wisconsin, Charles McCarthy, for the position as secretary.[37]

Procrastination appeared in another matter that developed in the summer of 1903. The Public Archives Commission of the American Historical Association, headed by Herman V. Ames of the University of Pennsylvania, inaugurated a program of state archival reports. Could Phillips suggest some competent person to serve as adjunct member of the commission to report on the nature and condition of Georgia's archives?[38] The letter was referred to Baldwin, who wrote Ames that reorganization of the society was not far enough along to permit designation of the appropriate person. If Ames would write him again next winter, he would then give attention to the matter.[39] Perhaps Ames sensed the inactive role Baldwin was playing, for he endeavored to enlist Phillips' services as temporary adjunct member for Georgia to survey Atlanta records. He wrote Baldwin that Phillips would be available after he completed his term at the University of Tennessee. The association would contribute twenty-five or fifty dollars toward approximately a hundred necessary to pay Phillips' expenses, and he hoped the Georgia society would pay a like sum. "He might be able to make a separate report to your society as well as ours, so that what we would publish would not be a duplicate of the report he would submit to you." Ames observed that the association would be "very fortunate if we are able to secure the services of so competent a scholar and investigator as Dr. Phillips."[40] Notwithstanding the fact that Phillips' services would be available only during the latter part of the summer, Baldwin wrote that after his vacation he would "press the matter" before the society at its next meeting.[41] Lack of cooperation did not stop historical wheels, however, for Phillips accepted the temporary assignment as Georgia adjunct, and with expenses paid by the American Historical Association he inaugurated the work in Atlanta.[42]

While working in the state capital, Phillips interviewed Governor Terrell and former Governor Candler. He wrote Baldwin that he inquired of the latter "concerning his work and plans as

Compiler of Records; and found that in truth the greater part of his activity in the office is expended in drawing his salary. He is about to print one or two volumes of documents; but nearly all of these documents have already been printed before, and most of the material of greatest importance historically is quite unknown to him or neglected by him. This is not through any special lack of industry, but is chiefly because of his entire lack of Training in historical work." Phillips explained this situation to Terrell, indicating that no improvement could be expected as long "as the work is entrusted to a political employee." * As a better alternative Phillips proposed that responsibility for publishing the records be assigned to the Georgia Historical Society. Some subterfuge could be invented, Phillips thought, to circumvent a constitutional provision forbidding "direct appropriations to the Society." The state could thus secure "expert and enthusiastic service," and the society would profit from its expanding functions. "Governor Terrell evidently took very kindly to the plan. And in general it appears that there is no insurmountable obstacle in the way of carrying out the plan, provided the moving force in your Society are disposed to exert themselves for its realization. . . . A great number of Georgia people with whom I have talked this summer

* Phillips wrote in 1905: "The State of Georgia has recently begun to publish its colonial, Revolutionary, and civil war records. The first two volumes (all so far published) show not the slightest attempt to aid the student in the use of the material, and they leave much to be desired in the quality of the book-making. Improvement is promised, however, for the rest of the series. The compiler of records has not begun to systemize the MS. records in the Georgia State capitol." Ulrich B. Phillips, "Documentary Collections and Publication in the Older States of the South," American Historical Association, *Annual Report,* 1905, I (Washington, 1906), 200–201. A more favorable view of Candler's work is presented by Theodore H. Jack in "The Preservation of Georgia History," *North Carolina Historical Review,* IV (July, 1927), 245–46: "He entered into arrangements for the copying of records in London, he began the collection of material throughout the State, he searched the State offices for documents long lost, he copied records in the court houses of the counties settled before the Revolution, he put every source of light then known under tribute. At the time of his death and in a period of less than ten years, Governor Candler had compiled material for more than fifty volumes in manuscript,—thirty-nine on the colonial period, five on the revolutionary epoch, seven on Georgia's part in the War between the States. In this relatively brief time and under such unfavorable conditions, he had put into print twenty-one volumes of Colonial Records, three of Revolutionary Records; and five on the Confederate Era in Georgia. Material for twenty-four additional volumes was left in manuscript. The Colonial and Revolutionary Records are fairly complete and the Confederate Records, though still incomplete, are fairly well advanced. It is impossible to overestimate the great service rendered the state of Georgia by Governor Candler in his work as Compiler, and his labors constitute by far the most effective work done for the collection and preservation of the records of the State."

have evinced interest in the movement for scientific historical study in the South." [43]

One could almost predict Baldwin's reply: a hearty endorsement of everything Phillips wrote and a decision to lay the matter before the board. "Your diagnosis of the situation in Atlanta confirms in every respect my own opinion and the suggestion you make appears to be most valuable." At the next meeting of the board he would promote the appointment of a committee "to take charge of the matter and push it to some definite conclusion, believing that a favorable outcome will result, as several of our Board are personal friends of Governor Candler, while others of my friends here are his political associates"! [44]

Meanwhile, Phillips continued to suggest a publication program for the Georgia Historical Society. The Draper Collection at the State Historical Society of Wisconsin did not provide a lasting interest, but in his early years at Madison he found some of the manuscripts inviting. In April, 1903, he wrote Boggs about an anonymous "account of the customs and institutions of the Creek Indians," probably written in the twenties or thirties by an educated half-breed or a white adoptee. Phillips would be glad to edit the document with introduction and notes for the *Collections of the Georgia Historical Society,* but his policy of thoroughness in everything he did would require a fifty-dollar fee. He preferred to edit the Lumpkin autobiography for the society.[45] Baldwin acknowledged Phillips' proposal with a promise to consider the Creek manuscript shortly and a notice that he had written the University of Georgia library about Lumpkin's autobiography.[46]

Correspondence between Phillips and Baldwin ceased for five years, to be revived in 1908 by Baldwin, who wanted Phillips to evaluate some letters of Don Manuel de Montiano, copies of which were in the Georgia Historical Society. If the documents were publishable, the society would have the services of Major C. DeWitt Willcox as translator and editor. Perhaps recalling Phillips' earlier effort to commercialize his talent, the society would pay a modest fee, for Baldwin hesitated to request Phillips' professional services because of his interest in the state's history.[47]

"The Montiano letters," Phillips replied, "are distinctly worth translation and printing. They probably tell most of the story of Georgia relations with Florida, from the Spanish point of view, and form an essential part of the record of Georgia's infancy. Your Society is remarkably fortunate in securing so excellent a translator and editor as Major Willcox." Phillips' counsel was of course provided "gratuitously." [48]

In the same letter Phillips notified Baldwin that he was presenting to the Georgia Historical Society copies of the Manigault records of a rice plantation on Argyle Island, a dozen miles from Savannah. Some extracts would appear in "Plantation and Frontier," Phillips' contribution to the ten-volume cooperative *Documentary History of American Industrial Society.* The whole collection merited publication, he advised, and he was placing it at the disposal of the society.[49]

Baldwin graciously thanked Phillips for reading the Montiano manuscript, which the society would publish; [50] congratulated him on his appointment at Tulane University, where the South would reclaim him even if his native locality could not; expressed delight with the author's *History of Transportation in the Eastern Cotton Belt;* and observed with regard to the Manigault Papers that his "personal inclination would be to make this our next work." [51]

The Baldwin-Phillips correspondence came to an end in 1910.[52] Many of their letters, particularly those of 1903, were concerned with significant matters relating to the Georgia Historical Society. They reveal a young, talented, ambitious historian, just out of his doctorate, eager for opportunity to establish a reputation in the historical world; eager also to promote historical consciousness in his native state. They disclose too the avocational interest of a middle-aged businessman who sensed that the Georgia Historical Society was not functioning properly, but who was unwilling to lead a revolution that would ignore conservative interests in the society. Phillips, who visualized rapid advancement to bring the state to the Alabama or Wisconsin level, could not adapt his ambitious career to a moribund organization.*

Most of Phillips' recommendations and suggestions were constructive; many of them were attainable. It is quite likely that a genuine revival would have occurred if he had returned to Georgia

* Nearly a decade passed before historical activity in the state experienced a major impetus. A rival Georgia Historical Association was inaugurated in 1917, largely by University of Georgia men. Three years later the new association and the old Georgia Historical Society were merged. Meanwhile, the *Georgia Historical Quarterly* had been founded. On the establishment of the association and its merger with the society, see *Proceedings of the First Annual Session of the Georgia Historical Association; Proceedings of the Second Annual Session of the Georgia Historical Association* (Atlanta, 1918) ; *Proceedings of the Third Annual Session of the Georgia Historical Association* (Atlanta, 1919) ; *Georgia Historical Quarterly,* IV (June, September, 1920) .

even on a part-time basis—if he had exhibited patience and the legislature had appropriated funds to promote the assembling, editing, and publishing of historical records. If it be asserted that Phillips was seeking selfish ends in his recommendations, one could reply that he had much to offer the society. What would have happened to his outlook and perspective if he had become absorbed in state and local history? Would he have been typed as a state historian, and therefore missed the opportunity to become a historian of the South?

These questions cannot be answered, but the historiographer can recall Phillips' dilemma of 1903—"it is hard to decide where to work or what crop to raise, or whom to engage as allies in the task"—and the way in which he resolved it. By 1910 or before, he had decided to continue in university work and raise a crop of southern plantations, with subsidiary attention to Negro slavery. He had formulated his basic ideas on these subjects before he left the South for the University of Michigan in 1911. In later books and monographs he would polish his words and refine his concepts, but he would develop no new ones. Nor would he again reside in his native Southland.

CHAPTER IX

Charles W. Ramsdell: Historian of the Confederacy

More than a score of years ago, Charles W. Ramsdell was invited to inaugurate the Walter Lynwood Fleming Lectures in Southern History at Louisiana State University.[1] A program of the first series, characterizing the lecturer as the "Dean of Southern Historians," reached him a few days before he left Austin for Baton Rouge. The well-merited designation brought a quick response from the historian who was modesty personified: "When I read that I could not refrain from saying to myself, 'My God! Has it come to that?' "[2]

It had, indeed, though it would be difficult to assign a monocause for the respect and esteem in which Ramsdell was held by the historical guild in the 1930's. He had, by that time, served as president of the Mississippi Valley Historical Association and of the newly established Southern Historical Association.* Faithful and competent member of the history faculty at the University of Texas since 1906, he had taught annual generations of undergraduate and graduate students for thirty years, and he had given generously of his time to directing master's theses and doctoral dissertations. His publication record—in pages he had put in print—was certainly not impressive. His only scholarly book at that time, *Reconstruction in Texas,* was his dissertation at Columbia University, printed in 1910. A score of articles and essays had appeared in such professional periodicals as the *Southwestern Historical Quarterly,* the *Mississippi Valley Historical Review,* the

* In addition to the presidencies of the two associations, Ramsdell gave other official services to professional societies: secretary-treasurer of the Texas State Historical Association, 1907–1942; associate editor of the *Southwestern Historical Quarterly,* 1910–1938; member executive council, Southern Historical Association, 1935–1939; member board of editors, *Journal of Southern History,* 1937–1940; member executive committee, Mississippi Valley Historical Association, 1928–1935; member board of editors, *Mississippi Valley Historical Review,* 1930–1933; member executive council. American Historical Association, 1931–1934.

Journal of Southern History, and the *American Historical Review.* Half a hundred appraisals of books had been contributed to scholarly journals. The *Dictionary of American Biography* had profited from his concise sketches.[3] Perhaps a few score of Ramsdell's southern contemporaries equaled his productive record, and many surpassed it.

The "deanship," nevertheless, was hardly a specious invention. Contemporaries in the guild, including his students, recognized the superior qualities of his mind, the logic of his thought, the soundness of his judgment. A younger member of the craft who listened spellbound as Ramsdell read his Mississippi Valley Historical Association presidential address, "The Natural Limits of Slavery Expansion," imagined the dignified Texan attired in judicial ermine. The neophyte was so awed that he could not muster the courage, after adjournment, to make his presence known to the association's retiring president. Five years would elapse before the anonymous admirer meekly sought Ramsdell's aid in organizing the Southern Historical Association and in launching its *Journal of Southern History.* To his amazement he discovered that the Texan was one of the most approachable men he had ever known. The self-depreciating scholar stood in sharp contrast with inhabitants of the historical world who wore their scholarship so conspicuously on their coat sleeves. He was very human, aware of his own limitations, eager to grasp further insight.

I

The year 1877 was significant in southern history as the end of Radical Reconstruction and in southern historiography as the beginning of Charles William Ramsdell. His birthplace was Salado in Bell County, Texas, where he attended the public schools and also the private Thomas Arnold High School.[4] The "classical course" at the University of Texas, where he received the bachelor of arts degree in 1903, included among other subjects Greek, Latin, German, and English, as well as history and political science. In most of his courses Ramsdell earned grades of A or B notwithstanding participation in football.[5] Collegiate experience on the gridiron later enhanced his value as a faculty member at his alma mater, for he understood "men and how to handle them," and "proved himself a very useful man on committees concerned with student activities."[6] Athletes were not subsidized in Ramsdell's undergraduate days. In the summer preceding his senior year, he wrote to George P. Garrison, head of the history department, indicating the need for employment to continue his quest for a degree. "Would the work that I might get on the *Quarterly* [of the Texas State Historical Association] amount to very much?" he inquired. While he preferred quarters where he could earn his board, he would labor at any task.[7] A fifth year at the university yielded the master's degree in 1904, with a thesis on presidential Reconstruction in Texas.

An enviable academic record led to a fellowship at Columbia University for the year 1904–1905.[8] Ramsdell kept Garrison informed of his progress, the academic opportunities at the university, the caliber of his instructors as scholars and teachers, and the extracurricular advantages of living in New York City. Despite the "strenuous life" imposed by his teachers, he found time to observe the great metropolis—"this noisy quarter of the world." The student attended the best operas and theaters, listened to well-known preachers, and visited "points of greatest interest from the Ghetto to the Metropolitan Museum of Arts."[9]

These diversions consumed only a minimal slice of his time budget. He was ever busy attending lectures and preparing term reports. His professors passed in review as he confided to his Texas mentor the nature of their courses and the measure of their personalities. He studied American constitutional history with John W. Burgess, who seemed "to stand afar off," though his lectures were excellent. John Bassett Moore, who guided his study of diplomatic history, was "a very pleasant man," and he liked him immensely. Herbert Levi Osgood "would be a fine man to know if one could get close to him." He was "above all things a *driver,* a worker." Ramsdell thought he "would have been a great success as a restless, bustling business man. The remorseless energy with which he can pile up millions of facts and hurl them at you is overwhelming." Like his volumes on *The American Colonies,* lectures were "wearisome in their particularity."[10] Students dreaded his rapidly delivered "paralyzing" performances. But they had "an immense respect for his scholarship," and they understood why he acquired recognition as "the first authority in Colonial History." Ramsdell's thesis-length term report, a history of the Committees of Correspondence, 1764–75, required more than a month, but he had his "reward in that Prof. Osgood seemed pleased and—which is not his habit at all—spoke of it in a rather complimentary way."

The Texan's favorites were James Harvey Robinson and William A. Dunning, both of them "charming men, not only scholarly and fine teachers, but they are very *approachable* and one can get a great deal from the personality of the men." The student was "particularly impressed" with Robinson and his course on the cultural history of western Europe. It was "the only thing of its kind offered in the country," Ramsdell reported. Members of the class acquired firsthand acquaintance "with every writer with any claim to prominence from Boethius to Erasmus." A new approach to the French Revolution reserved a semester for the old regime, for Robinson was convinced "that the real revolution was practically accomplished by 1789." Ramsdell's forty-page report on "The Republican Spirit in France before 1792" went slower than papers in other courses, as much of the evidence was in French. A formal statement of Robinson's New History would not appear until after Ramsdell left Columbia University, but the inspiring teacher gave the student a genuine love for modern European history and a desire to inaugurate work in that subject when he was offered an instructorship at the University of Texas.

As a master's candidate, Ramsdell had, as we have seen, investigated presidential Reconstruction in his native state, and he therefore felt much at home in Dunning's seminar. His report on "the legislative and constitutional history of the Civil Rights Bill" required another four or five weeks. Ramsdell was grateful for Dunning's "expression of pleasure in the paper." He was also indebted to his director for a part-time teaching position at Barnard College. As fellowships at Columbia University were not renewable for a second year, he faced the problem of continuing there until residence requirements were completed. It was Dunning, the student thought, who was chiefly responsible for providing the means—an assistantship created by the prolonged absence of James T. Shotwell in Europe. As there were other candidates for the position, Ramsdell was hard pressed to find a reason for his own selection. "It all means I suppose that Prof. Dunning wants that thesis on Reconstruction in Texas . . . finished." He would teach Barnard College classes in general history, and although the remuneration was not great, he would acquire valuable teaching experience, a "closer contact with the faculty," and an opportunity to observe "the inside workings of a great institution"; or, as Dunning whimsically phrased it, " 'in being a cog in the machine—*once in a while.*' " Ramsdell was so excited over the appointment that he required over a week for complete recovery of equilibrium.[11]

In his mature years, the former assistant of 1905–1906 humorously recalled his first class of girls at Barnard College. He labored assiduously in preparing lectures in advance and worked out material for at least three. The notes moved more rapidly than he anticipated, and he used all of them in the first half hour of his opening lecture. At this embarrassing point he decided that a summary of what he had said was in order. Time was still heavy on his hands, so he summarized the summary. As he had no heart for summarizing the summary's summary, he dismissed the class five minutes early.

II

Before Ramsdell's second year at Columbia University was well under way, glorious news arrived from Austin: a letter from Garrison offering him an instructorship in history at his alma mater. As the ambition of every transplanted Texan seems to be a return to Texas, the offer—though not the salary—was highly gratifying. He thought of all the reasons why he should receive $1,200 for fifteen or eighteen hours of teaching; but as that salary was not forthcoming, he accepted the position anyway.[12]

Thus began Ramsdell's career as a historian at the University of Texas, where he would continue until his death in 1942. The department of history then consisted of four members: Garrison, who was nearing the end of his period of service; Eugene C. Barker, who would continue at the university until his retirement nearly half a century later; Herbert E. Bolton, destined for a conspicuous career at the University of California after a period of seasoning; and Ramsdell, "the lowest in rank of the four men in the department," as the new appointee phrased it. Before Barker succeeded Garrison as chairman of the department a few years later, the neophyte taught ancient history, modern European history, and English history. In the last field he soon developed British Empire and period courses for advanced undergraduates and graduate students. The department's personnel expanded rapidly under Barker's leadership, and Ramsdell gradually shifted to United States history, Civil War and Reconstruction, and the Old South.[13]

Through no fault of his own, advancement came slowly in Ramsdell's early years at Texas. Despite his experience at Barnard College, the Texas authorities "considered him as in a measure untried." A new president with conservative notions of promotions and a governor who "pledged the Regents" to make no salary increases in return for a new library appropriation delayed his progress. And so the matter stood when Ulrich B. Phillips, another Dunning student, resigned his professorship at Tulane University in 1911 and sought to make Ramsdell his successor. But somehow Tulane's President Edwin B. Craighead got the impression that the Texan was "a factionalist and of malcontent disposition." [14] This misconception prompted a letter from Barker, full of honest if restrained commendation. "It would be hard to imagine a man further removed from the character of a factionalist than is Ramsdell," he wrote. He was "a conservative progressive" who talked little, and least of all "about his own grievances." Ramsdell was "a good teacher, not striking, but quite well up with the average, and perhaps a little better." As a man he was "plain, straight-forward, and likeable." If he lacked "brilliant qualities," he was nonetheless "perfectly solid." Barker hoped that Texas would be able to retain his services.* After five years as instructor, he was promoted to adjunct professor of American history.

In evaluating Ramsdell as a historian of Reconstruction, it is necessary to understand, first, that his only serious venture into this period was his dissertation at Columbia University; and, second, that it conformed rather rigidly to the generally accepted pattern of the time. As a product of the Dunning school, it was an adequate performance, though the doctoral candidate did not attain the broad perspective achieved by his contemporary, Walter L. Fleming, whose 800-page *Civil War and Reconstruction in Alabama* treated both controversial epochs on a substantial ante-

* Barker to Phillips, March 21, April 2, 1911, Eugene C. Barker Letters (Archives Collection, University of Texas, Austin, Tex.). When Dunning learned that Ramsdell might not be promoted in 1911, he wrote to a friend at Georgetown College in Texas: "If this is the case I think it is one of the greatest outrages, and worse than that; the greatest blunders ever made by an educational institution. I have the highest possible respect for Ramsdell as a man and as a scholar. . . . If there were a position open at Columbia we of the History Department would offer it to him in a minute, so sure are we of his powers to do good work." William A. Dunning to S. H. Moore, March 9, 1911, Barker Letters.

bellum base, and supplemented conventional approaches by incorporating a great mass of social and economic data in his narrative. Ramsdell's briefer *Reconstruction in Texas* devoted only sixteen pages to secession and the course of the Civil War in Texas. Primarily political and constitutional history, it provided only incidental consideration of social and economic aspects of the period. The brief presentation of labor conditions was certainly inadequate, and the state's history out of social context made the study less than comprehensive. The two-page bibliography indicated chief reliance upon Texas newspapers, convention and legislative journals, and correspondence of contemporaries.

Judging Ramsdell's performance in the conceptual framework of the Dunning school, it was on the whole an impartial effort at factual reporting. The historian frankly admitted, however, that he was "naturally drawn into a sympathetic attitude toward the people whose social and political system was being 'reconstructed.' " [15] Avoiding injudicious terminology throughout most of the book, Ramsdell's irritation occasionally came to the surface. He spared no words in excoriating the Radicals. "Never, perhaps, was punitive legislation founded upon a more distorted array of evidence, upon worse misrepresentation as to facts." Governor Edmund J. Davis was "self-willed, obstinate, pig-headed almost beyond belief, a most intense and narrow partisan." Ramsdell credited him with personal honesty, but he was associated with "a group of the most unprincipled adventurers that ever disgraced a government." The Radical governor's police included "the worst desperadoes in the state." With the badge of public authority, they "committed the most high-handed outrages: bare-faced robbery, arbitrary assessments upon helpless communities, unauthorized arrests, and even the foulest murders." Lawlessness was not confined to the Radicals, however, for "Texas was pre-eminently a frontier state," with rough and tumble means of settling disputes outside the law. The state's problem "was to endure as best she could the rule of a minority, the most ignorant and incapable of her population under the domination of reckless leaders, until time should overthrow it. Reconstruction had left the pyramid upon its apex; it must be placed upon its base again." [16] Whether in the period before Radical control began, or subsequent to it, Ramsdell defended Conservatives against charges of disloyalty and approved their means of restoring "home rule." [17]

Aside from the emphasis on political and constitutional history to the neglect of social and economic factors, the study's major imperfections lay, first, in the writer's inability to detach himself from the period's controversial events and personalities; and, second, in his acceptance of the contemporary view that the Negro was innately inferior. Southern writers, and northern historians too, had not yet taken the Negro seriously as a factor worthy of careful consideration. Another generation would pass before his part in Reconstruction would be fairly evaluated, or progressive and constructive implications of the period would be recognized and appreciated. Ramsdell understood the period only in part. Understanding eventually became a quality of his mind, but it would be directed mainly to the Civil War period and its antebellum background.

Before a history of the Confederacy could be written, its records must be assembled for the historian's use. The initial impulse at the University of Texas was supplied by Barker, with Ramsdell an enthusiastic coadjutor. The unfair accounts that came out of the North were not due to prejudice alone. The South was responsible in large part for the unbalanced history that was written, for the region had done little to make its records available. Barker's 1912 questionnaire to leading historians and librarians in the South provided a dismal picture of meager funds for acquisitions and inevitable paucity of materials for the teaching of southern history and slight incentive for writing it.[18]

The Littlefield Fund for Southern History was established by a Confederate veteran, Major George W. Littlefield. He donated $25,000 in 1914 for the purchase of southern records, provided special gifts totaling over $30,000 by 1920, and generously bequeathed an additional $100,000 to the endowment at his death in that year. From the early 1920's the fund yielded an annual income of about $4,000. Ramsdell became a member of the Littlefield committee in 1914 and negotiated for the acquisition of sundry important purchases from the beginning of his membership. He was immediately in charge of two of the three projects launched in 1937. One of them was a program of microfilming southern materials for the three score years from 1820 to 1880; the other was a proposal for writing a multivolume history of the South.[19]

As director of the microfilm project, Ramsdell arranged for a graduate student, Barnes F. Lathrop, and his wife, to tour the important depositories from Massachusetts to Louisiana, equipped with a Photorecord camera. For two years, 1937–39, and again in the summer of 1940, they photographed nearly forty thousand feet of film, representing approximately four hundred thousand pages of historical material. "The Ramsdell films," Lathrop reported, "constitute one of the most valuable additions to the Littlefield collection." [20]

The other Littlefield fund project was a history of the South, for the endowment contemplated the writing of the South's history as well as the assembling of its records. The Littlefield committee delegated Ramsdell to plan a series of volumes. At first he contemplated three, covering the period from the end of the Revolution to the close of Reconstruction. He later decided to add three more to include the earlier and later periods of southern history. It does not detract from the Texan's initial planning to understand that a somewhat more ambitious project was in an advanced stage at a neighboring university, and that its ten-volume proposal was eventually adopted as a joint endeavor of the Littlefield fund and the Louisiana State University Press. Ramsdell's capacity for adjustment and cooperation came to the surface in working out arrangements for a history that involved cooperation between the sponsoring institutions, between the coeditors, and among the contributors of the several volumes. The editorial correspondence is replete with evidence of Ramsdell's sound judgment in choosing authors and in establishing flexible objectives for the whole series.[21] Tragedy intervened to prevent him from writing the Confederacy volume or from witnessing the appearance of even the first published number, which materialized five years after his death. The planning stage of the cooperative work yields tangible evidence of Ramsdell's philosophy of history.

As anyone who knew the workings of Ramsdell's mind might expect, he was opposed to system builders—to great patterns or unifying themes. Using the history of the South as an example, he explained his view in unmistakable terms. As he contemplated the broad range of the South's past, he saw "a continuous evolution (mixed up with a certain amount of *devolution*), but it is too complex for my simple mind to reduce to a few simple factors. I am conscious of continuous change and a multiplicity of factors some of which are simple and evident, some of which I only partly understand, and others that I merely sense without being able to analyze them. Some are local, some are world-wide. There are intangibles that elude me, imponderables that I cannot weigh."

Ramsdell hoped that each contributor to the cooperative work would "avoid treating his volume as a mere cross-section of the South's history, but rather as a chapter in a continuous narrative; he should look both backward and forward in order that, while telling his portion of the story as completely and effectively as possible within the limits set for him, he may fit it into the larger unit." [22]

With Phillips' "most interesting paper" on "The Central Theme of Southern History," Ramsdell was "favorably impressed"; it was, he thought, "factually consistent" and "as valid as any." But he saw "an element of danger" in such a fascinating "intellectual exercise." "It could so easily be pushed too far." Writing to Avery Craven, who requested Ramsdell's view of the article, the Texan pointed out that it was difficult, "considering the complexity of conditions, interests and motives throughout the whole South during its whole history to select any one thing as *the* central theme. But if we must have one, I think the problem of racial adjustment or white control comes nearest being the one of universal interest." [23]

The amiable Ramsdell did not permit his charitable nature to dull the edge of critical appraisal. In reviews and in correspondence he defended Clio against assaults of historians who distorted facts, drew erroneous conclusions, or wrote unbalanced history. He could speak most authoritatively on the Confederacy period, and with some assurance on the Old South and the Civil War's aftermath. Phillips' primacy in the antebellum field did not overawe him. *Life and Labor in the Old South* was a "delightful and illuminating book," and it approached definitiveness in the author's main interest—"southern agriculture and agricultural society." But he protested neglect of the six million nonslaveholders and scant attention to business, industry, transportation, and education. Specialists in southern history had a right to expect answers to many questions which the book did not provide. Was the peculiar institution profitable? Did it actually oppress small farmers? "Barring the cataclysm of war," what was "the probable future of the institution?" What had agricultural reformers accomplished by 1860? And was the time propitious for a "fairly workable synthesis" of the Old South? [24]

Ramsdell's most caustic criticism was reserved for Frank L. Owsley's *State Rights in the Confederacy*. He disagreed with the book's thesis, that the Confederacy "Died of State Rights." The author did, of course, "find evidence that state authorities frequently hampered the Confederate government," and therein lay a "useful contribution." But Owsley "tried to prove too much," and he did so by mishandling evidence. Becoming enamored of his subject, he abandoned "his critical powers," he "accepted isolated and casual statements as bases for sweeping declarations," he "read into some of his sources statements that are not there even by implication," and he "ignored evidence that tends to disprove or to qualify materially portions of his general thesis." Owsley assigned southern governors—particularly Joe Brown, Zebulon B. Vance, and Francis R. Lubbock—to the "rogues' gallery," but he found no fault with any of the Confederate government's acts or policies or any of its officials' mistakes. The dissertation's thesis, Ramsdell thought, was more appropriate for the period after the military disasters of July, 1863, when the Confederacy was headed down hill; it could hardly apply to the first two years of the conflict.[25] While Ramsdell "tried to keep from saying anything positively offensive," he feared his constant "state of irritation" prevented success.[26]

Among nonprofessional historians who sought Ramsdell's counsel was George Fort Milton, who was writing a biography of Stephen A. Douglas. After *Eve of Conflict* appeared, Ramsdell wrote another reviewer that if he disliked the published work, he should have seen the manuscript. The Texan "wrote long protests and criticisms on nearly every chapter" that he read. "I warned him that he was allowing the partisan character of the Douglas correspondence to betray him into a one-sided story and that the critics would certainly pitch into him about it. He promised to tone down his statements in certain particulars, and he has, but not enough."

Milton's "inside story of party politics" was an excellent contribution, and Ramsdell was "temperamentally sympathetic with his central theme—that Douglas' plan offered the only peaceful solution for the territorial squabble, weak as it was in logic, if only emotional strain joined to the inevitable maneuverings of party politics had permitted it to be honestly tried." * Ramsdell's stock

* Ramsdell to Dwight L. Dumond, February 2, 1935, Charles W. Ramsdell Papers (in possession of Mrs. Ramsdell). See also Ramsdell to George Fort Milton, May 30, 1930, Ramsdell Papers, in which he explained the limits of slavery expansion and the problem of slave labor in Virginia's mining and milling industries. Slaveowners could not afford to support slave families and employ only the men in heavy industrial work. Only when they combined agriculture and industry could slave labor be used profitably "in any large scale industry."

phrase appeared again: Milton "tried to prove too much." He "underestimated the strength of popular sentiment North and South"; overestimated Douglas' "southern popular support"; and understood neither the "local factional jealousies" that prompted southern votes nor the Ultras who were committed to John C. Breckinridge.[27]

An appraisal of Ramsdell would be incomplete without some indication of his competence in the unrewarding task of refereeing papers submitted to scholarly reviews. Serving in that behind-the-scenes capacity for the *Journal of Southern History* in its early years, he demonstrated previously anticipated talent for separating papers with solid worth from others of questionable quality, and he readily recognized articles appropriate to newspaper Sunday supplements. Of one in the last category, the critic observed that "the only suggestion of a new approach" was contained "in the rather cleverly phrased title." [28] But he was genuinely interested in the paper that showed promise even though it was not a finished product in research and craftsmanship. His constructive, critical evaluations—often running to a thousand words or more—enabled young scholars to revise their work with improving effect.[29] His critical comments were often masterpieces of appraisal, and the managing editor might ponder whether historical scholarship would be better advanced by publishing the critiques rather than the articles.

III

If Ramsdell's critical thinking had a quality that distinguished it, *understanding* might be singled out as a special gift. He was not free of error—he might be wrong because he had not discovered all the evidence, even wrong in his speculative conclusions from the evidence before him. Yet it would be difficult to find in his thinking or writing either pettiness or sensationalism. He wore the historical ermine as befitted a man who conscientiously sought truth in appraising men who wrote history, or in presenting events and movements and men who formed its warp and woof. Perhaps no one was surprised when he reported unfavorably on Owsley's *State Rights in the Confederacy* or viewed sympathetically Douglas S. Freeman's *R. E. Lee.*[30] In the first instance, he saw the novice at work, misusing evidence to prove a thesis that had only limited validity; in the second, he observed the experienced master architect who built a magnificent house upon a firm foundation.

He took no pride in the first, and regretted the assignment; he regarded the second as an opportunity for self-enlightenment.

The magnum opus on the southern Confederacy was never completed; in fact, no chapters ever reached first draft. Readers of Ramsdell's briefer treatises, however, could visualize the nature of the Confederate history he would have written if time had permitted more years for the task. His paper on "Some Problems Involved in Writing the History of the Confederacy" presented at the first annual meeting of the Southern Historical Association in 1935, was a prospectus of the unfinished work. The problems were those that confronted Ramsdell. His discussion of them reveals his own comprehensive grasp of the Confederacy's main currents, his abundant knowledge of the documentary materials, his awareness of contributions scholars had made, and the innumerable gaps that awaited investigation before a definitive work could be written.

It was Ramsdell's habit to ask himself questions before he began to write, to weigh possible approaches, to state the broad plan, and to inventory his own equipment. He began: ". . . what we do *not* want is a history that lays undue emphasis upon any particular phase of the story, whether it be military operations, or the political and administrative policies and difficulties of the Confederate government, or the socio-economic conditions of the people." On the contrary, what we do want is "a full, comprehensive, well-balanced and articulated account that will give due weight to all discoverable factors in the struggle of the Southern people for independence and their failure to achieve it. Without sacrificing accuracy, it should have as much literary charm as the writer is capable of imparting to it." [31]

The Confederacy's historian could not begin his narrative with secession, for almost every problem had antebellum roots. Thanks to Phillips, the plantation and slavery background was well known, but the role of the small farmers, the bankers, the merchants, the factors, and the industrialists had received scant attention. Unless the historian understood southern businessmen and the South's "material resources," he could not hope to comprehend the problems that faced the Confederacy. There were few "searching studies of ante-bellum state politics." The historian would be severely handicapped if he did not understand "personal and factional rivalries," for "local ante-bellum political alignments and jealousies were carried over into the public affairs of the Confederacy."

In treating the war period, the historian could hardly ignore the Confederacy in battle array. Despite a tendency in the 1930's to relegate all military history to a subordinate position, "the fate of the 'revolution' " depended upon the success of the armies. The story of the supply services—the quartermaster's, subsistence, ordnance, and medical bureaus—was largely unknown. Wartime "mechanical industries," railroad transportation, financial problems, governmental measures that affected military operations, "the condition and attitudes of the people," were factors that must be weighed, and the historian would "find difficulty enough to challenge all his powers of analysis." Among the problems of government, the effective use of the Negro population and the disposition of such staples as tobacco and cotton would prove "troublesome." The influence of speculators and the blockade upon the Confederacy's fortunes, the privations endured by poor people, factionalism in Confederate politics, relief organizations, churches and hospitals, medical substitutes, foreign policy—these and countless other matters needed further investigation.

Ramsdell closed his prospectus with the significant observation that anyone who would "write a comprehensive history of the very complex life of the Confederacy must do a great deal of pioneer work for himself." [32] He was presenting problems of a quarter-century ago. The monographic studies that have appeared in the interim have solved many of them; some others still await scholarly treatment.

Much has been written on "The Changing Interpretation of the Civil War" since Ramsdell presented his presidential address on that subject before the Southern Historical Association in 1936. The most comprehensive of the studies, Thomas J. Pressly's *Americans Interpret Their Civil War,* surveyed with insight and understanding the conflicting viewpoints from the war period to the middle of the twentieth century. In briefer compass, Ramsdell viewed the evolution from apologias of contemporaries to the more objective accounts of the twentieth century's critical school. In presenting his conclusions, he differentiated between the two crises, secession and war. The first crisis, he thought, was inevitable, but the second was not—"unless those whose official positions gave them the power to choose war or peace were obliged to choose war for reasons of policy." [33] Admitting that both southern whites and Negroes were "better off with slavery gone," he was convinced that the institution "would have begun to decline" soon after 1860 "and eventually have been abolished by the Southerners themselves." Despite "substantial progress" of Negroes since Appomattox, he questioned whether "their condition is better now than it would have been had a more orderly process of social and economic change been followed." He was also certain that the outcome of the war had not benefited the "poor white" outcasts of the Old South. "This submerged class remains submerged."

Evaluating the results of the war, he found them wanting.

> Making all necessary allowances for our inability to weigh accurately the imponderables in the history of a great people [he wrote], can we say with conviction that this war accomplished anything of lasting good that could not and would not have been won by peaceful processes of social evolution? Is there not ground for the tragic conclusion that it accomplished little which was not otherwise attainable? Had the more than half a million lives and the ten billions of wasted property been saved, the wealth of the United States and the welfare of the people would not likely have been less than they are now. Perhaps some of the social and economic ills that have bedevilled us for the past fifty years would have been less troublesome.[34]

Ramsdell's speculations as to voluntary southern termination of slavery and the easier adjustment of social and economic problems through evolution rather than revolution were accepted in some quarters, questioned in others. Some eyebrows were lifted higher at the thesis of his "Lincoln and Fort Sumter" study, which concluded that Lincoln, through ingenious strategy, "maneuvered the Confederates into firing the first shot in order that they, rather than he, should take the blame of beginning bloodshed." He resorted to the maneuver after deciding "that there was no other way than war for the salvation of his administration, his party, and the Union." * If Ramsdell failed to prove his point convincingly, he exhibited rare talent for marshaling evidence and of piecing together the fragmentary contemporary information. In this premise the article has enduring merit as an example of meticulous inquiry, of search for obscure sources.†

* Ramsdell, "Lincoln and Fort Sumter," *Journal of Southern History,* III (August, 1937), 285. Near the beginning of the article on page 259 he wrote: "Whether the war was inevitable, in any case, is a question that need not be raised here. It has been the subject of endless disputation and is one to which no conclusive answer can be given. But even though it be conceded that if the conflict had not arisen from the Fort Sumter crisis it would have sprung from some other incident growing out of the secession of the 'cotton states,' the actual firing of the 'first shot' placed the Southerners under a great moral and material disadvantage."

† Unusual interest in the "Lincoln and Fort Sumter" article is indicated by excessive requests for reprints directed to the editorial office as well as to the author. "I expect a furious kick-back on this paper from various sources," Ramsdell wrote,

In the absence of a comprehensive work on the war years, one must turn to Ramsdell's Fleming lectures, *Behind the Lines in the Southern Confederacy,* for a basic interpretation of the Confederate States of America. Previous writers had indicated a variety of reasons for the failure of the stroke for independence—disparity in manpower, shortage of mechanical and military equipment, insufficient provisions, the northern blockade, faulty strategy, monetary problems, internal dissension on the issue of state rights, inferior statesmanship, a psychological spirit of defeatism, lack of will to win. "If I were asked what was the greatest single weakness of the Confederacy [Ramsdell wrote], I should say, without much hesitation, that it was in this matter of finances. The resort to irredeemable paper money and to excessive issues of such currency was fatal, and it weakened not only the purchasing power of the government but also destroyed economic security among the people. In fact, there seems to be nothing vital that escaped its baneful influence."

On the other hand, Ramsdell recognized the causative arc as well as the apexed culmination. While hopelessness of Confederate finances was the main root of the difficulty, there were other contributing factors to collapse, among them "industrial weakness," illegal trade with the enemy, and the transportation problem, which he ranked "next to finances in its deleterious consequences." [35]

Ramsdell's last "great adventure," as he called it, was an edition of the *Laws and Joint Resolutions of the Last Session of the Confederate Congress (November 7, 1864—March 18, 1865), Together with the Secret Acts of Previous Congresses.* The volume, published the year before he died, exhibits Ramsdell as the careful, thorough, and precise editor in search of the last scrap of evidence. The project was initiated by Duke University, which had acquired eighty-nine "manuscript enrolled acts and resolutions" of the Congress' final session, along with a few other acts and resolutions and "the official manuscript 'Register of Acts, C. S. A.'" The

---

"but I don't care as long as I believe I am right. I wish the thing were better written, however. Now that I have read it in type, I can see plenty of faults in the composition and in the presentation of the argument. But that has always been true of anything I have ever written." Of one modification in galley proof he said, "How in the world I could have left in the text such an asinine expression as 'strategic astuteness' I don't understand." Ramsdell to the writer, June 10, 1937, personal files. Many requests came also for reprints of Ramsdell's "The Changing Interpretation of the Civil War." Ramsdell to the writer, April 2, 1937, personal files.

editor searched elsewhere for other missing acts and resolutions—Richmond newspapers, John H. Reagan Papers, and the National Archives—with rewarding discoveries.[36] Here was a volume of solid worth, assembled and edited in authoritative manner.

IV

The historian's appraisals and articles of mature years manifested careful reading, cogent thinking, basic understanding, and clear expression. One of his pieces transcended his usual competence. The article, "Carl Sandburg's Lincoln," contributed to the *Southern Review,* indicates what Ramsdell could do with a theme that demanded perspective and inspired enthusiasm. The six-thousand-word essay was his last significant piece of writing. Craftsmanship attained literary distinction. Understanding promoted evaluation. Perspective assumed broad canvas. If only this essay survived, Ramsdell's mature historianship could be fairly evaluated. Sandburg and his Lincoln were mirrored against a mosaic of problems that faced the Civil War President as well as those that confronted the biographer. Of all the estimates of the poet's portrait, this one reveals better than any other the stature of the author, the subject—and the reviewer.

In well-turned sentences, Ramsdell painted the mythical and legendary Lincoln whose vitality found expression in "thousands of books, pamphlets, essays, poems, and stories," in "references to him as an authority on countless disturbing questions, in appeals to his name in behalf of all sorts of causes." Although "one does not usually expect a critical biography from the hand of a poet who writes of his life-long hero, or an adequate understanding of all the great problems and developments which impinged upon his subject's career, the reader of these volumes soon discovers that Mr. Sandburg has tried to do an extremely difficult job with entire honesty. His warm imagination, his gift for vivid and colorful description—so welcome and so rare among the 'professionals'—have not been allowed to run away with the evidence."

Sandburg had not escaped entirely the legend's "powerfully persuasive influence," for the poet "grew up in the midst of it" and "breathed its atmosphere all his life."

In words that command attention, the reviewer described Sandburg at his best.

Everywhere are men and women talking of some aspect of the war and commending or condemning the doings of "Old Abe." All this is unlike the ordinary biography: it is more like a vast moving picture with thousands of actors passing in and out, back and forth across half a continent for a stage, but with one central figure who gradually draws the confusion into a certain order, gives it meaning and direction and finally dominates every scene. Little by little, almost imperceptibly, the personality of Lincoln changes too. Losing nothing of his native shrewdness or his deft political touch, he seems to rid himself of the awkward manners which dismayed so many early White House visitors, to lay aside more and more the crude jocosity which shocked others, and to reveal a deeper and profounder spiritual quality as he approached the ultimate tragedy awaiting him.

In one respect, at least, Ramsdell's estimate of Lincoln was more tenable than Sandburg's. For the poet, like so many other admirers of the emancipator's humanitarian qualities, disliked to paint him as a politician. Although Sandburg did not ignore Lincoln's political genius, he seemed "less interested in the politician than in the statesman and less in the statesman than in the personality of the man." But, says the reviewer, "Lincoln himself would never have denied that he was a politician; on the contrary, he would probably have been surprised and pained to learn that the distinction was withheld from him, for he delighted in his skill as a political manager and felt no squeamishness about the business of political trading for support. The truth is that he loved the game and made no pretense that he did not."

Ramsdell was among the first "professionals" to welcome Sandburg into the historical guild. Contrast if you will his appreciation for the poet's talent for revealing the real Lincoln with the cold reception accorded the *Prairie Years* of the mid-twenties. A reviewer characterized the two-volume biography of the pre–Civil War Lincoln as "a literary grab bag into which one may reach and draw out almost anything." Much of it was "imaginative poetry and historical fiction" punctuated by passages of "driveling sentimentality." Emphasizing factual errors, he concluded that "whatever else it may be, it is not history." [37] Ramsdell devoted some space to imperfections that marred many pages of *The War Years,* but he lifted understanding above the stuff of which history is made to the meaningful and accurate portrait the artist painted. Despite the imperfections, Sandburg produced a monumental work. The great interest in Lincoln was chiefly explained by "the peculiar qualities of the man himself," and Sandburg's biography presented "an unforgettable picture." [38] The professionals might profit from the lesson.

Historians may have had the "Sandburg's Lincoln" article at attention's focus when they lamented the loss of so much unwritten history with Ramsdell's passing. He seemed always on the verge of the great work that was never born. One explanation was his time-consuming university duties and many oddments that complicated his life. Unsparing attention to graduate students obstructed the even flow of scholarly activity. He wrote of "bedevilment" with doctoral orals, dissertations, and theses. Once he "quake[d] with fear and dread at the thought that a pile of them" might descend upon him at any moment; and again he planned to hibernate in New England where he would be inaccessible to students. His letters were punctuated with mild complaints of incidents and accidents, of "odds and ends that seem to hit me every day." An overzealous maid destroyed some note cards, and he himself mislaid some notes that occasioned searching again for references. An "emergency matter" robbed him of "time and sleep"; "energy that was far below par" delayed his writing. Even after a task was finished, he was interminably busy "tinkering with sentences and paragraphs." [39]

Lured by modest fees, he wrote introductions and encyclopedia articles,* wasted endless hours editing a history of Bell County, collaborated on a school text, and embarked on another—a joint project with J. G. de Roulhac Hamilton and Franklin L. Riley—that was never finished. Before the contract was canceled after a biennium, Ramsdell used some picturesque language. He wrote to Hamilton: "If I ever get free of all the fool obligations I have gone into for the probability of making a little money, I promise myself that I shall spend the rest of my life in trying to live as I want to live—and that doesn't mean doing nothing."

A few weeks later he proposed to the same correspondent "a solemn compact and covenant . . . never to engage to write any future text book or any part thereof. This thing has taken all joy and freshness out of my young life." It would certainly "be the last 'pot boiler' " he would "ever undertake. I would much prefer to go back to the farm and raise pigs." [40]

* As an example, Ramsdell wrote an introduction for the second and third volumes of the *Standard History of the World* (10 vols.; New York, 1914), which Paul Leland Haworth was revising a decade later. Ramsdell wrote to the editor: "Of course, I know nothing about the history of the period . . . but as I would undertake to write a dissertation on Chinese history for $100.00, I have done what I could." He hoped that the two volumes would "never fall into the hands of any of my scholarly friends save yourself. Of you I expect discretion." Ramsdell to Haworth, June 8, 1926, Ramsdell Papers.

These were some of the complexities and weaknesses that impeded Ramsdell's writing, but they were not unlike the autobiography of other scholars who published more. Perhaps he became more of a slave to routine and let it interfere unnecessarily with obligations to himself and his craft. Even if he had systematized his way of work, it is unlikely that he would have turned out book after book. He needed the pressure of program committees to prepare manuscripts, the urgent solicitation of prodding editors to submit them for publication. He lacked an impelling obsession to speed his pen.

Two assumptions seem valid: first, that his storehouse held much historical knowledge in reserve; and, second, that the articles and reviews and books he put in print merely illustrated his comprehension of the critical years at mid-nineteenth century. The unwritten part of his learning, as well as his wise counsel and official services, contributed to his deanship of southern historians. How shall we evaluate his stature in the historical world?

First, he and his colleagues assembled a notable collection of printed, manuscript, and microfilm records at the University of Texas, making it a center where scholars may investigate nineteenth-century southern history.

Second, he gave liberally of his time to students who profited from his understanding of history and the congenial atmosphere of classroom, seminar, and conference. The investment yielded returns in competently trained students, some of whom became reputable historians. His influence as a teacher transcended formal instruction to include a widely scattered clientele whose relationships were informal and casual.

Third, he developed a personal philosophy of history based upon understanding as a major ingredient. While there was nothing new in the concept, it enabled him in teaching and writing to view history in terms of human complexity that no central theme or neat pattern could explain. Human behavior, whether of the individual or of collective society, was intricate and chaotic, and no simple explanation could account for a people's development.

Fourth, he expanded the frontiers of history by distilling a segment of it, more significant in quality than in quantity.

Finally, he bequeathed a body of challenging interpretations which are worthy of consideration by students who seek meaning in past events. Not all of them were original, but his analyses of basic historical survivals were a worthy contribution. Among them were the following:

> The institution of slavery had reached its natural limits before the crisis of 1860 arrived. Ultimate extinction was its destiny.
>
> The Civil War was not inevitable. It could have been avoided if an artificial issue—expansion of slavery into territory where natural causes excluded it—had not reached the stage of acrimonious political debate.
>
> The hopeless condition of Confederate finances was a major factor that led to Appomattox. It occupied a central position on the causative arc.
>
> Abraham Lincoln was an adroit politician whose growth under pressure of responsibility was a deciding factor in the struggle to preserve the Union. Evidence of this quality was apparent as early as the firing on Fort Sumter.
>
> The results of the war were negative. The submerged elements in the southern population—black and white—would be further advanced in the twentieth century if improved social and economic status had arrived through the processes of evolution. Half a million lives and billions of dollars in property were needlessly sacrificed.

This summarization suggests the validity of Barker's characterization of Ramsdell in 1913 as a "conservative progressive." The atmosphere of his formative years in Reconstruction's aftermath was conservative. The Texan's concept of history was stability tempered by change, or, as Ramsdell phrased it, "continuous evolution." He clung tenaciously to the fundamentals of the old while incorporating the new. The historian of Reconstruction in Texas who sought objectivity without attaining it advanced far along the road to liberal understanding in appraising Carl Sandburg and his Abraham Lincoln. Historiography to Ramsdell was sometimes confirmatory, often transforming.

CHAPTER X

Thomas M. Owen: Pioneer Archivist

Of the Alabama historians who attained recognition in the period of the pioneers, Thomas M. Owen was the only one without formal training in history.[1] Unlike George Petrie and Walter L. Fleming, both of whom acquired the doctorate and taught history at the college level, Owen held no academic position; and unlike William G. Brown, he had no unusual talent for writing. Like so many of his contemporaries in state historical activity, he entered the guild by way of the law. He compiled bibliographies, wrote a history of his state, edited publications of the Alabama Historical Society and the *Gulf States Historical Magazine,* but his great work was as a pioneer in archival organization and administration.

I

Born near Jonesboro on December 15, 1866, Owen attended Pleasant Hill Academy, taught by his uncle, Isaac W. McAdory.[2] The records of the University of Alabama, where he was a student from 1884 to 1887, show that he studied English, Latin, Greek, French, German, and chemistry, in all of which he excelled, but they do not indicate that he took history.[3] He graduated in 1887 with the A.B. and LL.B. degrees, and then practiced law at Bessemer, Carrollton, and Birmingham.

From 1894 to 1897 Owen served in Washington as chief clerk in the division of post office inspectors. This position had unusual significance in determining his subsequent career, for in the national capital he became acquainted with Colyer Meriwether and Stephen B. Weeks, both of whom had acquired the doctorate in history at the Johns Hopkins University, and also with Thomas Nelson Page. With these and other men Owen joined in forming the Southern History Association in 1896.[4] But the man who influenced him most in his transition from lawyer to historian was Dr. Ainsworth R. Spofford, librarian of Congress, who counseled the young Alabamian in his quest for historical knowledge. The clerkship in the Post Office Department became a means to an end, for Owen's leisure time was spent in the Library of Congress searching for materials on his section of the South and discussing historical sources with Spofford and other scholars who frequented the library.[5] This experience partly compensated for lack of formal training in history; it provided many of the lessons others learned in graduate school.

Tangible results of Owen's labors in the Library of Congress were his compilations of "A Bibliography of Alabama" (1898) and "A Bibliography of Mississippi" (1900), each of which was published in an annual report of the American Historical Association. The Alabama bibliography, 472 pages in length, listed titles of books and pamphlets, newspaper and periodical sketches, articles appearing in transactions and other publications of learned societies, maps of Alabama, and "official documents." "It therefore embraces," the compiler wrote, "not only the historical and biographical works relating to the State, its institutions, and its public men, but it includes as well the intellectual product of the literary and business life of the State." [6] The Mississippi publication, similar in design, ran to 196 pages.[7]

Owen's first significant accomplishment after his return to his native state was a reorganization of the Alabama Historical Society. Founded in 1850, this association led a precarious existence during its first half century.[8] Quiescent during the years of war and Reconstruction, it was revived in 1874 only to fall again into peaceful oblivion after a decade.[9] For its rebirth in 1898, Owen was almost solely responsible. At a meeting of the society, held at the University of Alabama, he was elected secretary, and immediately there was evidence that it had acquired a dynamic and energetic leader. He carried on copious correspondence with Alabamians, promoted effective publicity, secured an annual appropriation to publish the society's transactions, and in general made the state history-conscious. To Colonel John W. A. Samford of Montgomery he wrote in 1898: "Interest is now general all over Alabama. The press will be active in our behalf. Our officials are not merely nominal, but they are doing all they can for the Society." [10] Perhaps they were more genuinely interested in the welfare of the organization than their predecessors had been for many years, but the fact remains, as Mitchell B. Garrett phrased it, that "the Secretary was to become, to all intents and purposes, the Society." [11]

During his first half dozen years as secretary, Owen brought out four volumes of *Transactions of the Alabama Historical Society.** It is no disparagement of his efforts to say that many of the articles he published were of doubtful value, for that fault was common to most of the state historical society publications of his day, and to some in our own. A generous sprinkling of papers that appeared in the Alabama series had real merit, and others served a useful purpose in stimulating interest in the society. One could hardly expect, however, that all participants in annual meetings would present papers that actually contributed to knowledge. After reading the first volume of the transactions, George W. Hamner of Washington, a native Alabamian who graduated in law at the University of Alabama and took a doctorate in history at Columbia University, wrote Owen a critical appraisal of the work. He was "delighted with it" despite its "typographical errors, which seem to fill every book published in the State. . . . Mr. [Peter J.] Hamilton writes on ancient roads like a lazy South Alabamian writes for the newspapers, is not particular, exact or concise enough & adds little or nothing to what is already known of the Subject." Owen's work, Hamner thought, was "more creditable from a historical or a literary standpoint & shows a north Alabamian without a lazy bone in his body." General William F. Perry's "The Genesis of Public Education in Alabama" was "valuable," but it was "a pity he did not have more data to refresh his memory & give point & locality to his statements." Major Howell Tatum's "Topographical Notes and Observations on the Alabama River, August, 1814," edited by Hamilton and Owen, and Owen's "The Work of William Henry Fowler as Superintendent of Army Records, 1863–1865," were " 'the Stuff.' " The volume was, in Hamner's opinion, "a credit to the energy and enterprise of a native Alabamian." [12]

Although Owen did not comprehend fully all the functions that an editor should perform, he took his responsibilities seriously and supplemented the work of contributors. He thought it his duty to

* The Alabama Historical Society really ceased to function after 1905. The last annual meeting was held in that year, "though it did not formally disband." Its work was gradually absorbed by the state department of archives and history. See Allen J. Going, "Historical Societies in Alabama," *Alabama Review,* I (January, 1948), 45–46.

annotate fully by appending "bibliographical, critical and illustrative notes and comments." The society's members were, in a sense, "a body of students," and he would serve them as instructor. So, while "the text is the work of the contributor . . . *the notes are the work of the editor*"—except in the case of Hamilton, who did his own annotating.[13]

A radical change was noticeable in the third volume of the transactions, which covered the period 1899–1903. The scholarly activities of Petrie at Alabama Polytechnic Institute were bearing fruit. Petrie himself contributed two papers to this volume, "What Will Be the Final Estimate of Yancey?" and "William F. Samford, Statesman and Man of Letters." [14] Six more papers emanated from Petrie's seminar, and though most of them were clearly the product of immaturity, all demonstrate the constructive influence of trained historical scholarship. Outstanding in the group was Fleming's "The Buford Expedition to Kansas," [15] an expansion of his study which had already appeared in *The American Historical Review*. Of Gaius Whitfield's "The French Grant in Alabama, A History of the Founding of Demopolis," [16] Petrie had written Owen, "I consider it in some respects the best piece of historical work done here. It contains a number of extracts, laws, decrees etc. never before published." [17] Meritorious also were Toccoa Cozart's "Henry W. Hilliard," Shepherd H. Roberts' "Benjamin Fitzpatrick and the Vice-Presidency," Emma B. Culver's "Thomas Hill Watts, A Statesman of the old Regime," and J. E. D. Yonge's "The Conservative Party in Alabama, 1848–1860." [18] No longer was it necessary for the editor to document most of the studies he printed, for those from Petrie's "laboratory" had at least the outward appearance of scholarly paraphernalia.

Other Petrie students contributed to the fourth and last volume of transactions: George W. Duncan, "John Archibald Campbell," William Watson Davis, "Ante-Bellum Southern Commercial Conventions," and Dallas T. Herndon, "The Nashville Convention of 1850." [19] About half of the volume was contributed by men who had studied under Petrie.

The most valuable of the *Publications of the Alabama Historical Society* was Volume I, *Report of the Alabama History Commission to the Governor of Alabama,* issued in 1901. At the urgent solicitation of Owen, the legislature in 1898 passed an act providing for the appointment of a commission of five "to make a full, detailed and exhaustive examination of all the sources and materials, manuscript, documentary, and record of the history of Alabama from the earliest times, whether in domestic or foreign archives or repositories, or in private hands," and for the printing of the report at state expense.[20] The president of the society, Joseph F. Johnston, designated as members of the commission Owen, Peter J. Hamilton, Charles C. Thach, professor of English at Alabama Polytechnic Institute, Samuel W. John, a member of the legislature, and William S. Wyman, professor of Latin at the University of Alabama.[21]

The work of the commission was largely the work of its chairman. Between June, 1899, when three of the group assembled and adopted Owen's plan of organization, and December of the following year, the chairman with some help from other members collected a great mass of data which materialized in a volume of 447 pages. Part I surveyed manuscripts, papers, and documents pertaining to Alabama in foreign and federal offices and in the adjacent states of Florida, Georgia, Louisiana, Mississippi, South Carolina, and Tennessee; Part II gave an account of them in official Alabama repositories; Part III described Alabama materials in private possession; Part IV treated Alabama war records; and Part V surveyed aboriginal and Indian remains in the state. An interesting chapter in Part III described the holdings of private collectors and students, which is particularly significant for its catalogue of the extensive holdings of Owen, whose library grew to considerable size before its destruction by fire in 1906. The whole inventory was a useful guide, though perhaps Part I on Alabama sources outside the state was least well done.[22]

The commission's report was favorably received, beyond the limits of the state as well as in it. Fleming, then a graduate student at Columbia University, wrote that he had shown "the 'Blue Book' to Prof. Dunning. He thinks the Report a very valuable publication; and to the Southern History students it was a very pleasant surprise." [23] Franklin L. Riley, one of Herbert B. Adams' students who occupied the chair of history at the University of Mississippi and who served as secretary of the Mississippi Historical Society, wrote Owen after examining the report: "I do not hesitate to pronounce this the most important work your Society has ever done for the history of your State. It shows a wide range of research into every important phase of your history." [24]

But Owen was more interested in the impression made by the volume in Alabama, particularly on members of the legislature.

The report recommended the establishment of a department of archives and history which would serve as custodian of the "official archives" of the state and assemble "a State library, museum and art gallery." Beyond "sentimental and patriotic considerations," the recommendations stressed the "practical benefit" to all Alabamians, for "the entire body of the State archives would be given the attention befitting their priceless value, and they would be arranged and so indexed as to be available for almost immediate consultation by all interested parties." The department would also establish "a great reference historical library," it would assemble "the surviving letters and papers of our public men" as well as museum pieces and pictures, and it would collect and house the military records of Alabamians. Provision should also be made for the publication of state papers, the periodical compilation of an official register, and the marking of historic sites.[25]

The legislature responded favorably and passed a measure approved on February 27, 1901, creating a state department of archives and history, which began to function on March 2 with Owen as director. Lawmakers appropriated $2,500 to finance the new agency,[26] and the governor designated the senate cloakroom to house it. How Owen assembled records and expanded his quarters was ably if facetiously told in 1940 by R. D. W. Connor in an address dedicating the new home of the department: "His first drive was upon heads of executive and administrative departments to persuade them to transfer their noncurrent records to the archives department. From all sorts of sources he collected manuscripts, books, newspapers, museum objects, and portraits of famous Alabamians. Soon the senate cloakroom was bursting with Owen's collections and legislators were beginning to fear that unless they gave him more space, he would take over the halls of legislation and perhaps the offices of the governor and other officials. You may think this statement somewhat exaggerated, but how else, by any accepted canon of historical interpretation, can you explain the fact that in 1903 the alarmed lawmakers were induced to appropriate $150,000 for the enlargement of the capitol?" When the first new wing was completed, the archivist "with characteristic self-restraint took over *only* one-half of the basement for his archives and one-half of the second floor for his other activities." Perhaps "grateful officials" appreciated Owen's generosity in permitting several other departments to use the rest of it. At the end of "a decade the stream of material which continued to flow into the Department of Archives and History burst forth from its narrow confines in the capitol and overflowed into five buildings which then stood on the block now occupied by this building." [27]

In his dedicatory address Connor stated succinctly the importance of Owen's contribution to the preservation of historical records: "The Alabama department . . . was the first archival agency established in the United States as an official organ of a government." By 1940 almost every state as well as the central government had followed Alabama's example.[28] North Carolina did so in 1907, and after Connor's appointment as secretary of the state's historical commission, he "jumped the first train" for Montgomery to consult with Owen who received him "with all the kindness of an older brother." The archivist was "installed in his cramped quarters in the capitol, literally lost to view behind great mountains of disorderly masses of documents, which were piling up on him so rapidly and in such volume as would have discouraged a less determined man." It is not surprising that the North Carolinian learned nothing about "archival organization, arrangement, classification, or cataloguing." The interview was nonetheless rewarding, not because of what Owen had accomplished or what he said to his visitor, but rather because of "what he was. He was energy, he was enthusiasm, he was courage, he was vision, he was faith, he was inspiration." [29]

Owen's correspondence yields tangible evidence of an early realization that his new departure was worthy of emulation. Letters of inquiry poured into his Montgomery office, and invariably they brought courteous and helpful answers. A year after the establishment of the state's department, the Mississippi legislature copied the Alabama act almost verbatim. North and South Carolina soon modeled their historical commissions on the Alabama pattern. In Virginia and Tennessee efforts were made to follow Alabama's example, but without much success.[30] After Fleming transferred to Baton Rouge in 1907, he hoped to establish a department in Louisiana similar to Alabama's. He soon learned, however, that the Louisiana Historical Society would oppose such a project. In fact, Professor John R. Ficklin of Tulane University had, somewhat earlier, investigated the possibility of establishing a department of archives and history, but "he was so certain of opposition from La. Hist. Soc. (a wretched mess) that he never acted." [31]

Owen was justifiably proud of Alabama's accomplishment, and he insisted upon recognition of his state's priority when other commonwealths followed the Alabama pattern. Writing to William K. Boyd of Trinity College about the time the North Carolina department was established, Owen requested "that you give our State credit for being *the pioneer* in this *specific* form of institutional activity. We are not in competition with other States in the matter of development. I have on all occasions shown a willingness and desire to help others in the projection and development of plans, and in the solution of their problems. What we are proud of, is, however, the fact that Alabama is *the first* of all the States to undertake to care for and to meet the duty of the commonwealth both to the care of archives and its historical interests, through *a separate Department* of State, ranking in dignity with other State Departments." [32]

II

The success of Owen's experiment in state-supported archives brought immediate recognition within the South; the meeting of the American Historical Association jointly with the American Economic Association in a southern city in 1903 provided opportunity for scholars outside the region to recognize his statesmanlike undertaking.* Southern historians had been attempting since the turn of the century to persuade the national organization to encourage historical activity south of the Potomac by assembling on southern soil; and the appropriateness of commemorating the hundredth anniversary of the purchase of Louisiana by meeting in New Orleans assured the desired result.

The prospect of attending a meeting in "America's most interest-

* Owen's correspondence is a mine of information on a great variety of subjects, and it serves as an index to recognition of his accomplishments in history and in other fields. Among the historians with whom he corresponded were J. Franklin Jameson, Herbert B. Adams, Woodrow Wilson, Evarts B. Greene, Andrew C. McLaughlin, Reuben Gold Thwaites, Henry E. Bourne, Edward G. Bourne, Herman V. Ames, A. Howard Clark, Charles H. Haskins, James Ford Rhodes, George L. Beer, James M. Callahan, William A. Dunning, John S. Bassett, Ulrich B. Phillips, R. D. W. Connor, Alexander S. Salley, Jr., William K. Boyd, Walter L. Fleming, George Petrie, Franklin L. Riley, Dunbar Rowland, Peter J. Hamilton, William O. Scroggs, Frederick W. Moore, H. T. Quarles, Grace King, Joel C. Du Bose, John W. Du Bose, Alfred H. Stone, Allen D. Candler, Thomas C. McCorvey, Stephen B. Weeks, Lester G. Bugbee, and Robert A. Brock. Among the librarians were William Beer, Wilberforce Eames, John S. Billings, James W. Cheney, J. P. McLean, Robert H. Kelby, Arnold J. F. van Lear, and C. B. Tillinghast. He also corresponded with Warren K. Moorehead, anthropologist, and Edwin R. A. Seligman, economist.

ing city" and of vacationing in the South appealed to scholars in the East and West, and arrangements were made for special trains from New York and Chicago. The New York special planned brief stopovers in Richmond, Atlanta, Montgomery, and Mobile, and Owen corresponded with Edwin R. A. Seligman, president of the American Economic Association, relative to entertainment in the first capital of the Confederacy. The party would arrive in Montgomery on December 27, and Seligman requested that Owen "arrange to have the old capitol open and lighted up for us." [33] After returning to New York, Dunning reported to Fleming, who had not attended the meeting, that "your enterprising friend, Owen, at Montgomery, made a particularly good impression for himself; he treated us royally well. When the train stopped there at 9:30 in the evening, the historic old state house was very impressively and entertainingly exhibited by him, and his whole spirit, both there and at New Orleans, won him a host of friends in the Association and at the same time, I think won for the Association a very earnest friend in him." [34] And to John S. Bassett, kept away by illness, Dunning wrote that the travelers "were exceedingly pleased at the energy and thoughtfulness manifested in connection with our advent. Owen made a very favorable impression on everybody." [35]

Sundry letters of appreciation came directly to Owen after historians had returned to their homes. James Ford Rhodes recalled that "the History and Economic people have not yet got over talking of your speech in the moonlight on the Capitol," [36] and George L. Beer wrote Owen that "the memory of the Southern trip is a joy to all of us, and we shall not soon, believe me, forget that moonlight night in Montgomery and the guide who made the noble old city's past so charmingly alive for us." [37]

Despite the energetic effort of southerners to promote attendance, only twenty-one members from the South registered for the meeting—the same number that came from faraway Massachusetts. Two of the sessions had a southern theme: one of them consisted of papers relating to the Louisiana Purchase; the other, arranged by Dunning, considered "The Study and Teaching of History in the South," with brief papers by seven southerners—William E. Dodd of Randolph-Macon College, Alcée Fortier of Tulane University, Lillian W. Johnston of Nashville, Tennessee, Frederick W. Moore of Vanderbilt University, David Y. Thomas of the University of Arkansas, Franklin L. Riley of the University of Mississippi, and Thomas M. Owen. Owen responded to Dunning's invitation by proposing a paper on "state supported historical work in the South," a subject which seemed appropriate to the chairman of the committee.[38] Dunning's conference was well attended despite a paucity of members from the South, and, if letters from contemporaries may be believed, it was decidedly successful. Owen, so the report of the annual meeting recorded, discussed southern state aid in collecting, preserving, and publishing historical records. "Scarcely any States in the Union," he said, "are doing as much as are Alabama and Mississippi, where the State governments have established departments charged with the task of gathering and preserving valuable historical papers." Other states of the South were miserly in promoting historical activity. "In Texas a small appropriation has been made for the classification and translation of early Texas manuscripts, while the Texas Historical Association [*sic*], without material financial encouragement from the State, has been courageously undertaking the enormous task of bringing together the old records and miscellaneous papers bearing on the early history of the Southwest." [39]

The favorable impression which Owen made at the New Orleans meeting of the American Historical Association prompted an invitation to appear on the program at the Chicago meeting the next year. Addressing a round table conference, "On the Problems of State and Local Historical Societies," he described the organization of the Alabama department of archives and history, stressed the obligation of the state to preserve its records, and pointed to the necessity of placing them in charge of some one who appreciated their significance. In the past the responsibility had been assumed by state historical societies, but experience had shown that such organizations were "unable to care for the public records." Alabama's historical society had "decided to surrender to the State the task of collecting manuscripts, and to content itself with holding meetings, publishing material, and stimulating interest in history." [40]

Owen had already performed another function for the association. At the request of Herman V. Ames, chairman of the public archives commission, he prepared a report on "Alabama Archives" for publication in the association's annual report.[41] In his introduction Owen said that a "result of the establishment of the Department has been to dignify the hitherto neglected accumulations of old papers, denominated by many as so much worthless trash and rubbish." [42] He organized his report into five parts: state archives, county records, municipal records, records of federal offices in Alabama, and miscellaneous items.[43] The report was not wholly a new piece of work: the compiler rearranged and brought down to date the data he had previously assembled for the *Report of the Alabama History Commission.*

Further recognition came to Owen from the historical guild. In 1905 he succeeded George P. Garrison as a member of the American Historical Association's Historical Manuscripts Commission.[44] He was one of the pioneers in the Mississippi Valley Historical Association, and served as its second president, 1907–1908.[45]

During Owen's busy years in establishing the department of archives and history and in continuing the work of the Alabama Historical Society, he embarked upon another editorial project. In 1902 he and Joel C. Du Bose, principal of Du Bose's school for boys in Birmingham and writer of Alabama history on occasion, inaugurated *The Gulf States Historical Magazine.*[46] Owen served as editor and Du Bose as business manager of this bi-monthly journal concerned with the history of states from Florida to Texas. After a year Owen abandoned the magazine because of heavy duties in the department, and Du Bose carried on a second year as editor, at the end of which publication was discontinued largely because the magazine could not pay its way. Without subsidy or society behind it, the fate of the periodical had been determined at its inception.

During its brief existence, the magazine served as a medium for some scholarly studies as well as a vehicle for considerable trivia. Of the former, Fleming contributed some segments of his incipient dissertation on Alabama in Civil War and Reconstruction: "The Churches of Alabama during the Civil War and Reconstruction," "The Formation of the Union League in Alabama," "The Ku Klux Testimony Relating to Alabama," and "Conscription and Exemption in Alabama during the Civil War." [47] Ulrich B. Phillips published two unimportant papers in the journal: "Early Railroads in Alabama" and "Historical Notes on Milledgeville, Ga." [48] "Alabama and Territorial Expansion before 1860" was contributed by William O. Scroggs, and "The Diplomatic Struggle for the Mississippi River and the Southwestern Boundary" was contributed by David Y. Thomas.[49] Owen himself compiled several pieces for the magazine: "Colonel Edward Lacey of the Revolution and Some of

His Descendants," "The Fisher Family," "The Ross Family," "An Alabama Protest Against Abolitionism in 1835," "Emma Sansom, An Alabama Heroine," [50] and some lists of newspapers in various depositories.

As a productive historian Owen was a compiler and editor rather than a writer of history. His Alabama and Mississippi bibliographies, the *Report of the Alabama History Commission,* and the survey of "Alabama Archives" demonstrated considerable ability in inventorying records. His posthumous publication, a four-volume *History of Alabama and Dictionary of Alabama Biography,* was encyclopedic in nature and served as an indispensable reference work. Of several brief articles, five were genealogical,[51] three were biographical,[52] one was anthropological,[53] but the most important of the group was the paper he read at the Chicago meeting of the American Historical Association in 1904, "State Departments of Archives and History." [54] Owen also edited five departmental bulletins, three of which he compiled,[55] and he issued sundry other publications under the imprints of the society and the department.

Owen's compilations and edited works represent a creditable performance in value and volume, but they are secondary to his monumental work, the establishment of the first archival organization as a state agency. Had he accomplished nothing else in the quarter century prior to his death in 1920, this alone would place the historical guild under deep obligation.

CHAPTER XI

Twenty-five Years of Southern Historical Writing

The founding of the Southern Historical Association and the *Journal of Southern History* a quarter of a century ago marked an era in the South's historical development.[1] Susan M. Kingsbury and Elizabeth Donnan were publishing the fourth and final volumes of their documentary collections, *The Records of the Virginia Company of London* and *Documents Illustrative of the History of the Slave Trade to America;* and William C. Binkley was completing *The Official Correspondence of the Texas Revolution. The Antislavery Impulse* and *The Irrepressible Conflict,* new-departure studies by Gilbert H. Barnes and Arthur C. Cole, led some historians to revise their images of the abolitionists and the Civil War generation. Lewis C. Gray's *History of Agriculture in the Southern United States to 1860* brought acclaim as a sound work of reference, and Douglas S. Freeman's monumental *R. E. Lee* set a high standard for historical biography. An epoch-making article by J. G. Randall, "Has the Lincoln Theme Been Exhausted?" was answered by a resounding negative in years that followed; but Milo M. Quaife, who may not have recovered from Carl Sandburg's *Prairie Years,* protested that Civil War studies were already too plentiful. Within a year after the association got under way, William B. Hesseltine and R. S. Cotterill presented teachers of southern history with syntheses for their college courses. And it might also be recalled that the next decade saw publication of the *Horn Papers,* much trumpeted locally as a blasting blow at back-country misconceptions, and the discovery of forty-nine Dare Stones, the first of which was written up with all the trappings of critical scholarship in a piercing article that appeared in the *Journal of Southern History.* *

* Arthur P. Middleton and Douglas Adair, "The Mystery of the Horn Papers," *William and Mary Quarterly,* Ser. III, Vol. IV (October, 1947), 409–45. For the first

Except for the last two items, these are a few of the landmarks of the middle 1930's that indicate considerable maturity in southern history—a groundwork of research and writing necessary to the hundreds of special studies that emanated from the following quarter century. Some of the region's pioneer historians had passed from the scene or abandoned the profession; a few other stalwarts continued historical activity; but accelerated advancement was largely the work of young scholars who with discrimination accepted the credible heritage from their predecessors, but who also found new paths that led from and to the past. The founders of the association could hardly foresee the plethora of books and articles that expanded historical knowledge into avenues undreamed of a quarter century ago and that revised the interpretations and conclusions of the pioneers.

I

A survey of the intervening years' historical literature might well begin by inquiring whether southern historians have discovered any great theme or pattern of the past that accounts for unity and continuity, if such existed, that explains southern thought and action since colonial days, or at least since the South became conscious of itself. The present generation inherited from the past Ulrich B. Phillips' "Central Theme" of white supremacy; but some latter-day scholars have questioned its centrality and significance, and suggested its possible demise sometime in the future. In "The Central Theme Revisited," George B. Tindall concluded that the "day when white supremacy should be no longer the cardinal tenet and primary aim of white Southerners" would mark the end of Phillips' thesis—as a continuing identification. Only "a rash prophet . . . would forecast" the day, but Tindall believes that trends since 1928 "and the direction of public policy today" make that desideratum less improbable than it seemed in the late 1920's.[2] Years ago a younger contemporary of

Dare Stone, see Haywood J. Pearce, Jr., "New Light on the Roanoke Colony: A Preliminary Examination of a Stone Found in Chowan County, North Carolina," *Journal of Southern History,* IV (May, 1938), 148–63, and the managing editor's face-saving editorial, *ibid.,* 263. For descriptions of the forty-seven stones and some miscellaneous data, see H. J. Pearce, Sr., "The Dare Stones," *Breneau Bulletin,* XXXI, No. 17 (November 15, 1940), a pamphlet of sixteen unnumbered pages. Boynton Sparkes conducted a careful investigation and came up with some devastating observations and conclusions in "Writ on Rocke: Has America's First Murder Mystery Been Solved," *Saturday Evening Post,* CCXIII (April 26, 1941), 9–11, 120–22, 124–26, 128.

the Georgian, Charles W. Ramsdell, saw danger in a fascinating "intellectual exercise" that designated "any one thing as *the* central theme," for it might "easily be pushed too far."[3]

To this problem of pattern the original editors of the multi-volume "A History of the South" gave considerable thought while the project was aborning, and they decided against a system-building series. They recognized elements of continuity, but they also saw change; and they questioned whether a group of individualistic contributors, working with only a minimum of consultation, could mould intangibles and imponderables into an overarching theme that threads its way through three and one-half centuries of time. System-building with its tendency toward formulistic writing would have assured questionable simplicity and defeated comprehensiveness.

No one of the southern syntheses published during the period under review undertook a grand design, though each of them proposed an emphasis or theme. R. S. Cotterill sought "to relate as clearly as possible the story of the Old South; if there be a central theme at all, it is in the development of Southern nationalism." "The integrating theme" of Clement Eaton's *A History of the Old South* "is the emergence of a regional culture, created by all classes of Southern society rather than by an elite, aristocratic group." The design of William B. Hesseltine's first revision, *The South in American History,* is essentially the same as the 1936 publication: "The South is American: its problems have been the nation's; its social adjustments have been reflections of national society, its politics have found their orientation about the federal government, and its economics has been an integral part of the national economy." And Francis B. Simkins, in the 1953 revision of his 1947 publication, defines the South as "an attitude of mind and a way of behavior" as well as a territorial location. Whether in its alpha, "The Land and the Tradition," or in its omega, "The South Retains Its Past," the author consciously sought a continuum of thought in the "everlasting" quality of the region's life and structure.

The intangibles and imponderables that troubled the editors of "A History of the South" have not prevented a few writers from endeavoring to master them. These nebulae might contain the inner reality of that ephemeral unity and continuity that seem so difficult to isolate and comprehend. The South has often been defined as a state of mind, though always with the understanding that states of mind spring from geographical or environmental factors, economic or social impulses, local institutions or controversial pressures. If some poet, novelist, or historian, endowed with penetrating insight, could sense the main currents of thought, if he could comprehend the southern mind in its unchanging and enduring qualities that made inhabitants of the South southerners, he could write a rewarding essay on the timelessness of sectional or regional essence.

One of the latest writers to examine the imposing idea was Henry Savage, Jr. Vivid in preaching, livid in teaching, his *Seeds of Time: The Background of Southern Thinking* adds no more than an honest and sincere whit to southern understanding. The most ambitious undertaking of the sort was Wilbur J. Cash's provocative and stimulating *The Mind of the South.* Ignoring many of the region's best minds, Cash created a fictitious "basic Southerner" or "simple generic figure" whose reactions to the complex sea around him were essentially the same whether he resided in a frontier community or on a plantation, in the Old South of antiquated pattern or in the New South of the Industrial Revolution with its accent on Progress and with the factory "essentially indistinguishable in organization from the familiar pattern of the cotton fields." Civil War and Reconstruction wrought no revolutionary change, for the section's mind was continuous with the past, ever changing, the author admitted, but still basically the same. The shadowy threads of unity and continuity were etched too distinctly; nonconforming attributes too minimized and blurred.

If few historians have trailed the southern mind in search of a satisfying theme, many have sought more tangible identifying differentia. Over two decades ago, Avery Craven designated climate, ruralness, a country-gentleman ideal, and the Negro's presence as distinguishing features of the section.[4] From the perspective of a later present, C. Vann Woodward wrote with poise, balance, clarity, habitual caution, and in some instances with considerable philosophic insight in his essay, "The Search for Southern Identity." "Is there nothing about the South," he asks, "that is immune from the disintegrating effect of nationalism and the pressure for conformity? Is there not something that has not changed?" Only its history, he suggests; and among southerners' "collective experience" as a "basis for continuity of their heritage" he discovers several distinguishing factors: southerners were "People of Poverty" in contrast with "People of Plenty" in other parts of the country; they suffered "frustration, failure, and defeat" in a nation whose national "history *is* a success story"; they experienced evil in a land of legendary innocence; they embarked on an "un-American venture in feudal fantasy" in an America that was "born free"; and finally, southerners feared abstraction in a land that personified it.[5]

II

The great outpouring of books and articles on southern subjects during the past quarter century has been, as one would expect, of uneven quality. They range all the way from competent and significant contributions that extend the limits of knowledge and provide new insights and interpretations, through dull and pedestrian discourses of limited value, to the products of loquacious quacks who convert trivia into sensational disclosures.

As to distribution among periods and types of subject matter, the writer has only a subjective impression, for a quarter century of books on southern history and articles published in national, regional, and state reviews are too many to count and analyze in so brief a time. Chronologically, there has been a surprising amount of interest in the colonial period, considering the low estate into which that era fell some years ago; nearly as much in the epoch of the Revolution and the completion of independence. The middle period, which merges into the Civil War generation, has suffered no diminution in volume. The heaviest concentration has been on the war generation, and if studies and biographies involving the coming and the causes be included, this segment accounts for fully a third of the productivity; but the aftermath of the war has attracted only a limited number of contributors. The New South has competed with one of its component elements—the Negro—in producing much good writing and considerable new interpretation. In fact, the Negro, whether in slavery or in freedom, has elicited increasing attention as his struggle for human and civil rights continues with quickened pace. Military history has challenged the pre-eminence of political themes, cultural history still lags behind. Only a few of the many college and university histories, usually inspired by commemorative anniversaries, may be classified as cultural. Finally, the publication of useful bibliographies, catalogues, and guides to historical materials has greatly facilitated the work of research scholars. The most imposing of these is the monumental compilation of travel accounts, ably edited by Thomas D. Clark and a coterie of competent associates.[6]

The historiographical era under consideration witnessed the publication, in some instances the inauguration, of definitive editions of the works of great Americans, among them some prominent southerners. John C. Fitzpatrick's *The Writings of George Washington* and Roy P. Basler's *The Collected Works of Abraham Lincoln* were brought to completion; Julian P. Boyd's *The Papers of Thomas Jefferson,* with editorial policy that served as a model for other projects, reached an advanced stage. The Calhoun, Clay, and Madison papers [7] will have significance, like those of Washington and Jefferson, that transcends the South. Sam Houston's writings [8] were issued during the period under review, which also saw publication of the Weld-Grimké and the James G. Birney letters,[9] both influential in revision of abolitionism in sectional controversy. The papers of two southern literary figures, William Gilmore Simms and Sidney Lanier,[10] were published during the quarter century; and so was Edgar W. Knight's five-volume *Documentary History of Education in the Old South.*

In some cases publication of papers may not greatly alter portraits already in existence. Certainly the first volume of the Calhoun Papers does not materially change the image of the man recorded by Charles M. Wiltse. On the other hand, the Simms letters provide documentary evidence for a new concept of the South Carolina litterateur and proslavery advocate. William P. Trent's biography of nearly seventy years ago created a myth of a man of considerable talent who was snubbed by Charleston and other South Carolina aristocrats, and whose potential ability as a writer was blighted because of the slaveholding society in which he lived. The legendary Simms disappears; his replacement is a normal, wholesome personality who is at once a product of and a contribution to his society.

Myths and mythmakers have ever provided historians with convenient targets for their ammunition. Many of the books from the period here considered mar a myth or lay a legend. Occasionally a writer singles them out as a special theme. Bernard Mayo's *Myths and Men* is an inspiring example: a potpourri of glorifying and defaming myths that distorted the portraits of Washington and Jefferson and Patrick Henry, served up in delectable and felicitous style. On the other hand, the word might have been deleted from the title of Carl Bridenbaugh's *Myths and Realities: Societies of the Colonial South,* for while the book slays some myths and re-explodes some others, its great contribution lies in a positive defining and refining of societies, with much fresh material about them. It has an honest preface, in the Walter Webb manner, with text as well as preface shouting Eureka! too often.

III

Historians devoted much effort before as well as after the middle thirties in searching for roots of American democracy. When the writer took a first course in southern history a dozen years before the founding of the Southern Historical Association, the great revisionist of the day was Thomas Jefferson Wertenbaker, who was exploding myths perpetrated by Philip Alexander Bruce. Old Dominion plebeians of the seventeenth century were having a field day at the expense of the aristocracy, who would have to await the eighteenth before they inherited the earth, or at least Virginia's half of it. His pioneering studies and *The Old South* volume of his trilogy, *The Founding of American Civilization,* achieved considerable success as pathbreakers, but in later works Wertenbaker, like William E. Dodd, found too much democracy in the colonial period. Historians questioned the analogy between the crises of 1676 and 1776 in *Torchbearer of the Revolution; The Story of Bacon's Rebellion and Its Leader;* and they discounted the familiar theme in *Give Me Liberty; The Struggle for Self-Government in Virginia,* with its many incidents great and small from Jamestown to Jefferson paraded as miniature American Revolutions and its plethora of colonials dedicated to unfaltering liberty. Nor could they accept at face value the rival interpretation of 1676 in Wilcomb E. Washburn's *The Governor and the Rebel: A History of Bacon's Rebellion in Virginia,* which correctly deflated Bacon as torchbearer in political and humanitarian reform, but restored Berkeley to the stature of his earlier years in the governorship.

It is a relief to turn from pendulum-swinging interpretations to the more convincing and judicious evaluation of Wesley Frank Craven in *The Southern Colonies in the Seventeenth Century,* or to Charles Sydnor's realistic view of late eighteenth-century aristocracy and democracy in *Gentlemen Freeholders: Political Practices in Washington's Virginia.* While aristocracy persisted as a powerful factor in the Revolutionary era, Virginia's relatively democratic electorate gave lesser freeholders a definite responsibility in the choice of burgesses. The interplay of forces showed that democracy and aristocracy were neither mutually exclusive nor contradictory; and the combination, Sydnor concluded, was responsible for producing such able leaders in thought and action as Jefferson, Madison, Mason, Marshall, and Washington.

The search for more adequate knowledge of southern society's structure at mid-nineteenth century paralleled efforts to discover democratic foundations of earlier generations. One of the most significant revisions of the past quarter century is definitive proof of the existence of a strong yeoman class in the antebellum South. A long time before Frank Owsley began a systematic study of the southern social framework, perceptive historians rejected the old classification of planters, poor whites, and slaves, and suggested a more complex structure, but with insufficient data to make more than general revisionary statements. Some twenty years ago the Owsleys and sundry graduate students at Vanderbilt University began to exploit agricultural schedules from the manuscript census reports of 1850 and 1860, local tax records, and wills—all of which emphasized the importance of middle classes, especially small farmers and stock raisers, and relegated planters to a less significant position than tradition assigned them. Their findings resulted in new conclusions applauded by many historians, and also by sociologists, but with some reservations. Rupert Vance saw much merit in *Plain Folk of the Old South,* but it was not definitive, for it did not study all classes of southern society in their relationship to each other, and left society's "power structure" unexplained. Vance also found the author's knowledge of method deficient, for he presented only "the raw material of statistics." [11] But the method, as far as Owsley and his students carried it, convinced historians that advancement had been made in solving one of the region's important problems.

IV

The writer would like to report that such matters as the abolitionist crusade, the proslavery argument, the causes of the Civil War, and that conflict's meaning and aftermath had finally been resolved, and that historians might now turn their attention to less publicized but equally important facets of southern history. Thousands of books and articles on these subjects have been published during the last quarter century, and the generation preceding it had certainly not ignored the clash and conflict of the era. Biographers, historians, litterateurs, romancers, social scientists, journalists, lawyers, doctors, warriors, scientists, and unemployed women have scanned, less often searched, contemporary printed and manuscript sources, explored innermost depths of human minds for unrecorded thoughts and motives, conjured up assumptions, hypotheses, and theories, used historical, psychological, sociological, quantification, and literary methods to explain America's most controversial epoch and epic.*

Excluding from attention's focus the fly-by-night sensational pieces that pest control cannot eradicate, it is quite likely that there is less divergence of opinions and conclusions in the controversial literature of the years 1830 to 1877 than surface indications reveal. If the last antebellum decade may be isolated for examination, volumes and multivolumes present facts and personalities, rehash events and movements, reinterpret leadership or indicate lack of it, lay more emphasis here and less there—and come up with some good, albeit repetitious, history of the period, little of which is startlingly new. Historians have talked about symbols and symbolisms, of emotionalisms and hyperemotionalisms, of ideals and ideologies, of conflicting ways of life and work, of the political power struggle, of "the problem of slavery *with its complementary problem of race-adjustment*," of inevitability and needlessness, of disruption of national parties as bonds of union, and of a hundred and one clashes that created irreconcilable minds. If there is a tendency today, after reading books good and bad, to conclude that historians are still at swordplay, it is well to understand that much of the controversy lacks depth, and that semantics has not been very useful. Unfortunately, the ablest of these writers —shall we call them Mat, Marcus, Lucas, and Jonathan to avoid all suspicion of identity—got to reviewing each other's books, the appraisals employing as a springboard the author's rare scholarship. All that is needed to complete definitive consideration of the 1850's is another volume, "A Reconciliation of the Gospels."

Perhaps mid-nineteenth century history has suffered from too many theses. Some social science historians assert that only the

* Note the close resemblance between this literature of controversy and the controversy of cigarettes. Some are long and some are short, some are mild and some are pungent, some are filtered and some are raw, some are hardpacked and some are softbacked, some are toasted and some are roasted. One leaves behind a trail of *ifs*, the other a debris of *butts*. Supposedly both are cancerous, though one is cause, the other effect. In either case, the manufacturers and the publishers do the puffing. But the analogy must not be carried too far. One product is southern home grown, the other has a strong "foreign" flavor.

"systematic procedure" involving a problem derived "from knowledge" is justifiable; and they poohpooh the idea of embarking on an exploratory journey through documents in search of discoveries. The resultant disclosures may be more rewarding experiences than the foreordained problem yields. When such a period as the late antebellum years has been so meticulously investigated, the new thesis may degenerate into formulistic writing with all the hazards of pushing it too far, of selecting evidence that proves the thesis, of ignoring or minimizing whatever proves something else. Some doctoral candidates may therefore have Q.E.D.'ed rather than Ph.D.'ed and, having tasted forbidden fruit in Clio's Garden of Eden, may continue in maturity to *quod erat demonstradum*. Perhaps you will permit the observation that the years at mid-century are thesis-ridden to the point that suggests turning attention to virgin lands as a remedy for soil exhaustion and the production of more diversified crops. Speaking subjectively, it is quite likely that Clio has posted more theses on the fifties and sixties than Martin Luther nailed to a church door.

Yet not Clio, but the ministers here below who carry on in her name. For like England's queen, Clio reigns but does not rule. Actually, she has less authority than the aforesaid monarch, for she cannot perform even the perfunctory obligation of designating a new minister when an old one dies or no longer commands confidence. Fortunately, there is little regimentation in the choice of historical servants. The little manifests itself in the appointment of boards of editors, the selection of contributors to series of histories, and the guidance given graduate students in choosing research subjects. A tremendous responsibility rests with self-called ministers. The would-be author is free to accept whatever portfolio assignment he will; but searching introspection, a probing of conscience, should precede the volunteering for service. Obviously, some of the volunteers who have written on controversial aspects of southern and sectional history have not begun by determining whether they were competent to sit in judgment, or they would have recused themselves because they were already so committed that decisions would be unacceptable to the spirit we call Clio.

The story is told of a Georgia parson whose rural flock supplemented his meager income by contributions from the orchard and the garden, all of which he acknowledged from the Sunday morning pulpit. Imagine his dilemma when Brother Brown presented him with a gallon of his favorite beverage, peach brandy.

Not wishing to offend either the contributor or abstemious members of his congregation, he graciously thanked the donor for the peach juice, and especially for the spirit in which it was given. Whether the good parson realized it or not, he was subtly pulling one of the tricks of our guild, as old as history itself. He was withholding from his hearers the transforming processes of fermentation and distillation through which both the juice of the peach and the evidence of the event pass before they reach the ultimate consumer. Of the two products, the brandy may be the more palatable, for the seeds and the pulp will have been removed, while the corresponding undigestible ingredients of history often survive to give the printed page a stony and mucous character.

Some of these faults are readily detected by the discerning reader, whether in cultural centers like Athens or Oxford, or in less sophisticated towns like Forsyth or Juniper Grove. But the layman, and sometimes the professional, may not observe the simultaneous fermentation of the evidence *and* the writer's mind, which may become so intoxicated that he is incapacitated for sober historical research. Or how else can one account for some of the last quarter century's studies of the abolitionist crusade and the proslavery argument?

These passionate antagonisms have not been stilled after the lapse of a century. The persuasive *The Antislavery Impulse* was an exception, for some contemporaries thought Gilbert H. Barnes had settled certain aspects of the problem with considerable finality. The publication soon thereafter of the Weld-Grimké and Birney correspondence added documentary proof to the new interpretation of western responsibility and leadership, and further indicated the nature of the moral reform movement of the thirties and the transition to Birney's political antislavery after that decade. Despite widespread acceptance of the Barnes-Dumond thesis, other historians some years later would question the validity of western emphasis and present evidence that suggested a northeastern impulse.

Divergent thought found expression in two books published twenty years ago, Dwight L. Dumond's *Antislavery Origins of the Civil War in the United States* and Arthur Y. Lloyd's *The Slavery Controversy, 1831–1860*. To an outspoken critic it seemed that the one was a belated abolition tract and the other a delayed proslavery argument. "Each produces in the year 1939," said Theodore Clarke Smith, "an attitude that might have been expected in 1859 but cannot now be termed anything but archaic." The reviewer saw no value in either book. "What this period of American history needs," he said, "is not a recrudescence of sectional writing and apologetics but a study of the whole tragic drama from the standpoint of a broad and sympathetic approach to the human nature of all parties involved." [12]

This sweeping indictment, and some others published in historical journals, expressed disappointment that the lapse of a century had not provided sufficient remoteness to insure the detachment pioneers of an earlier generation anticipated. An elemental principle, well known in the breach thereof as well as in its application, disparages historical writing from a debater's brief. To recapture the spirit and meaning of abolitionist and advocate, the historian may legitimately mount the forum or ascend the pulpit to experience and recapture all the feelings and emotions that stirred men to irrational thought and precipitous action, and then with calm serenity resume his role as assessor, critic, and moderator. In another setting Richard Brownlee paraded Missouri guerrillas in partisan warfare; with past-minded intent he seemed to ride with Bob Anderson and Quantrill and Joe Porter, only to dismount immediately for a critical appraisal of their escapades.[13]

V

The extent of Civil War historiography is phenomenal. Never before has any period received so much attention or subject matter attracted so diverse and motley a crew of competent historians, gifted outlanders, pious exhorters, and nondescript interlopers. The volume of output has been explained by the epic qualities of the war and its central figure Lincoln, the existence and the merging of resulting cults, the supposed origins of the Modern World, the real and fancied relationships and analogies between then and now, and the present-day striving of Negroes for recognition as first-class citizens.

Out of all this mass of millions of words emerges a Lincoln shorn of much legend, attired in human habiliments, Olympian in his qualities of common sense, balanced judgment, understanding, devotion to democracy; a Lincoln of frustrated optimism, costly errors, mistaken confidences, human frailties and weaknesses. Many historians and biographers have contributed to this more realistic Lincoln, so many that a simple listing of their names and their works without critical evaluation would require many pages. Perhaps no one would be greatly amazed if this essay designated James G. Randall's *Lincoln the President* as the great work that best delineates the man and the president. If Randall's four volumes were the reader's first introduction to the person and his period, he could hardly foresee until the end the Lincoln of cherished memory, but he would sense continuous growth and development, an imperceptible unfolding as the emerging Lincoln met crises, weathered emergencies, and carried on with renewed hope and strength. If one cannot find the complete Lincoln in Randall's pages, perhaps he would superimpose upon the masterly portrait the poetic touches of Carl Sandburg, the prodigious research of William Hesseltine, the military perspective of Kenneth Williams, the correcting lines of Paul Angle. He might also turn the spotlight on some of the *Lincoln and* books: *the Radicals, the Generals, the Fifth Column, the War Governors, the Bluegrass, the Tools of War, the Baltimore Plot, the Patronage, the Press, the Party Divided,* or *His Party and the Secession Crisis.* If these were not enough for a satisfying picture, he could turn to the possessives: *Lincoln's Imagery,* his *Secretary,* his *Cabinet,* his *Navy,* his *Rise to Power,* his *Supreme Court,* his *Herndon,* his *Sons,* or his *Vandalia.* And if the reader were confused by the medley that seemed to fit no pattern, he could turn the microscope's high power on Benjamin P. Thomas' competent one-volume portrait, where the diverse fragments would fall logically into place as a reasonable and captivating likeness of the whole man.

But enough. The subject is inexhaustible and never completely satisfying, for there is also *The Lincoln Nobody Knows,* with Richard Current's "essay in the uncertain, the undecided, the unknown" a valuable contribution to an understanding of the controversial and disputed aspects of Lincoln's career, the existence of which precludes the package biography "to end all Lincoln biographies." There are questions concerning Lincoln that historians cannot answer, the Lincoln that doesn't emerge.

It is apparent also that writings of the past quarter century recognize more than one civil war. In addition to the war that no one will ever comprehend in its entirety, there is another that stands out with great clarity: the clash that ended an old era and began a new one; an inevitable controversy necessary to set the house in order so that a modern world could emerge; a conflict which, despite human carnage and material destruction, produced constructive gains in industry, science, transportation, and social organization that rounded out a wonderful century of development. And there is the blundering generation's needless, unnecessary war that accomplished little or nothing that could not, and would not, have come by a peaceful, evolutionary process, whether in material advancement or in human relations. Historians have speculated, and will continue to speculate, upon the possible fruits of the method that was not tried, but the questions involved will remain unanswered. We have before us only the actual course that was pursued.

VI

The period of southern history since Appomattox has not inspired the mass of writing comparable to the preceding generation's deluge, yet no era has been more expanded or revised. The lengthening New South is an important factor. What seemed recent to the pioneers now possesses sufficient remoteness to provide perspective for at least two generations of post–Civil War history; and a continuing series of crises that span the last quarter century have yielded a greater consciousness of a past that might explain them. It is significant, too, that much of the best writing about this era has been done by students whose professional careers began with the period under review, many of them rather late in the quarter century. Young men growing up in a climate of opinion that differed sufficiently from that prevailing before the 1930's looked at present and past issues through variant lenses. It is not surprising that they asked new questions of the records and found answers that modified well-established interpretations. This was a natural and normal development, duplicated many times by their predecessors; and they in turn may be regarded as tradition-bound old fogies by the exuberant youth of a future generation.

The age or degree of maturity is not always a controlling factor in determining the character of history. The nostalgic Nashville Agrarians of 1930 were no older than contributors to a 1960 publication, *The Southerner as American.* The new group of associated scholars were not afflicted by any nostalgic conception of the past, whether before or after 1865. And the collection of essays in *The Burden of Southern History* reveals not a trace of dead-past traditionalism, but rather, a tendency to reassess the Old South and the New with great respect for the evidence and with a consciousness of its meaning today. C. Vann Woodward seems to have no other purpose than a contribution "to an understanding of the collective experience and the distinctive character of the South," premised on the fact that "the South is obviously American as well as Southern." [14]

If the essays in *The Southerner as American* achieve collectively somewhat less success than those in *The Burden of Southern History,* it may be attributable in part to multiple authorship and in part to a controlling theme, with some straining for straws in a few essays and too much eagerness to prove the volume's major contention. It presents a tragic view of southern history, for the chief significance of that subject lies in what it does to or for a people; and the South's past gave it "a false image of itself," and therefore failed to aid southerners to resolve "their inner conflicts and escape their tragic dilemma." [15] In this sense, the book has much usefulness, and its essays merit careful reading and pondering.

We have come a long way in our concept of the period following 1877 since Holland Thompson published a little volume on *The New South* in "The Chronicles of America," a remarkable book considering the recency of the period, a hitherto uncharted course, and a climate of opinion now somewhat antequated. It would hardly be correct to say that the era's history has been rewritten; rather, it has been written and so has the history of much of the period since 1918. Many New South facets have been carefully explored: agricultural, industrial, and economic problems, the changing social order, the Negro's place in the scheme of life, the South's efforts to escape traditionalism, the new era's relationship to the past, the region's position in the national picture. For breadth as well as depth, Woodward's *Origins of the New South* is the major contribution of the past quarter century. It enlarges, it revises understanding. Beyond dynamic portrayals of the South's political, social, and economic life, the book also depicts the southern mind and the southern spirit with greater insight than Cash achieved a decade before. Ignoring the grooves into which thought had fallen, the writer's comprehensive examination gave the book a Prometheus Unbound character. The qualities of his mind and method had already appeared in *Tom Watson* and *Reunion and Reaction:* deep insight, human understanding, unwillingness to accept previous conclusions or to arrive at new ones without adequate research and testing of assumptions. A different agrarian rebel appeared, and also a different compromise of 1877.

The criticism has been made that when Negroes began participating in writing their history, they exaggerated contributions the race had made to American development, discovered too many talented members, and condemned the majority race too severely. In so far as this is true, it is understandable. Their purpose was not unlike that of white southerners in the generation before our own, who were convinced that nineteenth-century historians, most of them northerners, had either ignored the South or presented it wrongly. The pioneers set about to correct the imbalance and the errors. If Negro historians of the twentieth century's first half were endeavoring to establish the Negro's place in history by correcting misconceptions and by insisting upon more attention, they were performing according to the pattern of their white contemporaries. In recent years some have shared with other writers responsibility for good studies on the Negro in America, presented with due regard for standards of modern-day critical scholarship.

It is not unusual for scholars to differ widely in their appraisals of books. Nearly a score of years ago, Robert A. Warner published a volume entitled *New Haven Negroes: A Social History*. Reviews were, for the most part, favorable. In the judgment of Joseph C. Robert, "The Negroes of New Haven could hardly wish for a more sensitive and friendly chronicler." But in W. E. B. Du Bois's opinion, "The New Haven Negroes deserve better study than Mr. Warner has given them." The author impressed the reviewer "as writing of the Negro group from the outside looking in." Du Bois would not contend that only an Englishman could write of England or a citizen of Japan of his country, but he "would insist that if a person is writing of a group to which he is socially and culturally alien, he must have some extraordinary gifts of insight."[16] Actually, Du Bois's standard of qualification would exclude all or nearly all white historians, even professional crusaders with much surface sympathy. And, perhaps to a slightly lesser extent, it would exclude Negro historians from writing about white groups, and thus we would have the history of both peoples written in vacuums. It is a horrible thought.

A different concept now prevails. John Hope Franklin sensed the new order when he wrote in 1960: "Northerners with no particular brief for John Brown are studying the South. Southerners with no defense of slavery or the fire-eaters are among the most zealous students of the new history of the South. Negroes with no feeling of inadequacy are examining various phases of the South's history and are writing about whites as well as about

Negroes."[17] The two races have been, and still are, segregated in some parts of the world, but there are so many impacts, cross-currents, and mutually agreeable and profitable relationships that Du Bois's implication of segregation has no place in the present Republic of Letters.

VII

As one would expect, southern history writing during the last quarter century has been largely monographic in character. In this sense there has been no radical departure from performance in past periods: the pioneers, too, concentrated on articles and books that treated narrowly encompassed subjects. Like pioneers in the wilderness, they were transforming virgin land into some semblance of order and usefulness. Their best research studies, and those of their successors, were not devoid of interpretation, for evidence and import have never been mutually exclusive.

Some recent writers have posed an important question: Is there less need for the mill and more for the refinery? They suggest quiescence in research and an inventory of accumulated knowledge with attention to analysis and reconstruction. In the lead article of the October, 1960, *American Historical Review,* Woodward concerns himself with revolutionary events since World War II and the responsibility of historians to reinterpret the past for meaning that explains their impact "upon the present and the immediate future." He believes "that future revisions may be extensive enough to justify calling the coming era of historiography an age of interpretation." Such a development seems reasonable for writers who have the perceptive talent to sense what he calls "a revolution, or perhaps a set of revolutions" that "should raise new questions about the past and affect our reading of large areas of history."

Several recent examples of critical reassessment, in addition to the two already presented—*The Southerner as American* and *The Burden of Southern History*—illustrate a trend. An ambitious undertaking by Thomas Pressly, *Americans Interpret Their Civil War,* was a highly successful and rewarding adventure. Interpretation is a major purpose in Avery Craven's *Civil War in the Making,* Bruce Catton's *America Goes to War,* David Donald's *Lincoln Reconsidered,* Allan Nevins' *The Statesmanship of the Civil War,* and the multiauthored *Why the North Won the Civil War*—actually, why the southern Confederacy lost it.

More emphasis on interpretive works, the writer assumes, will not mean a moratorium on monographic studies in southern or other areas of history. Students will still have need of conventional subjects that lend themselves to mastery of methodology. And ripe scholars and epic poets may still aspire to a place in Fame's Hall comparable to that of Douglas Freeman, David Mays, Dumas Malone, J. G. Randall, or Carl Sandburg. For such aspirants Carl Becker gave wise counsel. As a prerequisite for writing a definitive biography of Jefferson, he recommended thorough knowledge of American and European intellectual, economic, and political history through three quarters of a century. "The course would consist in learning all that the printed books and unpublished manuscripts could tell about Thomas Jefferson's manifold interests and activities during a long life. . . . Having found out, any sensible person who had reached the age of discretion would abandon the task. . . . Fortunately," Becker observed, "not all scholars have reached the age of discretion," and of these, he hoped, some are not "sensible; so that one of them with adequate ability may someday be rash enough to enter this labyrinth. Well and good," he concluded, "but let him abandon all hope of ever getting out." [18]

If the men who entered the Revolutionary and Civil War labyrinths produced monumental works, as some reviewers have said, what qualities made them superior, and probably enduring? Years of study that provide profound knowledge of the period. Research in depth on the major figure and his contemporaries who shared the spotlight, or occasionally usurped it. Perception that penetrates the factors and forces that influenced the man, or that he helped to mould into a medley and a mosaic of epic proportions. A sympathy tempered by recognition of weaknesses and mistakes that make the subject human. Talent for lifting both the person and the period above the monotonous evidence compiled on note cards. Capacity for recapturing the past, or that portion of it that has survived the ravages of time. Absence of controlling thesis or formula with their narrowing attributes that circumscribe the writer's intellect and produce an apex rather than an arc. An imaginative mind and a facile pen that combine to insure rhythmic prose with change of pace, shadows and shadings, highlights and crises. The will to know, capacity to understand, perseverance to complete.

CHAPTER XII

A Quarter Century of American Historical Scholarship

Michel de Montaigne, in his delightful autobiography written as sixteenth-century French civil wars drew to a close, complained of the excessive number of literary critics who swarmed everywhere.[1] "There is more to-do about interpreting interpretations," he wrote, "than interpreting the facts themselves. There are more books about books than about anything else. We do nothing but make commentaries on one another." If he had been writing three and a half centuries later, he might have fired both barrels at the scholarly world of letters: at purported contributions to knowledge as well as critiques of them. With the wisdom of the wise, this "unpremeditated philosopher" might call for a moratorium on histories and biographies until historians and biographers found something new to write about. Certainly he would demand sharp curtailment in addresses before scholarly societies unless speakers had discovered significant new truth or insight. The Mississippi Valley Historical Association's functionary of the year will resort to the very thing that Montaigne condemned, hoping that the eminent essayist, making allowance for the ritual of the historical guild, will forgive a commentarial discourse. The pages that follow are a product of observation and experience among my colleagues at work during the past quarter century.

I

The discussion, it should be admitted at the outset, concerns only fragments of the total historiographical picture; and the quarter century under review is only in a very limited sense a well-defined period. Actually, there is no assurance that a new era began in the 1930's, or that an epoch approached an end in the 1950's. Generations have a way of beginning when a person reaches maturity. The end is in sight when hair loses its pigmentation or abandons its abode.

If Americans who walked the earth a century ago were to return in the 1950's, they would indeed find themselves in a strange land. They would recognize mountains and valleys, lakes and streams, ancient and modern classics, masterpieces of art and sculpture, and here and there an antebellum structure that had survived the ravages of time and man. Bombast and bunkum in political bodies, disrespect for Supreme Court decisions, parades of American ideals, much ado about little in college classrooms, polemical discussions of the role of education—all these would provide bridges to the past. But for the most part, these visitors from America of the 1850's would be strangers in an incredible world. If in nostalgic dilemma they sought memory's refreshment in current works of history and biography, some accounts of their generation might be as unfamiliar as skyscrapers, airliners, or atomic energy. Americans who departed this land with Abraham Lincoln might exclaim, "Is this I?"

History should have meaning for the present; in the words of a threadbare platitude, each generation must write its own history in terms comprehensible to that generation. And yet the world we picture should not do violence to the past. Within ever-present limits of man's ability to know and understand his yesterdays, the past should be readily recognizable by hypothetical Enoch Ardens, albeit we would be obligated to enlighten them on matters that were only vaguely comprehended in their era. Still, we have no right to twist and distort their institutions and conceptions to the point that they would not feel comfortably at home in the pages of our history. "I'll gladly come back from the other world," Montaigne admonished, "to give the lie to anyone who will shape me other than I was, even though to honor me." No one has ever stated more explicitly a past-minded purpose of history. Alas, no one has ever achieved the perfection he demanded.

Nevertheless, the essayist's point is well taken. No historical concept can justify license in wrongly reconstructing a past to explain something that is present. Tricks on the dead make the past unreal, its people imaginary. Tricks on the dead are also tricks on the living, for when the past is portrayed as something it was not, to explain a present cause, both present and past become never-never lands. The past is difficult enough to recover without consciously creating a land of make-believe.

The generation of historians that began early in the twentieth century witnessed the birth of presentism and relativism, and the decline of the scientific concept that dominated the preceding era. Presentists, whose conceptual views reached capstone structure in the 1930's, saw a new relationship between past and present and a personal equation that prevented attainment of objectivity. Neither past nor future involved reality, they said; a fictitious zone of time, the specious present, separated past and future yet united both in a continuum of thought and action. Human experience in the realm of man's memory involved another factor inseparably linked with the first. Beyond the continuities of history the "emergent event," something new, not anticipated in the natural course of events, entered the record to give history an ever-changing quality.

This presentist revolt brought problems in its wake. Designed to make history useful in advancing democracy and other elements of progressivism, actually it became an expedient to preserve accepted values, and negated the concept of change. Such an approach served to inhibit the historian's search for truth by transforming him into a person who already possessed it, thereby impeding new insights into society's complexities. Before presentism had opportunity to reach this status, one of its founders, Carl Becker, explained history as "the *sense of the past,* as the apprehension of events, true or false, that are thought to have occurred or to be occurring in distant places and times past." The historian's task lay in reconstructing those events and in making them "live again" through "imaginative insight and aesthetic understanding."

The student can learn a new language and, upon mastering it, can use it as a medium of thought. He does not need to translate it into his native tongue to comprehend meaning. It seems reasonable to suppose that the historian can learn the language of a past generation, and by long association with its people and its thoughts, dispel a large part of the gulf that separates two eras, and therefore have less need for the refracting medium by which presentists say we know the past. It seems reasonable also that the historian who journeys to a distant part of his country, or to another country, can adjust himself, though never perfectly, to a new land and its people. The degree of adjustment will depend upon related components: how long he lives there, how much provincialism he retains, the sincerity of his will to understand new attributes in a different context. In final analysis the will to understand is the dominant factor that determines the accuracy and the thoroughness of his comprehension. The human sea around us, the events of everyday experience, the visual perceptions of the physical world—these unlock the door to the past. It is the understanding of what lies beyond that differentiates the commanding view of the historian from the myopic vision of the amateur. The present may be a key to the past, but emergent thought and emergent event in the interim between then and now make it an imperfect key.

Some contemporary Civil War historians so completely live and move and have their being in the era of their investigations that they may need a refracting medium by which to know the present. One of them, admitting the "fanatic quality" of writers zealously devoted to the paradisaic cause, whether lost or regained, alludes to "this determined band who live most of their waking hours in the 1860's." They have geared their habits of life and mechanics of thought to the one decade in American history worth recording; and only such superficial vestiges as beardless chins, modest manners, and devotion to royalties remain to identify them with the generation into which they were unfortunately born.

Despite attention given to presentism in seminars and scholarly journals during the last quarter century, perhaps only a few historians have consciously done violence to the past out of their concern for the present. No historical journal became a crusader for a contemporary cause; and, if we may judge by those who reviewed books, the ideal of the historian continued to be a re-creation of the past. Reviewers reserved for superior biographies and histories the expressions "live again" and "come alive."

If we observe from the vantage point of today the course of the last quarter century, an era in which Andrews and Charles A. Beard and Becker were completing their productive careers, our failure to recognize presentism in all of its premises does not mean that the concept had no influence. Charles McLean Andrews, for example, once paraded as the personification of objectivity, was, according to his biographer, actually a relativist, influenced by his own day's climate of opinion. The nature of the subject matter with which craftsmen work, as well as the human qualities of historians, precludes absolute objectivity or complete re-creation. Consciously or unconsciously, the world in which historians wrote conditioned their thinking about the past and prompted new questions.

Though the historian acknowledges the reality of a limited present-mindedness, he may still do violence to both present and past by provincialism of mind or by prejudice under the guise of presentism. Whether the subject under investigation is broad or narrow, he must see it in terms of the whole present—and also the whole past. This requirement does not convert a monograph on a restricted subject into an earth-shaking affair, but it does encourage regard for perspective; it restrains the enthusiast in his parade of past ties with the present; and it curbs the reading of the present into the past.

Speculations of this nature, of course, touch on matters of theory and philosophy. It may be that the apparent inattention of the historical guild to this field of thought is not a serious defect. It is doubtful if most historians understand philosophy if expressed in philosophic phrase. They seem impelled to go directly to the sources in search of truth without pausing to consider a theory that may justify method or conclusion. Despite paucity of surface indication, it is quite likely that they gradually evolve a philosophy of history as a product of the personal equation, although they may have difficulty in stating it abstractly. If an example is needed, J. Franklin Jameson may serve better than any of the other reputable historians whose careers ended in the 1930's. He confessed repeatedly in correspondence of statesmanlike quality that he did not understand philosophy. Perhaps he understood it, shorn of its special vocabulary, better than he admitted. And if an instance from the other side of the Atlantic is appropriate, Marc Bloch disclaimed competence in the "specialized trade" of the philosopher.

II

If memory serves its proper function, historians of the 1930's marveled at the historiographical advancement made since last century's pioneers laid foundations for systematic historical scholarship. They pointed with justifiable pride to a broader concept of their subject; to methodology that discarded the passive role of their predecessors who endeavored to convert history into a science; to vast accumulations of manuscript and printed materials in archives and libraries; to shelves of contributions to knowledge and collections of documents; to partial escape from monographic dullness; to firm establishment of history in high school and college curriculums; in short, to recognition of their craft as a vital and respected part of American enlightenment. They were, it appears in retrospect, only on the threshold of great advancement, as craftsmen have ever been in their successors' appraisals.

The achievements of the last quarter century seem notable to historians whose experience bridges the years between the 1930's and today. Reminiscent of the Great Depression, the Federal Archives and Historical Records Surveys opened to the guild valuable, unexploited documents that lay buried in federal buildings, county courthouses, city halls, and churches. The National Archives, gift of the past generation to our own, assembled records invaluable to historians. The expanding usefulness of the Library of Congress through its *Printed Cards* brought America's largest library within bibliographical reach of all universities; microfilm and microcard made available to research libraries many rare and distant sources. Thanks to World War II, the quarter century witnessed accumulation and preservation of military records, from which many volumes were written. Oral history projects preserved for posterity memories of contemporaries that otherwise would have been lost to history. Greater attention to the interrelation of history and other disciplines encouraged a limited number of historians to acquire special skills on the periphery of historical methodology. The American Historical Association's Service Center for Teachers of History provided a "constructive assistance" program designed to narrow the gap between the specialist and the high school instructor.

Meanwhile, promotion of publication proceeded at accelerated pace. University presses antedated the 1930's; the past quarter century saw them develop as significant mediums for the publication of historical works. The American History Research Center, sponsored by the State Historical Society of Wisconsin, promoted local history by subsidizing the work of scholars and by publishing the results of their labors. New state and regional scholarly journals supplemented older quarterlies in printing an ever-expanding number of articles and reviews; and *American Heritage,* sponsored by the American Association for State and Local History and the Society of American Historians, popularized history for the enjoyment and instruction of thousands of laymen. Definitive editions of the works of George Washington and Abraham Lincoln appeared; publication of the Jefferson Papers in fifty volumes began at mid-century. Serving as cooperative middleman, the National Historical Publications Commission encouraged sundry organizations—federal, state, and local—to collect, preserve, and print letters, diaries, and other documents pertinent to an understanding of American history. Projects are under way to publish the Adams, John Carroll, Calhoun, Clay, Franklin, Hamilton, and Madison papers; some smaller works like the journal of Francis Asbury; and documentary histories of the Constitution's ratification and the first federal Congress.

These and other aids to research, writing, and publication were paralleled by a broadening and deepening of the study of American history; broadening in its social studies implications, deepening in its humanistic aspects. Business history, railroad history, cultural history, literary history, the history of science, the history of any of the arts—these are evidences of a comprehensive concept of history. Some of them are also evidence that the historian's education has been extended to a mastery of other crafts than his own.

Public citizens as well as historians continued to look upon history as a study useful in performing important functions. A backward look at the path we traveled might indicate tomorrow's course. "To get our bearings," Warren R. Austin wrote in an article on "The Road Ahead," "let us begin by recalling a few of the milestones along the way we have come to this critical fork in the road." And James G. Randall counseled from the ripeness of his study and observation, "Historical insight can become the truest foresight." On the other hand, Jacques Barzun pointed anew to the importance of history to the individual. It is significant, he said, not because of "what you can do with history but what history does to you." In this sense it is valuable "for dealing with life itself, every day; for spiritual balance, for political, artistic and social judgment, in a word for the conquest of provincialism—the provincialism of self, the provincialism of place, the provincialism of time." This concept of history for our sake assigns it a broad, uplifting role as an area of knowledge contributing to the individual's poise and equilibrium.

Main currents of historical activity follow the interests of society. Americanists of the past quarter century continued to give attention to hundreds of persons and periods and places, but some trends are observable. Intellectual history attracted an increasing number of younger historians as American culture approached maturity. Recent history became an inviting field; a series of international crises beginning with World War I and the economic and social problems arising soon thereafter focused attention upon the immediate past; and a plethora of circumstances combined to inspire the writing of southern history in greater quantity. But a trend more conspicuous than any of these was the manner in which so much historical interest concentrated upon the stirring events and conflicts that culminated in the Civil War—and in Abraham Lincoln.

III

Here we may well pause a moment and view the development of a spirit of dedication and increased devotion among writers on the Civil War period. By mid-twentieth century, military history, once a subject that shared the spotlight with the political chronicle, had regained lost prestige. World War II revived interest in writing and in reading it, and courses in the subject were introduced into college curriculums. This revival prompted new questions addressed to the records of the 1860's. The Civil War, we discovered, was our first modern war; here and there it was total war. Historians restudied it, not only with past-minded intent, but also to discover the origins of twentieth-century warfare. Views of armed conflict and its history were divergent: Randall believed that war should be presented as a great fraud; John Bowditch called it a normal "form of human activity" that should be studied as carefully as any other segment of history.

Present-mindedness suggested another reason for renewal of interest in the whole Civil War generation. The Negro, forgotten man of our century's first third, emerged in the era of Franklin Roosevelt as a more important factor in American life. Present-day interest in his welfare gave impetus to restudy and rethinking of our history a century ago. For whatever the causes of the Civil War, it could not have happened had there been no institution of slavery and no problem of race.

The revival of interest in military history, the increasing concern for human rights, the struggle of liberty and democracy to survive the onslaughts of authoritarianism are only parts of the story that account for tremendous interest in the Civil War generation. The approaching centennial of that conflict engendered much of the historical activity of the 1950's. In this respect, the history of the Civil War was hardly typical of the fourscore civil wars of the modern era; its history was as unique as the war itself. The English Civil War of the seventeenth century attracted scores of historians; controversies and conclusions were extensively paraded. But that civil conflict produced no such heroes as Lincoln or Lee. It ran its course two hundred years before our own began; but in three hundred years it stimulated less "literature" than our own in one century.

The word "cult" had originally a religious connotation: V. Ogden Vogt defined it in *Cult and Culture* as a "system of religious actions which comprise public worship." In our own century it came to mean homage or devotion to some person or thing "paid by a body of professed adherents or admirers." The word retains the moral and emotional meanings of its original religious context. For Civil War historiography, the word is altogether fitting and proper.

The hero in history, at least in American history, has inspired adoration of succeeding generations; seldom has the crisis that launched the hero won its own fanatic devotees. The American Civil War stirred emotions that combined rights, causes, and encroachments in a permanent pageant of the past. The South forged its own Lost Cause cult, born of rationalization of righteousness in defeat: the heroic efforts of a minority who experienced hardships and sacrifices beyond ordinary human endurance, who acquitted themselves magnificently against great odds, whose cause survived the carnage and devastation of battle, the cunning and mischief of politicians. Lee symbolized the victor in defeat; Davis, the unpopular victim of treasonable rebellion—until rescued by postwar efforts of southern women.

On the other side, from log cabin beginnings, as humble as the Bethlehem manger, Lincoln rose to the stature of savior of the Union and liberator of four million slaves. Right triumphed over the forces of evil through the combined services of the first Great Commoner as political leader and able strategist and the common man as both soldier and civilian. Sundry roads to reunion and much literary ingenuity provided glory enough for all.

The Civil War period offers a better opportunity to test our concepts of the nature of history than any other era in which Americanists have been interested. So many thousands of volumes have concentrated on the four-year war and the generation that preceded it, and so many hundreds of writers have entered the field in the last decade, that the historiographer has abundant advantage in observing disagreements and discrepancies, methods of work and habits of thought, potboiler flurries and serious research projects, antiquarian revelations and historical discoveries.

This interest in Lincoln and the war brought the enthusiasm of devoted American writers and their readers to cultic proportions. Cults do not begin abruptly, and it would be difficult to determine when the image of Lincoln's grandeur had its origin, or when it merged into the Civil War cult. The martyr of 1865 inspired worship as soon as myth supplemented his great human qualities. Lincoln literature increased in volume during the second postwar generation and reached greater magnitude in the third. Although publication restrictions during World War II curtailed production, since 1945 the output of Lincoln books has become enormous. Randall's penetrating article, "Has the Lincoln Theme Been Exhausted?" stirred writers to greater activity in examining forces and events that culminated at Appomattox, and the hundredth anniversary of the war has prompted publication of books on both Lincoln and the American conflict. Certainly by mid-century the war cult was readily recognizable, not only in accretions to Lincoln–Civil War titles every year but also in expanding sales of books, good and bad, and in activities of such organizations as Civil War round tables. Books that attracted little attention at publication dates in the thirties and forties were reissued a few years later for enthusiastic purchasers. A quarter of a century ago, the editor of a scholarly journal devoted to southern history declined to publish many Civil War diaries and letters because of the mistaken notion that a surfeit had been reached!

There have been other cults in American history, but none as all-embracing as the authorities and patriots who worship at the shrine of Abraham Lincoln and the crisis that made him martyr. Tangible gauges have been registered by quantification: the number of visitors at Lincoln's birthplace near Hodgenville, the House on Eighth Street in Springfield, the Abraham Lincoln Insurance Company at Fort Wayne, the Lincoln Memorial in the national capital. The use of special collections at the Illinois State Historical Library, the Huntington Library, the Lincoln Insurance Company, the Library of Congress, and many other private and public depositories is a partial measure of research activity. Visitors to battlefields on southern soil and at Gettysburg are further evidence that Americans at the middle of the twentieth century have tremendous interest in military events of the 1860's.

Cultic aspirations are reflected in the *Lincoln Herald* and in *Civil War History,* sponsored respectively by Lincoln Memorial University and the library of the State University of Iowa. Each serves a useful purpose; perhaps both transcend strict historianship in some of their pages. The first follows the curve of Lincoln publications with avid interest, rejoicing when the number is appreciable, lamenting when it declines. In its early issues the second anticipated "forthcoming titles in that stream of publications which has been called 'The Continuing War.' " Its section entitled "For Collectors Only" is a unique category in the annals of scholarly magazines. The unrestrained enthusiasm of the contributor of this feature in *Civil War History* reflects the climate of opinion in which he moves. He glories in the "Civil War revival," with works on that era "outselling all other books in both fiction and non-fiction fields." Momentum is terrific: two years ago Civil War books were published "at the staggering rate of more than a new title a week"; the Civil War book-of-the-month club had to determine whether to become a " 'book-of-the-week club' or reconcile itself to distributing what its editors believe are the better books." Times have changed. The contributor recalls when sales of 3,500 to 5,000 copies were "regarded as amazing," and when "classics" by Randall, Fletcher Pratt, and Sir Frederick Maurice "graced the 'remainder' lists."

Our informant, searching for origins and explanations, peered further into cultic mysteries. "What caused the present boom?" Cyclical interest in the Civil War? The approaching centennial? No, good writing that produced "*good* books" led to "the present happy state of Civil War affairs." Carl Sandburg's *Prairie Years* with its Carlylesque technique, "a combination of genius, curiosity and story-telling ability," launched the revolution, and Stephen Benet's *John Brown's Body* "helped stir the kettle." Very soon journalists were supplanting academicians: "The Civil War was just another 'beat' and they covered Grant and Lee, the Shenandoah Valley and Shiloh just as they had handled local crime, the world series or current politics." A medley of newspapermen, including Allan Nevins and MacKinlay Kantor, Douglas Freeman and Harnett Kane, Lloyd Lewis and Burke Davis, Bruce Catton and Robert Kincaid, enlisted recruits for that "vast army" that is "the modern literary equivalent" of the Grand Army of the Republic, the Loyal Legion, the Sons of Confederate Veterans, and the United Daughters of the Confederacy.

Newspapermen did more than enlist tens of thousands of recruits. They exerted noticeable influence on academicians, "and toward a good purpose," for some lost dullness in style that sprang from self-consciousness, while others, it is encouraging to note, escaped the malady entirely. The disquisition closes with the statement that "the professional writer and historian" contributed a major part to the Civil War revival through meritorious writing. Thus, a new dichotomy of craftsmen was born, and professionals were teaching historians a valuable lesson.

What motives prompt this search for peak production in Lincoln and Civil War studies? The era has attracted historians and novelists in part because it provides inspiring themes, but not all who aspire to use the epoch and its characters have the necessary imagination to exploit its epic qualities. Is there so great a need for more and more books on that limited segment of American history? Should history be self-impelling? Are there dangers, temporary or permanent, that arise from irresponsible attention to an era that attracts so heterogeneous a mass of "authorities"? Is this unnatural gold rush to Springfield, Gettysburg, Appomattox, and a hundred spots where clashes occurred, the result of talent for the field, the consequence of tons of new evidence, the neglect of significant persons and events? Are books reviewed as critically and dispassionately as Clio demands?

Read, if you will, a book a day on the Civil War period for a year or two, and for good measure include a few articles as a part of each day's labor. You may emerge from your self-imposed task with mingled feelings of weariness with humdrum monotony of thrice-told tales, of amusement at quibble and dribble, of amazement at transgressions committed in the name of history, of renewed respect and esteem for the march of historical intellect toward a Republic of Letters. From the welter of a hundred thousand pages or more, a few observations must suffice.

Among current Americana, the name Lincoln and the era Civil War are sufficient to attract, often artificially, a generous clientele of buyers and readers. An article in *American Heritage,* "Riding the Circuit with Lincoln," illustrates the tendency. Actually, Lincoln was riding the circuit with Judge David Davis, whose letters make the story a contribution to knowledge. In approved newspaper fashion, the newsworthy Lincoln is featured not only in the title but also in a full-page picture at the beginning of the article; a small pen-and-ink sketch of Davis appears in its continued section. Years ago a witticism went the rounds that reader interest would make the title, "Lincoln's Wife's Doctor's Dog," a best seller. The title would be inadequate today unless preceded by the more euphonious "Rendezvous with Rover."

Just when the reader believes a fact has been nailed down, permanently, another writer upsets his peace of mind. In a recent Pulitzer Prize selection, Ben Butler's "eyes refused to mesh." Elsewhere, with slight variation, he grinned "sardonically with eyes that did not mesh." Surely now we have a positive, unquestioned descriptive statement, and we can dismiss Butler as the general with the unmeshable eyes. Alas, not so, for in a meritorious study of Lincoln's generals, the "squat, squinty Butler," to quote a contemporary, "looked like a cross-eyed cuttlefish." In this prolific age of Civil War history, we may anticipate a volume in a unique frame of reference, "Lincoln's Cuttlefish Division; A Study in Comparative Anatomy."

Unevenness in quality of Civil War literature may be no greater than in other areas of American history. An illusion may be created by its great bulk as well as by the writings of antiquarians and collectors, some of whom, it should be added, make commendable contributions. Representative of the trivia is an eight-page article, "Discovered—An Authentic Lincoln Fingerprint," the only dactyl impression with lineage directly traceable to the Civil War hero. Its significance? "To Lincoln scholars it's like finding the solar boat at the Great Pyramid," or, as "one of that strange tribe" relates: "I consider this the greatest Lincoln find in recent years. I would rather have this item in my collection than the Gettysburg Address, for there are five copies of Gettysburg but there is only one authentic fingerprint of Lincoln's." The "discovery" might be relegated to the collector's trade except that it appears in a magazine of history. One may question the interest of "Lincoln scholars," or the FBI for that matter, in the ink smudge. It might be filed away with the theme of the University of Wisconsin freshman who wrote, "Abraham Lincoln . . . was born in a log cabin which he built with his own hands."

The essence of the great outpouring of books and articles on the era lies in the substantial quality of the painstaking contributions rather than in the trivia of marginal worth. The comprehensive knowledge and critical acumen of Paul Angle; the tolerant, human understanding, judicious insight, and master workmanship of J. G. Randall; the midwestern, common man presentation of Carl Sandburg; the superb, small-canvas portraiture by Benjamin P.

Thomas; the challenging interpretations of T. Harry Williams and David Donald; the humanizing and glorification of the common soldier by Bell Wiley and Bruce Catton; the discerning, illuminating, and critical judgment of the war and its aftermath by William B. Hesseltine; the painstaking search of official records by Kenneth P. Williams; the scholarly studies of Confederate military history by Douglas Freeman and Frank Vandiver; the penetrating analyses of antebellum sectional conflicts and partisan clashes by Avery Craven, Roy Nichols, and Allan Nevins; the explorations into slavery and the Negro by Kenneth Stampp and John Hope Franklin; the masterly essays on Civil War historiography by Thomas Pressly—these and other recent writings add immeasurably to the "come alive," "live again" recapture of a great American crisis.

It would be comforting to believe that historians of the period under review, or at least the quality writers among them, were in substantial agreement wherever their subjects overlap. Actually, the interpretations and directions that flow from the evidence are as varied as the colors of the spectrum. In this divergence, Civil War writers are not unlike reputable historians of other subjects and periods. When the notes are taken and the chips are down, the mind seeks meaning from the chaos and complexity that is life in all of its uniqueness—and in all of its human relationships. From the labyrinth of the war epoch's historiography, two historians posed the question, "Can Differences in Interpretations of the Causes of the American Civil War Be Resolved Objectively?" The answer is undoubtedly a negative, but confusion in conclusion inspires a search for a solution that will make historiography more cumulative and less innovative. A few illustrations of divergence may serve a useful purpose.

We have been taught by sundry historians during the past fifteen years to believe that Radicals in Lincoln's own party stood in his way and handicapped the war effort through the press, the Joint Committee on the Conduct of the War, and obstructionist tactics on House and Senate floors. A critic of this view asserts that the Radicals now play the role formerly assigned to Jefferson Davis, Stephen A. Douglas, or the Democratic party. They are the new villains, he says. Historians are still writing history and biography with a hero-villain approach, and the Radicals—a whole flock of them—provide the necessary pawns to lift Lincoln to more heroic proportions. As evidence of the misconception, he points to

Charles Sumner to prove that, although he and Lincoln differed on many issues, they understood each other and worked together. The reviser emphasizes the complexity of politics and the error of simple categorizing.

Investigations of the abolitionist crusade symbolize oscillations of the historical pendulum. In the generation of Jesse Macy, Garrisonian emphasis was the accepted word. Two or three decades ago historians "proved" that the antislavery impulse was western: that the Tappan brothers, Charles Grandison Finney, Theodore Dwight Weld, and other dynamic New York and Ohio leaders gave impetus to the crusade. More recently an analysis of abolitionist leadership "confirms the traditional identification of radical anti-slavery with New England."

As the Civil War receded into the past and a new generation of northerners and southerners looked more dispassionately upon the leaders of the tragic quadrennium, Lincoln and Lee received more universal acclaim than other heroes of the period. Lee's personal qualities and his military genius were widely recognized. With fewer soldiers and inadequate economic support, he successfully defied Union generals until finally the most competent of them, Ulysses S. Grant, overcame the thinning gray lines that personified the Confederacy. Now it would seem that all of this is wrong. In a recent notable volume, Grant becomes a greater general than Lee; but Lincoln, the commander in chief, surpassed all the Union generals, including Grant, as master strategist. A critic questions the correctness of the conclusion, although "the growing disposition to glorify Lincoln and to transform him into an Olympian figure," he says, favors acceptance, for readers are "willing to accept as sound fact almost any claim or assertion made in his favor. To discover that he was a military genius is, therefore, only a logical step in the growth of the Lincoln myth." Lee personified a dying civilization as well as a lost cause. His type of strategy was passing into limbo; Grant's inaugurated modern warfare. In becoming the alpha of a new era, he superseded the omega of the old.

IV

It is a commonplace that history reflects the interests of the age in which it is written. Unfortunately, it is also true that the age's interests often color the past with unhistoric hues. A present view, a present cause, needs historic support. From a narrow segment of life today, the writer gazes into a corresponding segment of the past to find explanation and justification. Indeed, zeal for a subject may lead the historian beyond the limits of strict historianship. A crusade may be skillfully and subtly imbedded in fairly sound history; it may be expressed openly in private correspondence. Some young southerners trained at Columbia University in the early years of the twentieth century embarked upon a project to correct the history of the United States that had been written by northeasterners in the generation between the Civil War and the turn of the century. Among them was Ulrich Phillips, who, in personal letters, asserted that Harvard University historians in particular had distorted American history, although southerners were responsible for neglect in providing materials from which balanced history could be written. And Walter Fleming, a few years later, wrote of the younger generation in the South growing up on "prejudiced accounts written in Mass. or Ohio." Southern enthusiasts brought sectional history into better balance, but they, like their predecessors, neglected the role of the Negro, and very early in their careers closed their minds to anthropological scholarship. The thinking of Fleming, Phillips, and some other writers of the period was conditioned by their own present, the past of the eighties and nineties, which they understood only in part; and they failed to see the whole past of an earlier era.

The history of the South attained estimable stature in the years since the early thirties, though in the writer's judgment a recent trend overuses presentism in an effort to adjust the imbalance that remains unresolved. A study of the militant South promises in its preface consideration of one attribute of the Old South exhibited in proper context. Attention is focused upon military-mindedness, tangibly and correctly illustrated by military schools, citizen soldiers, state militias, personal encounters, expansionist activities, slavery defense, growing unity—all culminating in military preparedness for the inevitable war that began at Fort Sumter. By directing attention toward one quality of some southerners, the work creates the impression that violence was the major ingredient. The method produces a shuddering sensation as one contemplates the possibility of companion pieces on "The Provocative North" or "The Fanatical East." The complex and well-rounded lives of Americans can easily appear ridiculous if the historical spotlight is focused for three hundred pages upon a single component, without benefit of perspective. Southern militancy is a valid theme if other factors in a vast mosaic are intermittently on the periphery of attention.

Present-day climate has produced another venture into the realm of the peculiar institution. Phillips' study of slavery needed to be redone; despite some excellent qualities of his work, the author saw the institution from the plantation house, very imperfectly from the slave cabin. An analysis of the institution that neglected the viewpoint of cabin inhabitants could hardly be called definitive. The preface to the newer study recognizes past-mindedness—"knowledge of the past is a key to understanding the present"—though it hastens to assure the reader that the historian's "knowledge of the present is clearly a key to his understanding of the past." The statement is correct, of course; the present is a key. But understanding is the door through which the historian can view the past. And the door must be opened wide to permit a view of the whole past against which the segment is mirrored. The historian should endeavor to place what he sees in the context of its time. To transport it into the 1950's would do as much violence to history as removal of Lincoln's log-cabin birthplace to Times Square.

Neither the study of the region's militancy nor its institution of slavery is a history of the antebellum South, and it would be grossly unfair to criticize either because it treats only one segment of Old South history. But we have a right to demand of history that it do no violence to the total picture. The spirit of the present, whether the closing years of the nineteenth century or the middle of the twentieth, creates a South that differed so radically from reality that few contemporaries—North or South—would have recognized it.

Expressions have been invented in recent years to disparage historians who seek to understand the South in context of time and place. They are stigmatized as apologists for slavery, apologists for the Negro, apologists for conservatism, apologists for radicalism. Such epithets are more appropriate to political hustings or polemical tirades than to sober historical thought. The medievalist who endeavors to understand serfdom in past-minded context is not reproached as apologist for serfdom; nor are the motives of the modernist impugned if he presents historically the English problems that delayed universal manhood suffrage.

Marc Bloch put in trenchant language the purpose of the historian. "When all is said and done," he wrote, "a single word, 'understanding,' is the beacon light of our studies. Let us not say that the true historian is a stranger to emotion: he has that, at all events. 'Understanding,' in all honesty, is a word pregnant with difficulties, but also with hope. Moreover, it is a friendly word. Even in action, we are far too prone to judge. It is so easy to denounce. We are never sufficiently understanding." When the prejudices of the present invoke the passions of the past, history ceases to be an avenue to understanding.

History is too much a record of clash and conflict, of people on militant parade; too little a matter of harmonious living, of affairs great and small that affect daily lives more tangibly than political and constitutional issues. A clash and conflict emphasis in the writing of history, whether of the South or of any other part of the world, produces a distorted picture. Studies of the Civil War generation that concentrate upon clashes of rival partisans, the question of slavery and the problem of race, competition of agriculture and industry, the struggle between moderatism and fanaticism are important segments of history, but the reader may conclude that Americans of a century ago gave little attention to other aspects of human endeavor. Except for the abnormal sixties, they led normal, wholesome lives as they went about their daily tasks of plowing and planting and harvesting, of manufacturing and mining and transporting, of teaching and preaching and playing, of the hundred and one items that combine into a mosaic of individuality or of collective society. Southerners have been personified in terms of conflict: nullification, sectionalism, slavery, secession, civil war, hooded orders, the race problem. Many have worn such clothing, but it is not workaday apparel. Controversial issues are sometimes at attention's focus, more often on its periphery. Yet clash and conflict form the warp and woof of much history, of even more popular conception.*

Clash and conflict have been exaggerated; nevertheless, violence has ever been an imperfection in civilization. In America we have been taught that the frontier obstructed advancement in the arts; that cultural maturity could not arrive until war with nature ceased. The American frontier disappeared; and the Great Frontier of the European Metropolis, a recent writer says, soon followed it into oblivion. Competition for exploring and exploiting an

* This paragraph is adapted from the writer's *The South Lives in History: Southern Historians and Their Legacy* (Baton Rouge, 1955), ix–x. His obligations are legion, but only one will be recorded: He is indebted to Harold Bauman, "Some Aspects of Presentism in American Historiography" (M.A. thesis, University of Oregon, 1957), for a few of the statements on p. 237.

outer space frontier has begun; so has discussion of learning to live perpetually with limited warfare. Whether we accept the inevitability of clash and conflict or seek to reduce their impact, another look at the function of history in an ever-expanding knowable universe might be profitable. Obviously, harmonious living, like objectivity in history, is an unattainable goal: the time will never arrive when peace and quiescence reign in local, state, and international communities, when literati constitute a majority, and when leisure is devoted to the enjoyment of whatever is the ultimate in cultural advancement.

Some Americanists have been so absorbed in making history as social study useful to society that they may have neglected other purposes the subject might serve. The noble dream of the presentists, a better world through the instrumentality of a past absorbed in the present, was not an unrewarding chimera. Society's doctor, like the individual's, may justifiably inquire into the patient's past to prescribe for present pain to promote future health. But while society may be ill, unique individuals may enjoy relatively good health, and may therefore turn to history for some other immediate reason than society's reform. The thousands of our contemporaries who read Civil War history may do so for a variety of reasons, certainly among them the desire to know our past, if not for its own sake then for the reader's individual sake. History as heritage, the property of every person, may be the motive that prompts many historians to write it and many persons to read it. What history does to the individual may be more important than what history does for society, though the indirect influence may be considerable. But in either case, the portrayal of time's hinterland should be synonymous with understanding.

The historian's obligation is twofold: to another day's events and persons whom he is investigating and to readers for whom he is writing. This bifurcated responsibility produces a complex problem indeed: to integrate past-mindedness and present-mindedness, to make history less an autobiography of the mind and more an effort to find reality, and in doing so to wear the historical ermine with dignity and poise. But if historiography serves as a guide, historians in perpetuity will be looking backward to our own feeble efforts and pointing up the fallacies of assumptions and methods. Lest we take ourselves and our work too seriously, it is well to recall how imperfectly our historiographical ancestors served us and our generation.

Notes

INTRODUCTION

1 Walter P. Webb, *An Honest Preface and Other Essays* (Boston, 1959), 61–65.
2 This paragraph is adapted from the writer's *The South Lives in History: Southern Historians and Their Legacy* (Baton Rouge, 1955), 65–66.
3 Guy Stanton Ford, *On and Off the Campus* (Minneapolis, 1938), 314.
4 *Ibid.*, 301.

CHAPTER I

1 Originally published in the *Journal of Southern History,* XII (August, 1946), 315–44.
2 Albert B. Hart to Brown, September 28, 1903, January 2, 1906, Brown Papers.
3 Jeremiah Smith to Brown, December 4, 1900, Brown Papers. Smith was writing of Brown's *Andrew Jackson.*
4 Edward G. Lowry to Francis G. Caffey, April 7, 1911, Brown Papers. Lowry was Washington correspondent for the New York *Evening Post.*
5 J. Franklin Jameson to Brown, October 7, 1904, Brown Papers.
6 Andrew C. McLaughlin to Brown, April 12, 1905, American Historical Association Papers, Review Correspondence (Manuscript Division, Library of Congress, Washington, D.C.).
7 For sketches of Brown's career, see Francis G. Caffey, "William Garrott Brown," *Dictionary of American Biography* (20 vols. and index; N.Y., 1928–1936), III, 158–59; Edward S. Martin, "William Garrott Brown," *Harvard Graduates' Magazine,* XXII (December, 1913), 255–57; Thomas M. Owen, *History of Alabama and Dictionary of Alabama Biography* (4 vols.; Chicago, 1921), III, 237; Bliss Perry, "Tribute to William Garrott Brown, '91," *Harvard Alumni Bulletin,* XVI (Boston, 1913), 88–89; John S. Bassett, "My Recollections of William Garrott Brown," *South Atlantic Quarterly,* XVI (April, 1917), 97–107.
8 His diploma is preserved in the Brown Papers. He was appointed to the Gambrill Scholarship during his senior year, took "Highest Honors" in history, was elected to Phi Beta Kappa, and gave one of nine commencement orations. *Harvard College, Class of 1891, Secretary's Report, No. 1* (Cambridge, 1892), 28, 34, 36, 56.
9 Brown to Thayer, March 14, 1900, William Roscoe Thayer Manuscripts (Harvard College library, Cambridge, Mass.).
10 For Brown's trips to Europe, see Brown to Thayer, May 29, 1906; March 1, 1907, Thayer Manuscripts; and January 10, 31, 1913, Brown Papers.
11 *The Harvard University Catalogue, 1891–92* (Cambridge, 1891), 82, 84, 85, 227.
12 *Harvard College, Class of 1891, Secretary's Report, No. 2* (Boston, 1895), 13.
13 *Ibid.; Harvard College, Class of 1891, Secretary's Report, No. 3* (Boston, 1899), 9; *The Harvard University Catalogue, 1893–94* (Cambridge, 1893), 48; *The Harvard*

University Catalogue, 1896–97 (Cambridge, 1896), 50; *The Harvard University Catalogue, 1899–1900* (Cambridge, 1900), 15.

14 William G. Brown, *A List of Portraits in the Various Buildings of Harvard University* (prepared under the direction of the late Justin Winsor, Librarian), in William C. Lane (ed.), "Library of Harvard University, Bibliographical Contributions," No. 53 (Cambridge, 1898), 4.

15 *The Harvard University Catalogue, 1901–02* (Cambridge, 1901), 18, 365.

16 Charles M. Thompson to Bassett, June 12, 1917, Brown Papers.

17 William G. Brown, "An Opportunity," *Harvard Graduates' Magazine,* VIII (June, 1900), 490–94. See also Brown to Thayer, March 9, 14, May 17, 1900, Thayer Manuscripts; Smith to Bassett, December 28, 1916, Brown Papers. Brown alluded to the Dorman B. Eaton professorship to which A. Lawrence Lowell was appointed.

18 *American Historical Review,* XI (October, 1905), 181–86. For Brown's review of Volumes VI and VII, see *American Historical Review,* XII (April, 1907), 680–84. He called them "the best history yet written of Reconstruction," but he added that this statement must be discounted as very little on that period had been published. William A. Dunning, *Reconstruction, Political and Economic, 1865–1877* (New York, 1907), had not yet appeared.

19 Brown to James Ford Rhodes, March 22, 1905, Brown Papers. See also Rhodes to Brown, March 25, October 9, 1905, Brown Papers.

20 Brown, "The Problem of the American Historian," *Atlantic Monthly,* XCII (November, 1903), 654.

21 The manuscript is in the Brown Papers.

22 William G. Brown, *A History of Alabama, For Use in the Schools, Based as to Its Earlier Parts on the Work of Albert J. Pickett* (New York, 1900), 6.

23 Bertha C. Clement to Bassett, May 6, 1917, Brown Papers. See also Miss Clement to Bassett, December 27, 1916, Brown Papers. Miss Clement was Brown's nurse for two and one-half years.

24 Brown to Bassett, February 25, 1907, Brown Papers.

25 William G. Brown, *Andrew Jackson* (Boston, 1900).

26 Also published as "Lincoln's Rival," *Atlantic Monthly,* LXXXIX (February, 1902), 226–36.

27 William G. Brown, *Stephen Arnold Douglas* (Boston, 1902).

28 Brown to Thayer, May 23, 1906, Thayer Manuscripts.

29 William G. Brown, "The Early Life of Oliver Ellsworth," *American Historical Review,* X (April, 1905), 534–64; "A Continental Congressman: Oliver Ellsworth, 1777–1783," *American Historical Review,* X (July, 1905), 751–81; McLaughlin to Brown, April 12, 1905, American Historical Association Papers, Review Correspondence.

30 Andrew C. McLaughlin, review of Brown's *The Life of Oliver Ellsworth,* in *American Historical Review,* XI (April, 1906), 691.

31 William G. Brown, *The Life of Oliver Ellsworth* (New York, 1905).

32 Caffey, "William Garrott Brown," *Dictionary of American Biography,* III, 159.

33 William G. Brown, *The Lower South in American History* (New York, 1902), vii.

34 William G. Brown, "The Orator of Secession: A Study of an Agitator," *Atlantic Monthly,* LXXXIII (May, 1899), 605–17; "The Ku Klux Movement," *Atlantic Monthly,* LXXXVII (May, 1901), 634–44: "The Resources of the Confederacy," *Atlantic Monthly,* LXXXVIII (December, 1901), 827–38.

35 Brown, *Lower South in American History,* 27–40.

36 *Ibid.,* 94.

37 *Ibid.,* 34–40, 44, 57–58.

38 *Ibid.,* 88.

39 *Ibid.,* 117, 124–31, 134, 138, 142, 147–48.

40 *Ibid.*, 158, 185–86.
41 *Ibid.*, 192–95, 196–97, 223–25.
42 Brown to "Dear Frank" (Francis G. Caffey), May 14, 31, August 23, 1898, Brown Papers; Brown to Thayer, December 21, 1899, February 4, 1900, Thayer Manuscripts; *Harvard College, Class of 1891, Secretary's Report, No. 3,* p. 9.
43 Brown, *Lower South in American History,* 229–44.
44 *Ibid.*, 247–71.
45 Walter H. Page to Brown, August 9, 1900, Brown Papers.
46 William G. Brown, *A Gentleman of the South: A Memory of the Black Belt* (New York, 1903), 9–10.
47 Thayer to Brown, November 27, 1900, Brown Papers. See also Brown to Thayer, May 14, 1905, Brown Papers.
48 Brown to Thayer, May 23, June 1, 1906, Thayer Manuscripts.
49 Hart to Brown, September 28, 1903, Brown Papers; Harper and Brothers to Brown, October 12, 1903, Brown Papers.
50 Caffey to Brown, December 23, 1910, Brown Papers.
51 Ellery Sedgwick to Brown, December 16, 1905, Brown Papers. Sedgwick, editor of the magazine, suggested articles of 8,000 to 10,000 words to begin in the November, 1906, issue and end in the December, 1907, issue.
52 Caffey, "William Garrott Brown," *Dictionary of American Biography,* III, 159.
53 Jeanne Mitchell, Lynwood, Nottingham, to Brown, April 23, 1903, Brown Papers. See also "A Woman," Berlin, to Brown, April 25, 1903, Brown Papers. This was a seven-page letter. The article appeared in the *Atlantic Monthly,* XCI (April, 1903), 480–94; and in the *Fortnightly Review,* N.S., LXXIII (April, 1903), 646–64. It was reprinted as the title essay in *The Foe of Compromise and Other Essays* (New York, 1903), 11–64. For correspondence relative to publication in the *Fortnightly Review,* see W. L. Courtney, London, to Brown, January 9, February 28, April 6, 1903, Brown Papers.
54 [Paul E. More], editorial in the *Independent,* LV (April 2, 1903), 812; More to Brown, April 9, 1903, Brown Papers.
55 Vincent J. Walsh to Brown, April 8, 1903, Brown Papers.
56 William G. Brown, "Golf," *Atlantic Monthly,* LXXXIX (June, 1902), 725–35. For comment by a Canadian golfer, see T. Arnold Hamilton, Toronto, to Brown, July 6, 1902, Brown Papers. On June 5, 1902, Brown signed a contract with Houghton Mifflin and Company to reprint the article as a booklet, *Golf* (Boston, 1902). The author would receive a royalty of 10 per cent on all copies sold up to 5,000 and 15 per cent on all sold over that number. The contract is in the Brown Papers.
57 Frank B. Tracy to R. L. O'Brien, February 10, 1904, Brown Papers; Tracy to Brown, February 10, 1904, Brown Papers.
58 Tracy to Brown, February 8, 1904, Brown Papers; Boston *Evening Transcript,* February 27, 1904.
59 Boston *Evening Transcript,* February 27, 1904.
60 Tracy to Brown, February 9, 10, 1904, Brown Papers; Tracy to O'Brien, February 10, 1904, Brown Papers.
61 The itinerary, the dates of the letters, and the issues of the Boston *Evening Transcript* in which they were published follow: Washington, D.C. (February 25), February 27, 1904, p. 20; Richmond, Va. (March 1), March 5, 1904, p. 20; Durham, N.C. (March 3), March 9, 1904, p. [14]; Pinehurst, N.C. (March 9), March 12, 1904, p. 20; Columbia, S.C. (March 14), March 19, 1904, p. 12; Jacksonville, Fla. (March 21), March 26, 1904, p. 20; Orlando, Fla. (March 23), March 30, 1904, p. 16; Marion, Ala. (March 26), April 2, 1904, p. 20; Birmingham, Ala. (April 1), April 13, 1904, p. 16; Jackson, Miss. (April 2), April 20, 1904, p. 18; Greenville, Miss. (April 4), April 23, 1904, p. 26; Vicksburg, Miss. (April 7),

April 27, 1904, p. 18; New Orleans, La. (April 8), April 30, 1904, p. 26; Houston, Tex. (April 12), May 4, 1904, p. 18; College Station, Tex. (April 14), May 7, 1904, p. 26; Santa Gertrudes Ranch, Tex. (April 16), May 11, 1904, p. 8; Austin, Tex. (April 19), May 18, 1904, p. 18; Cleburne, Tex. (April 28), May 21, 1904, p. 36; Cleburne, Tex. (May 14), May 28, 1904, p. 27; St. Louis, Mo. (May 28), June 1, 1904, p. [24].

62 *Evening Transcript,* June 1, 1904.

63 *Evening Transcript,* February 27, 1904.

64 *Evening Transcript,* March 9, 26, 1904.

65 *Evening Transcript,* April 30, May 4, 7, 11, 18, 21, 28, 1904.

66 *Evening Transcript,* March 26, April 23, 1904.

67 *Evening Transcript,* May 28, 1904.

68 *Ibid.*

69 *Harvard College, Class of 1891, Secretary's Report, No. 2,* p. 13; *Harvard College, Class of 1891, Secretary's Report, No. 3,* pp. 9–10.

70 Brown to Martin, July 2, 1910, Brown Papers.

71 *Harper's Weekly,* LIII (March 6, 1909), 7, 9. These articles were reprinted in William G. Brown, *The New Politics and Other Papers* (Boston, 1914), 197–205, 206–15.

72 Photostat of letter, "Mark" to "Dear Colonel," *Harper's Weekly,* LIII (March 20, 1909), 6. George Harvey appended a note: "We did not write the articles so highly and so justly commended by Mr. Clemens. Both were composed by Mr. William Garrott Brown, a frequent and esteemed contributor to these columns."

73 *Harper's Weekly,* LVII (March 1, 1913), 6–7; *Harper's Weekly* (March 8, 1913), 7. These articles were reprinted in Brown, *New Politics and Other Papers,* 216–25, 226–35.

74 *Harper's Weekly,* LIII (February 6, 1909), 4; *Harper's Weekly,* LIII (March 20, 1909), 4; *Harper's Weekly,* LIII (May 29, 1909), 4; *Harper's Weekly,* LIII (June 5, 1909), 4; *Harper's Weekly,* LIII (November 13, 1909), 4–5; *Harper's Weekly,* LIV (August 13, 1910), 4. See also William G. Brown, "President Taft's Opportunity," *Century,* LXXVIII (June, 1909), 252–59, reprinted in Brown, *New Politics and Other Papers,* 165–94.

75 *Harper's Weekly,* LII (November 7, 1908), 4; *Harper's Weekly,* LII (November 28, 1908), 4–5.

76 *Harper's Weekly,* LIII (January 9, 1909), 5; *Harper's Weekly,* LIV (January 15, 1910), 4–5; *Harper's Weekly,* LIV (February 26, 1910), 5; *Harper's Weekly,* LIV (April 16, 1910), 4; *Harper's Weekly,* LIV (May 21, 1910), 4–5; *Harper's Weekly,* LIV (June 11, 1910), 5; *Harper's Weekly,* LIV (July 9, 1910), 5; *Harper's Weekly,* LIV (August 13, 1910), 4; Brown to Martin, July 2, 1910, Brown Papers; Brown to John M. Morehead, July 4, 1910, Brown Papers; Brown to Eugene L. Brown, July 4, 1910, Brown Papers; A. Piatt Andrew to Brown, September 19, 1910, Brown Papers.

77 Thomas Settle to Brown, March 4, 1910, Brown Papers; Morehead to Brown, March 10, April 16, May 25, 1910, Brown Papers.

78 *Harper's Weekly,* LIV (August 20, 1910), 4; Gilliam Grissom to Brown, July 23, 1910, Brown Papers; Settle to Brown, July 27, August 3, 1910, Brown Papers; Morehead to Brown, August 3, 1910, Brown Papers; Brown to Morehead, October 21, 1910, Brown Papers; Brown to Andrew, September 22, 1910, Brown Papers.

79 *Harper's Weekly,* LIV (November 26, 1910), 4.

80 Andrew to Brown, September 19, 28 (telegram), 29 (telegram), 1910, Brown Papers; Brown to Andrew, September 22, 1910, Brown Papers.

81 William H. Taft to Brown, November 3, 1910, Brown Papers. See also, for Brown's interviews and correspondence with Taft's secretary, Brown to More-

head, October 21, 1910, Brown Papers; Andrew to Brown, November 3, 1910, Brown Papers. For reply to the President's letter, see Brown to Taft, November 7, 1910, Brown Papers.

82 Brown to Taft, May 30, 1911, Brown Papers.

83 Brown to Andrew, May 30, 1911, Brown Papers; Brown to Henry C. Lodge, May 30, 1911, Brown Papers; Brown to Samuel W. McCall, May 30, 1911, Brown Papers; Lodge to Brown, June 1, 1911, Brown Papers.

84 Charles D. Hillis to Brown, June 17, 1911, Brown Papers.

85 Brown to editor of the New York *Times*, January 3, 1911, Brown Papers.

86 Brown to Martin, November 27, December 6, 1911, Brown Papers; Martin to Brown, December 4, 1911, Brown Papers; Rollo Ogden to Brown, December 11, 1911, Brown Papers.

87 Brown to Martin, May 19, 1909, Brown Papers.

88 Martin to Brown, November 8, 1911, Brown Papers.

89 Brown to Woodrow Wilson, October 30, 1911, Brown Papers. Writing to Andrew about his Wilson letter, Brown said: "The La Follette crowd are going to make Taft wish he had taken me seriously." Brown to Andrew, November 2, 1911, Brown Papers.

90 Wilson to Brown, November 7, 1911, Brown Papers.

91 Brown to Martin, November 10, 17, 1911, Brown Papers. See also Brown to Andrew, November 10, 1911, Brown Papers, in which Brown wrote: "You never saw a franker, manlier letter."

92 House to Brown, December 7, 14, 1911, Brown Papers; William F. McCombs to Brown, December 20, 1911, Brown Papers.

93 Martin to Brown, January 5, 1912, Brown Papers; Brown to Martin, January 7, February 8, 1912, Brown Papers; Eugene L. Brown to Martin, January 24, 1912, Brown Papers.

94 Smith to Brown, January 11, 1912, Brown Papers.

95 Brown to Smith, May 5, July 3, 1912, Brown Papers.

96 House to Brown, March 18, 1912, Brown Papers. See also House to Brown, April 9, December 8, 1912; February 28, March 15, 21, April 10, 1913, Brown Papers.

97 Brown to Martin, January 23, 1913, Brown Papers.

98 Brown to Martin, January 30, 1913, Brown Papers.

99 Brown to Martin, March 2, 1913, Brown Papers.

100 Brown to Martin, April 3, 17, 1913, Brown Papers; House to Brown, April 10, 23, 1913, Brown Papers.

101 Brown to Andrew, December 7, 1911, Brown Papers.

CHAPTER II

1 Originally published in the *Maryland Historical Magazine,* XLII (March, 1947), 1–20.

2 A possible exception to this statement was Charles E. A. Gayarré, whose *History of Louisiana* (4 vols.; New York, 1854–1866), possessed considerable literary charm.

3 *Southern Historical Society Papers* (Richmond, 1876–1910; 1914——).

4 See Wendell H. Stephenson, "A Half Century of Southern Historical Scholarship," *Journal of Southern History,* XI (February, 1945), 4–8.

5 Colyer Meriwether, in *Publications of the Southern History Association* (Washington, 1897–1907), V (1901), 448.

6 New York *Evangelist,* March 29, 1900, reprinted in Johns Hopkins University *Circulars,* XX, No. 149 (January, 1901), 23. A portion of the statement also ap-

peared in *Twenty-Sixth Annual Report of the President of the Johns Hopkins University . . . 1901* (Baltimore, 1901), 31–32.

7 *Eleventh Annual Report of the President of the Johns Hopkins University . . . 1886* (Baltimore, 1886), 16. For a sketch of the university's founder, see Broadus Mitchell, "Johns Hopkins," *Dictionary of American Biography,* IX, 213–14.

8 *Eleventh Annual Report of the President of the Johns Hopkins University . . . 1886,* pp. 13, 16.

9 New York *Evangelist,* March 29, 1900, reprinted in *Circulars.* The figures in this paragraph must be discounted, as it cannot be assumed that all residents of Maryland and other states south of the line were actually southerners.

10 *Ibid.*

11 *Sewanee Review,* VIII (April, 1900), 248.

12 Burr J. Ramage, "Professor Herbert Baxter Adams," *Herbert B. Adams: Tributes of Friends; with a Bibliography of the Department of History, Politics and Economics of the Johns Hopkins University, 1876–1901* (Baltimore, 1902), 63; hereinafter cited as *Herbert B. Adams: Tributes of Friends.*

13 For biographical data, see John M. Vincent, "Herbert B. Adams, A Biographical Sketch," *Herbert B. Adams: Tributes of Friends,* 9–23; Richard T. Ely, "A Sketch of the Life and Services of Herbert Baxter Adams," *Herbert B. Adams: Tributes of Friends,* 27–49; John M. Vincent, "Herbert B. Adams," Howard W. Odum (ed.), *American Masters of Social Science* (New York, 1927), 97–127, a rewriting of Vincent's earlier sketch; John S. Bassett, "Herbert Baxter Adams," *Dictionary of American Biography,* I, 69–71.

14 Vincent, "Herbert B. Adams, A Biographical Sketch," *Herbert B. Adams: Tributes of Friends,* 21.

15 Ely, "Sketch of the Life and Services of Herbert Baxter Adams," *Herbert B. Adams: Tributes of Friends,* 35, 41–42.

16 Frederick J. Turner to William E. Dodd, October 7, 1917, William E. Dodd Papers (Manuscript Division, Library of Congress, Washington, D.C.). See also Wendell H. Stephenson, "The Influence of Woodrow Wilson on Frederick Jackson Turner," *Agricultural History,* XIX (October, 1945), 252.

17 Quoted in Ely, "Sketch of the Life and Services of Herbert Baxter Adams," *Herbert B. Adams: Tributes of Friends,* 45.

18 Quoted *ibid.,* 46.

19 Herbert B. Adams, *The Study of History in American Colleges and Universities* (Washington, 1887), 171–99, including pictures and floor plan of the historical seminary; *The Johns Hopkins University . . . Register for 1896–97* (Baltimore, 1897), 100–108; Vincent, "Herbert B. Adams," in Odum (ed.), *American Masters of Social Science,* 106–108; W. Stull Holt (ed.), *Historical Scholarship in the United States, 1876–1901: As Revealed in the Correspondence of Herbert B. Adams* (Baltimore, 1938), 18; hereinafter cited as *Historical Scholarship in the United States.*

20 *Johns Hopkins University . . . Register for 1896–97,* p. 105; Vincent, "Herbert B. Adams," in Odum (ed.), *American Masters of Social Science,* 124–25.

21 "Johns Hopkins University Historical Seminary Records," 1877–1901 (Johns Hopkins University library, Baltimore, Md.). The first volume covers the period, 1877–1892; the second, 1892–1901.

22 Compiled from *Herbert B. Adams: Tributes of Friends,* bibliographical section, 3–160.

23 Ray A. Billington to the writer, and enclosure, July 30, 1963. The enclosure consists of excerpts from Dr. Billington's notes on F. J. Turner's appraisals of Turner's work at the Johns Hopkins, for which the writer is most grateful. See also Merle E. Curti, *Historiadores de America: Frederick Jackson Turner* (Mexico, D.F., 1949), 16–17.

24 *Johns Hopkins University . . . Register for 1896–97,* pp. 105–107.

25 *Ibid.*, 106.

26 W. Stull Holt, "John Thomas Scharf," *Dictionary of American Biography*, XVI, 420. See also, for the Birney and Scharf collections, *Sixteenth Annual Report of the President of the Johns Hopkins University . . . 1891* (Baltimore, 1891), 14–17.

27 Quoted in William K. Boyd, "Southern History in American Universities," *South Atlantic Quarterly*, I (July, 1902), 240.

28 *Eighteenth Annual Report of the President of the Johns Hopkins University . . . 1893* (Baltimore, 1893), 89; *Nineteenth Annual Report of the President of the Johns Hopkins University . . . 1894* (Baltimore, 1894), 113; *Twenty-Third Annual Report of the President of the Johns Hopkins University . . . 1898* (Baltimore, 1898), 89; *Twenty-Fourth Annual Report of the President of the Johns Hopkins University . . . 1899* (Baltimore, 1899), 88, 94; *Twenty-Fifth Annual Report of the President of the Johns Hopkins University . . . 1900* (Baltimore, 1900), 97, 99; *Twenty-Sixth Annual Report of the President of the Johns Hopkins University . . . 1901* (Baltimore, 1901), 26, 109; *Johns Hopkins University . . . Register for 1896–97*, p. 105.

29 The librarian reported as early as 1892 that the collection of materials on southern history contained 3,000 volumes. *Seventeenth Annual Report of the President of the Johns Hopkins University . . . 1892* (Baltimore, 1892), 85.

30 "Johns Hopkins University Historical Seminary Records." 1877–1901, *passim.*

31 *Sixteenth Annual Report of the President of the Johns Hopkins University . . . 1891* (Baltimore, 1891), 10, 60; *Twenty-Sixth Annual Report of the President of the Johns Hopkins University . . . 1901*, p. 81. John S. Bassett to Adams, June 21, October 23, November 14, December 15, 1899; April 1, November 2, 1900, Adams Papers. Bassett to John M. Vincent, February 5, 1900, January 15, 1901, Adams Papers.

32 *Twenty-Third Annual Report of the President of the Johns Hopkins University . . . 1898*, pp. 63–64.

33 *Twenty-Eighth Annual Report of the President* [*of the Johns Hopkins University*] *. . . 1903* (Baltimore [1903?]), 56. Sometime during the 1902–1903 session, George Petrie of the Alabama Polytechnic Institute "exhibited his collection of the manuscripts of William L. Yancey to the students and discussed their use."

34 *Twenty-Sixth Annual Report of the President of the Johns Hopkins University . . . 1901*, p. 83.

35 See *Report of the President of the Johns Hopkins University . . . 1904* (Baltimore, 1904), 61; and the report for each year to 1913. Occasionally neither course was offered.

36 Wendell H. Stephenson, "History of the South in Colleges and Universities, 1925–1926," *Historical Outlook*, XVII (November, 1926), 319–22.

37 Holt (ed.), *Historical Scholarship in the United States*, *passim;* and sundry letters in the Adams Papers not included in the Holt volume.

38 *Publications of the Southern History Association*, V (1901), 501.

39 *Herbert B. Adams: Tributes of Friends*, bibliographical section, 3–160.

40 Boyd, "Southern History in American Universities," *South Atlantic Quarterly*, I (July, 1902), 241.

41 Notes on Johns Hopkins men have been compiled from sketches in *Dictionary of American Biography*, *passim;* the bibliographical section of *Herbert B. Adams: Tributes of Friends*, 3–160; *Who Was Who in America . . . 1897–1942* (Chicago, 1942), *passim; Who's Who in America*, XXIII (Chicago, 1944), *passim;* and the private papers of several of them.

42 William A. Dunning to Bassett, January 18, August 25, September 6, October 1, 1903, John Spencer Bassett Papers (Manuscript Division, Library of Congress); Ira Remsen to Bassett, August 8, 31, 1903, Bassett Papers; Bassett to Remsen,

August 24, 1903, Bassett Papers; Frederic Bancroft to Bassett, August 28, 1903, Bassett Papers.

CHAPTER III

1 Originally published in the *Journal of Southern History,* XV (May, 1949), 151–77.
2 William P. Trent's work as a historian is discussed briefly in Wendell H. Stephenson, "A Half Century of Southern Historical Scholarship," *Journal of Southern History,* XI (February, 1945), 12–15. Franklin T. Walker, "William Peterfield Trent—A Critical Biography" (Ph.D. dissertation, George Peabody College for Teachers, 1943), is a meritorious study of his whole career. For a bibliography of Trent's writings in the period covered by this essay, see *Herbert B. Adams: Tributes of Friends, with a Bibliography of the Department of History, Politics and Economics of the Johns Hopkins University, 1876–1901* (Baltimore, 1902), bibliographical section, 135–39. For a critical view of Trent's appraisal of William Gilmore Simms, see Mary C. Simms Oliphant *et al.* (eds.), *The Letters of William Gilmore Simms* (5 vols.; Columbia, 1952–1956), I, xxxiii–xxxvi.
3 "Johns Hopkins University Historical Seminary Records," 1877–1892, (Johns Hopkins University library), 395–99.
4 Herbert B. Adams, *Thomas Jefferson and the University of Virginia* (Washington, 1888), 150–75, 218–25.
5 "Johns Hopkins University Historical Seminary Records," 1877–1892, pp. 562–63.
6 William P. Trent, *English Culture in Virginia* (Baltimore, 1889), 7–8, *et passim.* For Trent's method of treatment, see Trent to Herbert B. Adams, December 9, 1888, Herbert Baxter Adams Papers (Johns Hopkins University library, Baltimore, Md.).
7 "Johns Hopkins University Historical Seminary Records," 1877–1892, pp. 483–91. On March 1, 1894, a few years after Trent joined the faculty of the University of the South, he addressed the seminary on some current historical works. "Johns Hopkins University Historical Seminary Records," 1892–1901, p. 113.
8 *University of the South Papers,* Ser. B, No. 41, *Calendar for 1888–89* (Sewanee, 1888), 42–43, and subsequent catalogues.
9 Trent to Adams, June 9, 1890, Adams Papers. At this time he was also teaching classes in French and German for a colleague on leave.
10 Trent to Adams, November 13, 1890, in W. Stull Holt (ed.), *Historical Scholarship in the United States, 1876–1901: As Revealed in the Correspondence of Herbert B. Adams* (Baltimore, 1938), 142. See also Trent to Adams, November 24, 1890, April 17, 1891, Adams Papers; William E. Boggs to Trent, November 20, 1890, Adams Papers.
11 Trent to Adams, March 10, 1893, Adams Papers.
12 See E. Merton Coulter, "What the South Has Done About Its History," *Journal of Southern History,* II (February, 1936), 24.
13 William P. Trent, "Notes on the Outlook for Historical Studies in the South," in American Historical Association, *Papers* (5 vols.; New York, 1885–1891), IV, 381–91.
14 William P. Trent, "Notes on Recent Work in Southern History," *Collections of the Virginia Historical Society* (Richmond, 1892), N.S., XI, 59.
15 *Ibid.,* 54.
16 *Ibid.,* 55–56.
17 *Ibid.,* 57–58.

18 William P. Trent, "The Study of Southern History," in Vanderbilt Southern History Society, *Publications* (Nashville, 1895), I, *passim*.
19 J. Franklin Jameson (ed.), *Essays in the Constitutional History of the United States in the Formative Period, 1775–1789* (Boston, 1889), 186–262.
20 William P. Trent, "The Case of Josiah Philips," *American Historical Review*, I (April, 1896), 444–54, see 444–45. See also Trent to Adams, February 25, 1890, April 24, 1894, Adams Papers.
21 Trent to Adams, September 30, November 14, 1890, Adams Papers.
22 William P. Trent, *William Gilmore Simms* (Boston, 1892), v.
23 Trent to Adams, March 5, 1891, Adams Papers.
24 Trent, *William Gilmore Simms*, 333–42.
25 Trent to Adams, June 9, September 30, November 14, 1890, March 5, April 17, 1891, Adams Papers.
26 Trent to Charles D. Warner, June 11, 1892, in Walker, "William Peterfield Trent," 135.
27 Trent, *William Gilmore Simms*, vi–vii.
28 *Ibid.*, 36–37, 147–48.
29 *Ibid.*, 37, 39, 41.
30 *Ibid.*, 56, 104–105.
31 *Ibid.*, 169.
32 *Ibid.*, 289–90.
33 Trent appended a footnote to this statement: "Poe is excepted, as the South's claim to him is not unimpeachable." *Ibid.*, 44.
34 *Ibid.*, 75–76, 88, 101, 143, 236, 321–22, 330–32.
35 Charleston *News and Courier*, March 31, 1892.
36 *News and Courier*, April 18, 1892.
37 *News and Courier*, May 30, 1892.
38 *News and Courier*, July 25, 1892. See also *News and Courier*, August 20, 1892; an article on "'Writing Down' the South," Baltimore *Sun*, quoted in Charleston *Sunday News*, September 4, 1892; Richmond *Times*, July 24, 1892; [Virginius Dabney], "Liberal of the Nineties," an editorial in the Richmond *Times-Dispatch*, December 9, 1939; Virginius Dabney, *Liberalism in the South* (Chapel Hill, 1932), 226.
39 [Theodore Roosevelt], "Recent Biography," *Atlantic Monthly*, LXIX (June, 1892), 838–40.
40 Brander Matthews, "Two Studies of the South," *Cosmopolitan*, XIV (November, 1892), 125, 127.
41 Trent to Brander Matthews, October 25, 1892, Brander Matthews Collection (Low Memorial Library, Columbia University, New York).
42 William P. Trent, *Southern Statesmen of the Old Régime* (New York, 1897), vii.
43 *Ibid.*, x–xiv, 50, 96.
44 See especially *ibid.*, 18–19, 22–23, 32, 42–43.
45 *Ibid.*, 49–50, 60, 67–69, 78, 83. Trent correctly assigned the Kentucky and Virginia Resolutions more significance as political documents than as constitutional interpretations. *Ibid.*, 75.
46 *Ibid.*, 91.
47 *Ibid.*, 155, 158, 169–71, 191.
48 *Ibid.*, 199.
49 *Ibid.*, 259, 261–62.
50 *Ibid.*, 181.
51 William P. Trent, *Robert E. Lee* (Boston, 1899), ix–x.
52 *Ibid.*, 31–34, 36.
53 John B. Henneman, "Ten Years of the Sewanee Review: A Retrospect," *Sewanee Review*, X (October, 1902), 478.
54 *Ibid.*, 478–79.

55 Quoted in Alice L. Turner, *A Study of the Content of the Sewanee Review, with Historical Introduction* (Nashville, 1931), 3–4.
56 For an appraisal of the *Sewanee Review,* 1892–1902, see Edwin Mims, "Literary Notes," *South Atlantic Quarterly,* II (July, 1903), 290–94; for a more recent estimate, Dabney, *Liberalism in the South,* 227.
57 *Sewanee Review,* VIII (October, 1900), 512. See also Turner, *Study of the Content of the Sewanee Review,* 12.
58 Turner, *Study of the Content of the Sewanee Review,* 8–9, 108.
59 William P. Trent, "A New South View of Reconstruction," *Sewanee Review,* IX (January, 1901), 13–29. This was a lecture delivered before the Vassar Brothers Institute, Poughkeepsie, N.Y., March 6, 1900.
60 Walter H. Page to Trent, August 22, 1896, Walter H. Page Collection (Houghton Reading Room, Harvard College library, Cambridge, Mass.)
61 William P. Trent, "Dominant Forces in Southern Life," *Atlantic Monthly,* LXXIX (January, 1897), 42–53; and, by the same author, "Tendencies of Higher Life in the South," *Atlantic Monthly,* LXXIX (June, 1897), 766–78.
62 Trent to Adams, January 8, 1898, Holt (ed.), *Historical Scholarship in the United States,* 249–50.
63 Trent to Yates Snowden, May 6, 1913, Yates Snowden Collection (South Caroliniana Library, University of South Carolina, Columbia, S.C.).
64 Trent to Snowden, March 23, 1915, Snowden Collection.
65 Trent to John S. Bassett, April 12, 1900, John Spencer Bassett Papers (Manuscript Division, Library of Congress, Washington, D.C.).
66 Trent contributed an introduction to a new edition of Frederick L. Olmsted, *A Journey in the Seaboard Slave States, In the Years 1853–1854, With Remarks on Their Economy* (2 vols.; New York, 1904). The introduction is not meritorious.

CHAPTER IV

1 Originally published in the *North Carolina Historical Review,* XXV (July, 1948), 289–317.
2 See Chapter II.
3 Transcript memoir, John Spencer Bassett Papers (Manuscript Division, Library of Congress, Washington, D.C.).
4 John S. Bassett to Herbert B. Adams, July 31, 1895; January 16, 1896; November 15, December 16, 1898; April 3, 1899; December 7, 1900, W. Stull Holt (ed.), *Historical Scholarship in the United States, 1876–1901: As Revealed in the Correspondence of Herbert B. Adams* (Baltimore, 1938), 238–39, 242–43, 256–59, 261–62, 269–71, 291–92; hereinafter cited as *Historical Scholarship in the United States.* Bassett to Adams, January 24, April 17, 18, May 12, 1898; June 13, 21, October 23, December 15, 1899; April 1, May 27, June 17, November 2, 1900; February 3, 17, March 5, April 21, 1901, Herbert Baxter Adams Papers (Johns Hopkins University library, Baltimore, Md.). Adams to Bassett, May 15, November 27, 1896; January 14, 1897. June 19, 1900; February 27, May 9, 1901, Bassett Papers.
5 Bassett to Adams, February 17, 1901, Adams Papers.
6 Bassett to Adams, January 16, 1896, Holt (ed.), *Historical Scholarship in the United States,* 243.
7 Adams to Bassett, May 15, 1896, Adams Papers.
8 Adams to Bassett, November 27, 1896, Bassett Papers.
9 Adams to Bassett, January 14, 1897, Bassett Papers.
10 Bassett to Adams, January 24, 1898, Adams Papers.
11 Bassett to Adams, May 27, 1900, Adams Papers.

12 Bassett to Adams, November 15, 1898, Holt (ed.), *Historical Scholarship in the United States,* 256–57.
13 Bassett to Adams, January 24, 1898, Adams Papers.
14 Charles C. Weaver to Bassett, November 24, 1897, Bassett Papers. See also Bassett to Adams, January 24, April 17, 1898, June 13, 1899, Adams Papers; Bassett to Adams, April 3, 1899, Holt (ed.), *Historical Scholarship in the United States,* 270.
15 Mrs. N. B. McDowell to Bassett, February 11, 1897, Bassett Papers.
16 Quotations are from Bassett to Adams, January 24, 1898, May 27, 1900, Adams Papers. See also Bassett to Adams, June 17, 1900, April 21, 1901, Adams Papers; Adams to Bassett, June 19, 1900, May 9, 1901, Bassett Papers.
17 Nat C. Newbold to Bassett, March 4, 1897, Bassett Papers.
18 J. A. Baldwin to Bassett, March 22, 1897, Bassett Papers; Edward S. Yarbrough to Bassett, April 10, 1897, Bassett Papers.
19 R. E. Hunt to Bassett, February 13, 1897, Bassett Papers.
20 Bassett to William E. Dodd, February 2, 1904, William E. Dodd Papers (Manuscript Division, Library of Congress, Washington, D.C.).
21 Trinity College *Catalogus for the Year 1896–'97* (Durham, 1897), 50, 63; *Catalogus for the year 1897–'98* (Durham, 1898), 53.
22 Address to the society, October 13, 1904, Nannie M. Tilley, *The Trinity College Historical Society, 1892–1941* (Durham, 1941), 49–50.
23 Trinity College *Catalogue for the Year 1899–1900* (Durham, 1900), 61; *Catalogue for the Year 1901–1902* (Durham, 1902), 66.
24 Quoted in Tilley, *Trinity College Historical Society,* 12–13.
25 *Ibid.,* 26–27.
26 *Ibid.,* 29 n, 37, *et passim.*
27 Bassett to Adams, April 17, May 22, 1898; June 13, 1899; November 2, 1900, Adams Papers. Bassett to Adams, December 7, 1900, Holt (ed.), *Historical Scholarship in the United States,* 292.
28 Bassett to Adams, January 16, 1896, Holt (ed.), *Historical Scholarship in the United States,* 242–43. See also *Publications of the Southern History Association* (Washington, 1897–1907), I (1897), 234.
29 Bassett to Adams, September 26, 1897, Holt (ed.), *Historical Scholarship in the United States,* 246.
30 The speech is quoted in Tilley, *Trinity College Historical Society,* 51–59.
31 Transcript memoir, Bassett Papers.
32 Bassett to John M. Vincent, November 27, December 8, 1901, Adams Papers.
33 Bassett to Vincent, November 2, 1902, Adams Papers.
34 Bassett to Henry G. Connor, November 12, 1901, Henry G. Connor Papers (University of North Carolina library, Chapel Hill, N.C.); Bassett to Vincent, December 8, 1901, Adams Papers; "Editor's Announcement," *South Atlantic Quarterly,* I (January, 1902), 1–3.
35 Charles L. Raper to Bassett, February 2, 1902, Bassett Papers; Dodd to Bassett, February 6, 1902, Bassett Papers; Burr J. Ramage to Bassett, May 1, 1902, Bassett Papers. Raper was piqued at Bassett because of an unfavorable review of his *North Carolina: A Royal Province, 1729–1775* (Chapel Hill, 1901). See *South Atlantic Quarterly,* I (January, 1902), 93–94.
36 Edwin A. Alderman to Bassett, October 19, 1903, Bassett Papers.
37 Charles M. Andrews to Bassett, May, 1902, Bassett Papers.
38 See, for example, W. Roy Smith to Bassett, February 13, 1902, Bassett Papers; Dodd to Bassett, April 28, 1902, February 5, 1903, Bassett Papers; Thomas M. Owen to Bassett, July 14, 1902, Bassett Papers; Bernard C. Steiner to Bassett, July 15, 1902, November 2, 1903, Bassett Papers; Franklin L. Riley to Bassett, November 10, 1902, Bassett Papers; Charles F. Smith to Bassett, November 22, 1902,

Bassett Papers; *American Historical Review,* VII (July, 1902), 822; *Sewanee Review,* X (April, 1902), 251–52.

39 [John S. Bassett], "The Bottom of the Matter," *South Atlantic Quarterly,* I (April, 1902), 99–106.

40 [John S. Bassett], "The Problems of the Author in the South," *South Atlantic Quarterly,* I (July, 1902), 201–208.

41 [John S. Bassett], "The Reign of Passion," *South Atlantic Quarterly,* I (October, 1902), 301–309.

42 [John S. Bassett], "Stirring Up the Fires of Race Antipathy," *South Atlantic Quarterly,* II (October, 1903), 297–305.

43 This subject is discussed more fully in the following chapter.

44 William E. Dodd, "Some Difficulties of the History Teacher in the South," *South Atlantic Quarterly,* III (April, 1904), 117–22.

45 [John S. Bassett], "The Task of the Critic," *South Atlantic Quarterly,* III (October, 1904), 297–301.

46 *South Atlantic Quarterly,* I (January, 1902), 73–81; *South Atlantic Quarterly,* II (April, 1903), 107–13; *South Atlantic Quarterly* III (April, 1904), 99–108; *South Atlantic Quarterly,* III (October, 1904), 370–76.

47 *South Atlantic Quarterly,* I (April, 1902), 107–17.

48 *Ibid.,* 156–61.

49 *South Atlantic Quarterly,* II (April, 1903), 114–24; *South Atlantic Quarterly,* II (July, 1903), 246–60.

50 *South Atlantic Quarterly,* II (July, 1903), 231–36; *South Atlantic Quarterly,* III (January, 1904), 1–10.

51 *South Atlantic Quarterly,* II (October, 1903), 346–58; *South Atlantic Quarterly,* III, (January, 1904), 39–51.

52 *South Atlantic Quarterly,* IV (January, 1905), 71–77.

53 *Ibid.,* 91.

54 American Historical Association, *Annual Report,* 1894 (Washington, 1895), 141–212. For Bassett's brief paper, "Suffrage in the State of North Carolina," see *Annual Report,* 1895 (Washington, 1896), 269–85.

55 Johns Hopkins University *Studies in Historical and Political Science,* XII (Baltimore, 1894), no. 3.

56 *Studies in Historical and Political Science,* XIV (Baltimore, 1896), nos. 4–5.

57 *Studies in Historical and Political Science,* XVI (Baltimore, 1898), no. 6.

58 *Studies in Historical and Political Science,* XVII (Baltimore, 1899), nos. 7–8.

59 John S. Bassett, "The Regulators of North Carolina," American Historical Association, *Annual Report,* 1894, pp. 141–43, 211.

60 J. Franklin Jameson to Bassett, April 19, 1901, Bassett Papers.

61 Albert B. Hart to Bassett, October 22, 1904, Bassett Papers.

62 Hart to Bassett, October 10, 1905, Bassett Papers.

63 Hart to Bassett, November 4, 1904, Bassett Papers.

64 William MacDonald, in *American Historical Review,* XVII (April, 1912), 625.

65 William A. Dunning to Bassett, December 15, 1911, Bassett Papers; Bassett to Dunning, December 18, 1911, Bassett Papers.

66 American Historical Association, *Annual Report,* 1902 (Washington, 1903), I, 38; Charles H. Haskins to Bassett, January 6, 1902, Bassett Papers.

67 Bassett to Adams, December 18, 1900, Holt (ed.), *Historical Scholarship in the United States,* 292–93. See also Frederick W. Moore to Bassett, December 11, 1900, Bassett Papers.

68 Bassett to Haskins, November 13, 1901, "A. H. A., Invitations from Various Organizations for the Annual Meeting," American Historical Association Papers (Manuscript Division, Library of Congress, Washington, D.C.); Haskins to

Bassett, December 7, 1901, Bassett Papers. See also Henry E. Bourne to Bassett, October 6, 1903, Bassett Papers, for request asking Bassett's help in increasing membership in the South.

69 Jameson to Bassett, April 29, 1901, Bassett Papers.

70 Haskins to Bassett, July 15, October 4, November 9, 1901, Bassett Papers; Bassett to Lyon G. Tyler, August 18, 1901, "A. H. A. Programmes of Annual Meetings and Correspondence, 1896, '97, '99, 1900–1906," American Historical Association Papers; Charles H. Haskins, "Report of the Proceedings of the Seventeenth Annual Meeting of the American Historical Association," American Historical Association, *Annual Report,* 1901 (Washington, 1902), I, 29–31.

71 Dodd to Bassett, November 1, 1901, Bassett Papers; David Y. Thomas to Bassett, December 19, 1901, Bassett Papers.

72 Moore to Bassett, January 4, 29, July 8, September 17, 1902; January 23, 1903, Bassett Papers. Charles H. Haskins, "Report of the Proceedings of the Eighteenth Annual Meeting of the American Historical Association," American Historical Association, *Annual Report,* 1902, I, 31–32; Frederick W. Moore, "The Teaching of History in the South," *Vanderbilt University Quarterly* (1903), 8–27.

73 Frederick W. Moore, "The Status of History in Southern Colleges," *South Atlantic Quarterly,* II (April, 1903), 169–71.

74 Dunning to Bassett, March 9, October 21, 1903, January 6, 1904, Bassett Papers; Dodd to Bassett, March 23, 1903, February 11, 1904, Bassett Papers; Bassett to Dodd, March 25, November 9, 1903, Dodd Papers; Brevard Nixon to Bassett, January 3, 1903 [1904?], Bassett Papers.

75 Charles D. Hazen to Bassett, April or May, May 10, 15, 1906, Bassett Papers; Bassett to Hazen, May 3, 12, June 8, 10, 1906, Bassett Papers; Bassett to Julius Seelye, May 30, 1906, Bassett Papers. For Bassett's resignation at Trinity College, see Bassett to John C. Kilgo, May 30, 1906, Bassett Papers.

76 Dunning to Bassett, May 14, 1900, Bassett Papers.

77 Dunning to Bassett, May 19, 1906, Bassett Papers.

78 Bassett to Walter H. Page, May 29, 1906, Bassett Papers.

79 Bassett to William G. Brown, February 15, 1907, Bassett Papers. For Brown's reply, see Brown to Bassett, February 25, 1907, William Garrott Brown Papers (Duke University Library, Durham, N.C.); and for the reaction of two North Carolinians to Bassett's resignation at Trinity College, see J. G. de Roulhac Hamilton to Bassett, June 18, 1906, Bassett Papers; Bassett to Connor, June 11, 1906, Connor Papers.

80 Bassett to Boyd, October 11, 1908, Bassett Papers.

81 John S. Bassett, "Literary Record, October 4, 1917—Aug. 1, 1922," Bassett Papers.

82 Interviews with Mrs. Bassett, November 12–25, 1944.

CHAPTER V

1 Originally published in the *North Carolina Historical Review,* XXV (October, 1948), 427–41.

2 Typescript memoir, John Spencer Bassett Papers (Manuscript Division, Library of Congress, Washington, D.C.).

3 John S. Bassett to Herbert B. Adams, June 21, 1899, Herbert Baxter Adams Papers (Johns Hopkins University library, Baltimore, Md.).

4 Bassett to Adams, October 23, 1899, Adams Papers.

5 Bassett to Adams, December 7, 1900, W. Stull Holt (ed.), *Historical Scholarship in the United States, 1876–1901: As Revealed in the Correspondence of Herbert B. Adams* (Baltimore, 1938), 291; hereinafter cited as *Historical Scholarship in*

the United States. For other correspondence relating to the lectures, see Bassett to Adams, November 14, December 15, 1899, April 1, November 2, 1900; February 3, 1901, Adams Papers; Bassett to John M. Vincent, February 5, 1900, January 15, 1901, Adams Papers; Adams to Bassett, November 17, 1900, Bassett Papers.

6 [John S. Bassett], "The Negro's Inheritance from Africa," *South Atlantic Quarterly,* III (April, 1904), 99–108.

7 Bassett to Vincent, March 13, 1901, Adams Papers.

8 John S. Bassett, *Slavery and Servitude in the Colony of North Carolina* ("Johns Hopkins University Studies in Historical and Political Science," XIV [Baltimore, 1896]), nos. 4–5, pp. 12, 17.

9 John S. Bassett, *Slavery in the State of North Carolina* ("Johns Hopkins University Studies in Historical and Political Science," XVII [Baltimore, 1899]), nos. 7–8, pp. 10, 47, 90–91, 102.

10 Helper is discussed in John S. Bassett, *Anti-Slavery Leaders of North Carolina* ("Johns Hopkins University Studies in Historical and Political Science," XVI [Baltimore, 1898]), no. 6, pp. 11–29. For Hedrick, see *ibid.*, 29–47, especially 35, 42. For correspondence relating to publication of the monograph, see Bassett to Adams, January 24, April 17, 1898, Adams Papers.

11 Bassett to Adams, November 15, 1898, Holt (ed.), *Historical Scholarship in the United States,* 257–59.

12 Bassett to Adams, November 15, December 16, 1898, *ibid.*, 259, 261.

13 Bassett to Adams, May 27, 1900, Adams Papers.

14 [John S. Bassett], "Two Negro Leaders," *South Atlantic Quarterly,* II (July, 1903), 267–72.

15 *South Atlantic Quarterly,* I (April, 1902), 107–17.

16 *South Atlantic Quarterly,* I (July, 1902), 265–68.

17 *South Atlantic Quarterly,* III (October, 1904), 356–60.

18 *South Atlantic Quarterly,* II (October, 1903), 369–85.

19 [John S. Bassett], "Stirring Up the Fires of Race Antipathy," *South Atlantic Quarterly,* II (October, 1903), 297–305.

20 *Ibid.*, 299.

21 For "The Statement of the Trustees," "Memorial from the Faculty to the Trustees," and "Editorial in the Archive," the last representing student opinion, see "Trinity College and Academic Freedom," *South Atlantic Quarterly,* III (January, 1904), 62–72. See also Josephus Daniels, *Editor in Politics* (Chapel Hill, 1941), 428–37; Edwin Mims, *The Advancing South: Stories of Progress and Reaction* (Garden City, N.Y., 1926), 147–57; Virginius Dabney, *Liberalism in the South* (Chapel Hill, 1932), 339–41; "A Notable Victory for Academic Freedom," *World's Work,* VII (January, 1904), 4284–87; "In Memoriam—John Spencer Bassett," *South Atlantic Quarterly,* XXVII (April, 1928), 114–15.

22 Bassett to William K. Boyd, October 11, 1908, Bassett Papers.

23 Bassett to Edwin Mims, January 1, 1909, Bassett Papers.

24 Bassett to Charles Francis Adams, November 3, 1911, Bassett Papers.

25 See Chapter I.

26 Wendell H. Stephenson, "A Half Century of Southern Historical Scholarship," *Journal of Southern History,* XI (February, 1945), 12.

27 Bassett to William E. Dodd, May 7, 1907, Bassett Papers.

28 Bassett to Boyd, October 11, 1908, Bassett Papers.

29 Bassett to Boyd, January 2, 1912, Bassett Papers.

CHAPTER VI

1 Originally published in the *Alabama Review,* I (July, 1948), 164–79. This chapter is an expansion of part of a paper read before the Alabama Historical Association at Montgomery, April 17, 1948. The other segments considered Walter L. Fleming, Thomas M. Owen, and William Garrott Brown.
2 Thomas M. Owen, *History of Alabama and Dictionary of Alabama Biography* (4 vols.; Chicago, 1921), IV, 1351.
3 *Dictionary of American Biography,* XVI, 423–24; V, 140–41; XIX, 245–46. For these and other professors at the University of Virginia under whom Petrie studied, see Philip A. Bruce, *History of the University of Virginia, 1819–1919* (5 vols.; New York, 1920–1922), III–IV, *passim.*
4 Jack Dalton, associate librarian, University of Virginia, to the writer, April 17, 1948. An enclosure lists the courses Petrie took, arranged by sessions, and the faculty members who taught them.
5 For graduate work in history at Johns Hopkins University, see Chapter II.
6 Irene M. Davis, registrar, Johns Hopkins University, to the writer, April 6, 1948, and enclosure.
7 Interview with George Petrie, October 2, 1944, recorded in Wendell H. Stephenson, "Diary of a Research Tour of the South and East, 1944–1945" (2 vols; unpublished) I, 19–20.
8 Davis to the writer, April 14, 1948, and enclosure.
9 Interview with Petrie, October 2, 1944, recorded in Stephenson, "Diary of a Research Tour of the South and East," I, 20–21.
10 "Johns Hopkins University Historical Seminary Records," 1877–1892 (Johns Hopkins University library, Baltimore, Md.), 696–99, 723–26. The dates of these meetings were April 11 and October 31, 1890.
11 *Ibid.,* 701–706, 707, 716.
12 *Ibid.,* 796–98.
13 Interview with Petrie, October 2, 1944, recorded in Stephenson, "Diary of a Research Tour of the South and East," I, 22.
14 *Catalogue of the State Agricultural and Mechanical College of Alabama, 1884–'85* (Auburn, n.d.), 5, 22.
15 *Catalogue of the State Agricultural and Mechanical College, Alabama Polytechnic Institute, 1885–'86* (Auburn, n.d.), 27.
16 *Catalogue of the State Agricultural and Mechanical College, Alabama Polytechnic Institute, 1886–'87* (Auburn, n.d.), 6, 42.
17 *Catalogue of the State Agricultural and Mechanical College, Alabama Polytechnic Institute, 1892–'93* (Montgomery, 1893), 64. A similar statement had appeared in the catalogue during Petrie's first year at Alabama Polytechnic Institute. See *Catalogue of the State Agricultural and Mechanical College, Alabama Polytechnic Institute, 1887–'88* (Auburn, n.d.), 45. Petrie's career is treated briefly in Wendell H. Stephenson, "A Half Century of Southern Historical Scholarship," *Journal of Southern History,* XI (February, 1945), 15–16.
18 *Catalogue of the State Agricultural and Mechanical College, Alabama Polytechnic Institute, 1885–86* (Auburn, n.d.), 27.
19 *Catalogue of the Alabama Polytechnic Institute . . . 1900* (Montgomery, 1900), 67–68.
20 *Catalogue of the Alabama Polytechnic Institute . . . 1901* (Montgomery, 1901), 77.
21 *Catalogue of the Alabama Polytechnic Institute . . . 1900,* pp. 67–68.
22 Summary of students at Alabama Polytechnic Institute, compiled from the College catalogues, 1891–1911:

Year	*Total*	*Subfreshman*	*History*	*Latin*
1891–1892	225	30	137	72
1892–1893	213	30	124	84
1893–1894	236	20	152	76
1894–1895	252	19	144	103
1895–1896	265	32	178	106
1896–1897	314	43	196	144
1897–1898	312	29	168	141
1898–1899	318	38	181	157
1899–1900	346	38	205	137
1900–1901	357	55	208	119
1901–1902	348	58	227	101
1902–1903	337	57	233	103
1903–1904	425	55	276	119
1906–1907	543	57	342	124
1908–1909	701	..	379	111
1909–1910	760	..	368	92
1910–1911	737	..	365	110

23 *Catalogue of the Alabama Polytechnic Institute . . . 1911* (Opelika, 1911), 4–5.

24 See Petrie's article, "What Will Be the Final Estimate of Yancey?" *Transactions of the Alabama Historical Society, 1899–1903* (Montgomery, 1904), IV, 307–12. This paper was reprinted in *Studies in Southern and Alabama History: Papers by Members of the Historical Seminary, Alabama Polytechnic Institute, Auburn* (Alabama Polytechnic Institute "Historical Papers," Ser. I [1904]), 163–68.

25 For correspondence relative to his own and his students' contributions to publications mentioned in this paragraph, and participation in programs of the Alabama Historical Society, see Petrie to Owen, December 17, 1898; February 4, 7, April 30, 1900; February 25, April 24, May 9, June 1, 1901; May 20, 1902; March 15, April 17, 1903; February 2, March 16, May 12, 1904, Owen Papers. Owen to Petrie, March 5, 1902, December 19, 1903, June 25, 29, September 9, December 20, 1904, Owen Papers; Toccoa Cozart to Owen, August 27, 1901, September 27, 1903, Owen Papers; Owen to Cozart, October 2, 1903, Owen Papers; Birmingham *News,* May 6, 1904, clipping enclosed in Petrie to Owen, May 12, 1904, Owen Papers.

Among Petrie's students who contributed to one or more of these publications in the early years of the century were Walter L. Fleming, Gaius Whitfield, Toccoa Cozart, Shepherd H. Roberts, Emma V. Culver, J. E. D. Yonge, George W. Duncan, William Watson Davis, Dallas T. Herndon, and William O. Scroggs.

26 Alfred W. Reynolds, "Auburn Historians (1896–1941)," *Auburn Forum,* II (November, 1941), 9–10, [21].

27 *Alabama Polytechnic Institute Bulletin,* XXXVIII (October, 1942), *passim.*

CHAPTER VII

1 This paper was read at the forty-eighth annual meeting of the Mississippi Valley Historical Association at St. Louis, April 28, 1955.

CHAPTER VIII

1 Originally published in the *Georgia Historical Quarterly,* XLI (June, 1957), 103–25.

2 Susan B. Keane, reference secretary, Tulane University, to the writer, October 8,

1954, and enclosure, Florence Toppino, registrar, to Miss Keane, October 6, 1954.

3 *Annual Announcement of the University of Georgia with a Catalogue of the Officers and Students*, 1893–1894 (Atlanta, 1894), 10–11, 12–17, 18, 26.

4 John H. T. McPherson to Herbert B. Adams, March 28, 1891, Herbert Baxter Adams Papers (Johns Hopkins University library, Baltimore, Md.).

5 Adams' recommendation of McPherson, April 13, 1891, Adams Papers.

6 McPherson to Adams, October 4, 1891, W. Stull Holt (ed.), *Historical Scholarship in the United States, 1876–1901: As Revealed in the Correspondence of Herbert B. Adams* (Baltimore, 1938), 166–67.

7 *Ibid.*, 167.

8 *Ibid.*, 167–68.

9 *Ibid.*, 170.

10 *Annual Announcement of the University of Georgia with a Catalogue of the Officers and Students*, 1893–1894, p. 38.

11 *Ibid.*, 6; *Annual Announcement of the University of Georgia with a Catalogue of the Officers and Students*, 1898–1899 (Atlanta, 1899), 9–10.

12 University of Georgia, transcript of record, 1893–1897, provided through the courtesy of W. N. Danner, registrar, April 9, 1954, in possession of the writer.

13 *Annual Announcement of the University of Georgia with a Catalogue of the Officers and Students*, 1894–1895 (Atlanta, 1895), 22, 25; *Annual Announcement of the University of Georgia with a Catalogue of the Officers and Students*, 1896–1897 (Atlanta, 1897), 29.

14 *Annual Announcement of the University of Georgia with a Catalogue of the Officers and Students*, 1897–1898 (Atlanta, 1898), 19, 32; *Annual Announcement of the University of Georgia with a Catalogue of the Officers and Students*, 1898–1899 (Atlanta, 1899), 17, 21; *Annual Announcement of the University of Georgia with a Catalogue of the Officers and Students*, 1899–1900 (Atlanta, 1900), 17, 19.

15 *Annual Announcement of the University of Georgia with a Catalogue of the Officers and Students*, 1897–1898, p. 19; Danner to the writer, May 3, 1954, personal files.

16 "Graduate Examination in European History. Exam. no. 6. 1815 to the present, May 14, 1897"; "Graduate Examination (Final in Universal History), June 4, 1898" (University of Georgia library, Athens, Ga.), used by the writer through the courtesy of E. Merton Coulter.

17 Ulrich B. Phillips, "The Passing of a Crisis. A Study of the Early History of the University," *Pandora*, XII (Athens, 1899), 11–20, *passim*.

18 Ulrich B. Phillips, "Report on the Local Archives of Georgia: The University of Georgia" (University of Georgia library), used through the courtesy of E. Merton Coulter. Penciled marginal notes appear in the handwriting of R. P. B. (Robert Preston Brooks). The report is 133 half-size legal pages, some manuscript, others typewritten, but pages 7–22 are missing.

19 Phillips to Lucien H. Boggs, February 23, 1903, George J. Baldwin Papers (University of North Carolina library, Chapel Hill, N.C.), microfilm in possession of the writer.

20 Boggs to Phillips, February 26, 1903, Baldwin Papers.

21 Phillips to Boggs, March 3, 1903, Baldwin Papers.

22 Boggs to Phillips, March 23, 1903, Baldwin Papers.

23 Thomas M. Owen, "A Bibliography of Alabama," in American Historical Association, *Annual Report*, 1897 (Washington, 1898), 777–1248; "A Bibliography of Mississippi," *Annual Report*, 1899, I (Washington, 1900), 633–828. For an appraisal of Thomas M. Owen, see Chapter X.

24 Wilson Lumpkin, *The Removal of the Cherokee Indians from Georgia*, ed. by Wymberley Jones De Renne (2 vols.; privately printed, New York, 1907).

Actually the work covered Lumpkin's whole career, and contained public papers, speeches, and letters. See Haywood J. Pearce, Jr., "Wilson Lumpkin," *Dictionary of American Biography* (20 vols.; N.Y., 1928——) , XI, 504.

25 Phillips to Boggs, March 26, 1903, Baldwin Papers.
26 *Who Was Who in America,* 1897–1942 (Chicago, 1942) , I, 50.
27 Phillips to George J. Baldwin, April 17, 1903, Baldwin Papers.
28 Baldwin to Phillips, April 28, 1903, Baldwin Papers.
29 Phillips to Baldwin, May 2, 1903, Baldwin Papers.
30 Phillips to Baldwin, May 4, 1903, and enclosure, Baldwin Papers; Owen to Phillips, May 2, 1903, Baldwin Papers.
31 Baldwin to Phillips, May 4, 1903 (telegram) , Baldwin Papers.
32 Phillips to Baldwin, May 5, 1903, Baldwin Papers.
33 Baldwin to Phillips, May 6, 1903, Baldwin Papers.
34 Phillips to Baldwin, May 9, 1903, Baldwin Papers.
35 Baldwin to Phillips, May 12, 1903, Baldwin Papers.
36 Baldwin to Phillips, June 10, 1903, Baldwin Papers.
37 Implied in Baldwin to Phillips, June 19, 1903, Baldwin Papers.
38 Herman V. Ames to Phillips, June 16, 1903, Baldwin Papers.
39 Baldwin to Ames, July 9, 1903, Baldwin Papers.
40 Ames to Baldwin, July 15, 1903, Baldwin Papers.
41 Baldwin to Ames, July 18, 1903, Baldwin Papers.
42 Phillips to Baldwin, September 26, 1903, Baldwin Papers. The survey was published in two segments: Ulrich B. Phillips, "The Public Archives of Georgia," American Historical Association, *Annual Report,* 1903, I (Washington, 1904) , 439–74; "Georgia Local Archives," *Annual Report,* 1904 (Washington, 1905) , 555–96. The first report consisted of state archives (records of the state and executive departments at Atlanta) and local archives (records of Baldwin County and Milledgeville) ; the second consisted entirely of local archives (Oglethorpe, Habersham, and Clarke counties and Athens) .
43 Phillips to Baldwin, September 26, 1903, Baldwin Papers.
44 Baldwin to Phillips, October 1, 1903, Baldwin Papers.
45 Phillips to Boggs, April 10, 1903, Baldwin Papers; Phillips to Baldwin, April 17, 1903, Baldwin Papers.
46 Baldwin to Phillips, April 28, 1903, Baldwin Papers.
47 Baldwin to Phillips, July 7, 1908, Baldwin Papers.
48 Phillips to Baldwin, July 11, 1908, Baldwin Papers.
49 *Ibid.*
50 *Letters of Montiano, Siege of St. Augustine,* trans. and ed. by C. DeWitt Willcox (Savannah, 1909) . The thirty-six letters, November 11, 1727—January 2, 1741, were published as *Collections of the Georgia Historical Society,* VII, Pt. 1.
51 Baldwin to Phillips, July 15, 1908, Baldwin Papers. See also Baldwin to Phillips, July 17, 1908, Baldwin Papers; Baldwin to William Harden, July 25, 1908, Baldwin Papers.
52 Early in April, 1909, Phillips gave a lecture to the Georgia Historical Society. See Baldwin to Phillips, March 17, 1909, Baldwin Papers. Correspondence in 1910, last in the series, was concerned with *The Alexander Letters,* 1787–1900 (privately printed for George J. Baldwin, Savannah, 1910) , which Phillips reviewed for the *American Historical Review,* XVI (July, 1911) , 830–32. See Baldwin to Phillips, June 22, 29, 1910, Baldwin Papers.

CHAPTER IX

1 Originally published in the *Journal of Southern History,* XXVII (November, 1960) , 501–25.

2 Charles W. Ramsdell to the writer, April 11, 1937, in writer's personal files.
3 For "A Bibliography of the Writings of Charles W. Ramsdell," see Charles W. Ramsdell, *Behind the Lines in the Southern Confederacy,* edited with a foreword by Wendell H. Stephenson (Baton Rouge, 1944), 123–36. Two other books had appeared by 1937: *A School History of Texas,* in collaboration with Eugene C. Barker and Charles S. Potts (Chicago, 1912) and *The History of Bell County* (San Antonio, 1936), under Ramsdell's editorship. Two more were published subsequently: *Laws and Joint Resolutions of the Last Session of the Confederate Congress (November 7, 1864—March 18, 1865), Together with the Secret Acts of the Previous Congresses* (Durham, 1941) and his Walter Lynwood Fleming Lectures in Southern History, *Behind the Lines in the Southern Confederacy.* A few articles and reviews also appeared after 1937.
4 [Charles W. Ramsdell] to the University of North Carolina Press, October 23, 1933, Charles W. Ramsdell Papers (in possession of Mrs. Ramsdell).
5 Transcript of record, University of Texas.
6 Eugene C. Barker to Ulrich B. Phillips, April 2, 1911, Eugene C. Barker Letters (Archives Collection, University of Texas, Austin, Tex.).
7 Ramsdell to George P. Garrison, July 18, 1902, in George P. Garrison Papers (Archives Collection, University of Texas, Austin, Tex.).
8 *Columbia University Catalogue and General Announcement, 1904–1905* (New York, 1905), 495.
9 Ramsdell to Garrison, April 17, 1905, Garrison Papers.
10 See account, from which the quoted words are taken, in Dixon Ryan Fox, *Herbert Levi Osgood, An American Scholar* (New York, 1924), 47, 146–49.
11 Ramsdell to Garrison, December 11, 1904; April 17, 1905, Garrison Papers.
12 Ramsdell to Garrison, November 12, December 8, 19, 1905, January 24, February 18, April 4, 1906, Garrison Papers.
13 *Bulletin of the University of Texas . . . Catalogue* (title varies), 1907–1941 (Austin, 1908——), *passim.*
14 Phillips to Barker, March 30, 1911, Barker Letters.
15 Charles W. Ramsdell, *Reconstruction in Texas* (New York, 1910), 8.
16 *Ibid.,* 148, 317, 302, 127, 292.
17 *Ibid.,* 66–67 *et passim.*
18 Returned copies of the questionnaire and correspondence relating to it are in the Barker Letters; transcripts in possession of the writer. See also Barker to the editor of the *Nation,* May 1, 1914, New York *Nation,* July 2, 1914.
19 [Barker] to Major George W. Littlefield, April 16, 1914; April 6, 1915; "about April," July 18, 1917. Littlefield to Barker, October 16, December 2, 1914; April 7, 1915; March 5, 1917. [Barker] to Clarence Ousley, chairman, and the board of regents, April 11, 1914 in the Barker Letters. [Barker] to F. W. Cook, chairman board of regents, April 26, 1915; [Barker] to President W. J. Battle, April 21, 1916; [Barker] to President R. E. Vinson, April 23, 1917 Barker Letters. J. E. Goodwin, Librarian's Report on Expenditures for the Littlefield Collection for Southern History, Barker Letters, all in Barker Letters. See also Paul W. Schroeder, "The Littlefield Fund for Southern History, I. A History of the Littlefield Fund," *Library Chronicle of the University of Texas,* VI, No. 1 (Spring, 1957), 3–23; Thomas F. Harwood, "The Littlefield Fund for Southern History, II. Catalogued Books and Pamphlets on the Negro, Slavery, and the Civil War," *Library Chronicle of the University of Texas,* VI, No. 2 (Spring, 1958), 3–16.
20 Barnes F. Lathrop, "Microfilming Materials for Southern History," *Journal of Documentary Reproduction,* II (June, 1939), 91–108.
21 Correspondence of Ramsdell and the writer, personal files.
22 Ramsdell to the writer, June 16, 1939, personal files.

23 Ramsdell to Avery O. Craven, October 29, 1928, Ramsdell Papers.

24 Ramsdell's review of Ulrich B. Phillips, *Life and Labor in the Old South* (Boston, 1929), in *Mississippi Valley Historical Review,* XVII (June, 1930), 160–63.

25 Ramsdell's review of Frank L. Owsley, *State Rights in the Confederacy* (Chicago, 1925), in *Mississippi Valley Historical Review,* XIV (June, 1927), 107–10.

26 Ramsdell to Milo M. Quaife, January 2, 1926, Ramsdell Papers. The reviewer added in his covering letter: "To have called attention to all the errors would have required a book as long as Owsley's."

27 Ramsdell's review of George Fort Milton, *The Eve of Conflict: Stephen A. Douglas and the Needless War* (Boston, 1934), in *Mississippi Valley Historical Review,* XXII (June, 1935), 105–106.

28 Ramsdell to the writer, December 19, 1938, personal files.

29 As examples, Ramsdell to the writer, April 17, 1935, April 25, 1937, personal files.

30 Ramsdell's review of Douglas S. Freeman, *R. E. Lee: A Biography* (4 vols.; New York, 1934–1935), *Journal of Southern History,* I (May, 1935), 230–36.

31 Charles W. Ramsdell, "Some Problems Involved in Writing the History of the Confederacy," *Journal of Southern History,* II (May, 1936), 133–34.

32 *Ibid.,* 133–47.

33 Ramsdell does not clarify this statement in the pages that follow, but at this point he cites his "Lincoln and Fort Sumter" paper, subsequently published *Journal of Southern History,* III (August, 1937), 259–88.

34 Charles W. Ramsdell, "The Changing Interpretation of the Civil War," *Journal of Southern History,* III (February, 1937), 1–25.

35 Ramsdell, *Behind the Lines in the Southern Confederacy,* chap. iii.

36 Ramsdell (ed.), *Laws and Joint Resolutions of the Last Session of the Confederate Congress,* ix–xv.

37 Milo M. Quaife's review of Carl Sandburg, *Abraham Lincoln, The Prairie Years* (2 vols.; New York, 1926), *Mississippi Valley Historical Review,* XIII (September, 1926), 287–91.

38 Charles W. Ramsdell, "Carl Sandburg's Lincoln," *Southern Review,* VI (Winter, 1941), 439–53.

39 For these complaints, see Ramsdell to the writer, May 29, 1935; April 1, July 2, December 14, 1936; March 1, June 13, 20, 30, 1937; December 9, 1938, personal files.

40 Ramsdell to J. G. de Roulhac Hamilton, January 26, February 20, April 13, 1918, J. G. de Roulhac Hamilton Papers (University of North Carolina library, Chapel Hill, N.C.). See also, for this project, Ramsdell to Hamilton, January 9, 1917, Hamilton Papers; Ramsdell to Franklin L. Riley, April 17, 1918, forwarded to Hamilton, Hamilton Papers. The sad experience of 1917–18 did not cure Ramsdell of the malady, as indicated in the footnote on page 202.

CHAPTER X

1 Originally published in the *Alabama Review,* II (January, 1949), 45–62. Much of the correspondence used in this chapter was drawn from the Alabama Historical Society Papers and, beginning in 1901, from the departmental correspondence (Manuscripts Division, State Department of Archives and History, Montgomery, Ala.). For the sake of convenience, all are cited as Thomas M. Owen Papers.

2 For a brief sketch of Owen's career, see Thomas M. Owen, *History of Alabama and Dictionary of Alabama Biography* (4 vols.; Chicago, 1921), IV, 1310–11.

3 William F. Adams, dean of admissions, University of Alabama, to the writer, March 30, 1948, personal files.
4 *Publications of the Southern History Association* (Washington, 1897–1902), I (1897), pp. 1–11. Owen served as first treasurer of the association.
5 R. D. W. Connor, "Dedication of the Archival Section of the Alabama World War Memorial Building," *American Archivist,* IV (April, 1941), 78.
6 American Historical Association, *Annual Report,* 1897 (Washington, 1898), 799.
7 American Historical Association, *Annual Report,* 1899, I (Washington, 1900).
8 *Transactions of the Alabama Historical Society . . . July 14, 1851* (Tuscaloosa, 1852).
9 For the early history of the society, see Allen J. Going, "Historical Societies in Alabama," *Alabama Review,* I (January, 1948), 39–43; Mitchell B. Garrett, "The Preservation of Alabama History," *North Carolina Historical Review,* V (January, 1928), 4–7.
10 Thomas M. Owen to John W. A. Sanford, August 15, 1898, Owen Papers.
11 Garrett, "Preservation of Alabama History," 9.
12 George W. Hamner to Owen, August 8, 1899, Owen Papers.
13 *Transactions of the Alabama Historical Society* (Tuscaloosa, Montgomery, 1898–1906), II, 6. There is no Volume I of this series of the transactions, and the four volumes (II–V) are referred to in the text of this chapter by their correct designations, first, second, third, and fourth.
14 *Transactions of the Alabama Historical Society,* IV, 307–12, 465–85.
15 *Ibid.,* 167–92.
16 *Ibid.,* 321–55.
17 George Petrie to Owen, May 20, 1902, Owen Papers.
18 *Transactions of the Alabama Historical Society,* IV, 277–99, 357–64, 415–39, 501–26.
19 *Transactions of the Alabama Historical Society,* V, 107–51, 153–202, 203–37.
20 *Report of the Alabama History Commission,* I (Montgomery, 1901), 7–8. This volume was designated as *Publications of the Alabama Historical Society, Miscellaneous Collections,* I.
21 *Ibid.,* 13.
22 *Ibid., passim.*
23 Walter L. Fleming to Owen, October 8, 1901, Owen Papers.
24 Franklin L. Riley to Owen, April 16, 1901, Owen Papers.
25 *Report of the Alabama History Commission,* I, 36–44.
26 For the text of the act, see *The Establishment, Organization, Activities and Aspirations of the Department of Archives and History of the State of Alabama,* Department of Archives and History *Bulletin,* No. 1 (Montgomery, 1904), 2–6; *Laws Governing the Department of Archives and History, Bulletin,* No. 4 (Montgomery, 1907), 5–9. The director's salary was fixed at $1,800 and maintenance at $700.
27 Connor, "Dedication of the Archival Section of the Alabama World War Memorial Building," 80–81.
28 *Ibid.,* 77.
29 *Ibid.,* 82.
30 Owen to William K. Boyd, November 22, 1907, William K. Boyd Correspondence (Duke University Library, Durham, N.C.).
31 Fleming to Owen, December 18, 1907, Owen Papers.
32 Owen to Boyd, November 22, 1907, Boyd Correspondence.
33 Edwin R. A. Seligman to Owen, December 9, 1903, Owen Papers. See also Owen to Seligman, October 15, 1903, Owen Papers.
34 Excerpt from a letter, William A. Dunning to Fleming, February, 1904, Owen Papers.

35 Dunning to John S. Bassett, January 6, 1904, John Spencer Bassett Papers (Manuscript Division, Library of Congress, Washington, D.C.).

36 James Ford Rhodes to Owen, March 10, 1904, Owen Papers.

37 George L. Beer to Owen, February 20, 1904, Owen Papers.

38 Dunning to Owen, March 9, 20, 1903, Owen Papers; Owen to Dunning, March 12, 13, 1903, Owen Papers.

39 Charles H. Haskins, "Report of the Proceedings of the Nineteenth Annual Meeting of the American Historical Association," American Historical Association, *Annual Report,* 1903, I (Washington, 1904), 27. See also *American Historical Review,* IX (April, 1904), 444.

40 Charles H. Haskins, "Report of the Proceedings of the Twentieth Annual Meeting of the American Historical Association," American Historical Association, *Annual Report,* 1904 (Washington, 1905), 24; Thomas M. Owen, "State Departments of Archives and History," American Historical Association, *Annual Report,* 1904, pp. 237–57.

41 See Owen to Herman V. Ames, February 1, 1904, March 8, 1905, Owen Papers.

42 Thomas M. Owen (comp.), "Alabama Archives," American Historical Association. *Annual Report,* 1904, p. 488.

43 *Ibid.,* 487–553.

44 Charles H. Haskins to Owen, January 12, 1905, Owen Papers; Owen to Haskins, January 18, 1905, American Historical Association Papers (Manuscript Division, Library of Congress, Washington, D.C.); American Historical Association, *Annual Report,* 1904, p. 54.

45 *Proceedings of the Mississippi Valley Historical Association for the Year 1907–1908* (Cedar Rapids, 1909), I, 15, 17.

46 For notice of its inception, see *Sewanee Review,* X (October, 1902), 509–10.

47 *Gulf States Historical Magazine,* I (September, 1902), 105–27; *Gulf States Historical Magazine,* II (September, 1903), 73–89; *Gulf States Historical Magazine,* II (November, 1903), 155–60; *Gulf States Historical Magazine,* II (March–May, 1904), 310–25.

48 *Gulf States Historical Magazine,* I (March, 1903), 345–47; *Gulf States Historical Magazine,* II (November, 1903), 161–71.

49 *Gulf States Historical Magazine,* II (November, 1903), 172–85; *Gulf States Historical Magazine,* II (March–May, 1904), 343–63.

50 *Gulf States Historical Magazine,* I (July, 1902), 41–44; *Gulf States Historical Magazine,* I (September, 1902), 134–38; *Gulf States Historical Magazine,* I (November, 1902), 207–11; *Gulf States Historical Magazine,* II (July, 1903), 26–34; *Gulf States Historical Magazine,* II (March–May, 1904), 364–71.

51 "Bryant Lester, of Lunenburg Co., Va., and His Descendants," *Publications of the Southern History Association,* I (1897), 127–37; "William Strother, of Virginia, and His Descendants," *Publications of the Southern History Association,* II (1898), 149–73; *A Genealogy of the Kelly Family* (Carrollton, Ala., 1900); *A Genealogy of the Lacy Family* (Carrollton, 1900); *A Genealogy of the Stansel Family* (Carrollton, 1900).

52 "Dr. Basil Manly, The Founder of the Alabama Historical Society," *Transactions of the Alabama Historical Society,* IV, 125–40; "Emma Sansom, An Alabama Heroine," *Gulf States Historical Magazine,* II (March–May, 1904), 364–71; "Colonel William Eaton, of Granville County, North Carolina," *Davidson College Magazine,* XVI (1899), 14–19.

53 "Notes on Alabama Mounds and Antiquities," *Transactions of the Alabama Historical Society,* IV, 235–41.

54 American Historical Association, *Annual Report,* 1904, pp. 237–57.

55 *The Establishment, Organization, Activities and Aspirations of the Department of Archives and History of the State of Alabama,* Department of Archives and

History, *Bulletin*, No. 1; *Check List of Newspaper and Periodical Files in the Department of Archives and History of the State of Alabama, Bulletin*, No. 3 (Montgomery, 1904); *Revolutionary Soldiers in Alabama, Bulletin*, No. 5 (Montgomery, 1911).

CHAPTER XI

1 This essay was read at the twenty-sixth annual meeting of the Southern Historical Association, Tulsa, Oklahoma, November 11, 1960. The program committee requested a forty-five-minute "analysis stressing principal interpretations and developments," not a catalogue or bibliography of authors and titles. Much to the writer's regret, time and space excluded scores of important works.

2 George Tindall, "The Central Theme Revisited," Charles G. Sellers, Jr. (ed.), *The Southerner as American* (Chapel Hill, 1960), 125.

3 Charles W. Ramsdell to the writer, June 16, 1939, in personal files.

4 Avery Craven, *The Repressible Conflict, 1830–1861* (Baton Rouge, 1939), 11–27.

5 C. Vann Woodward, *The Burden of Southern History* (Baton Rouge, 1960), 15–25.

6 Thomas D. Clark (ed.), *Travels in the Old South: A Bibliography* (3 vols.; Norman, 1956, 1959), I (1527–1783), comp. by A. B. Thomas, Hugh Lefler, and Lester J. Cappon; *Travels in the Old South: A Bibliography*, II (1750–1825), comp. by John D. Barnhart, William B. Hamilton, Walter B. Posey, and Culver H. Smith; *Travels in the Old South: A Bibliography*, III (1825–1860), comp. by James W. Patton, Charles S. Sydnor, Robert G. Lunde, and F. Garvin Davenport. The fourth (unnumbered) volume appeared first: E. Merton Coulter (ed.), *Travels in the Confederate States: A Bibliography* (Norman, 1948). The fifth and sixth (unnumbered) volumes were published as *Travels in the New South: A Bibliography* (2 vols.; Norman, 1962), I (1865–1900), comp. by Fletcher M. Green and Thomas D. Clark; *Travels in the New South: A Bibliography*, II (1900–1955), comp. by Rupert B. Vance (English-speaking travelers) and Lawrence S. Thompson (foreign-language accounts).

7 Robert L. Meriwether *et al.* (eds.), *The Papers of John C. Calhoun* (Columbia, 1959——); James F. Hopkins *et al.* (eds.), *The Papers of Henry Clay* (Lexington, 1959——); William T. Hutchinson and William M. E. Rachal (eds.), *The Papers of James Madison* (Chicago, 1962——).

8 Amelia W. Williams and Eugene C. Barker (eds.), *The Writings of Sam Houston, 1813–1863* (8 vols.; Austin, 1938–1943).

9 Gilbert H. Barnes and Dwight L. Dumond (eds.), *Letters of Theodore Dwight Weld, Angelina Grimké Weld, and Sarah Grimké, 1822–1844* (2 vols.; New York, 1934); Dwight L. Dumond (ed.), *Letters of James Gillespie Birney, 1831–1857* (2 vols.; New York, 1938).

10 Mary C. Simms Oliphant, Alfred T. Odell, and T. C. Duncan Eaves (eds.), *The Letters of William Gilmore Simms* (5 vols.; Columbia, 1952–1956); Charles R. Anderson *et al.* (eds.), *The Centennial Edition of the Works of Sidney Lanier* (10 vols.; Baltimore, 1945).

11 Rupert B. Vance's review of Frank L. Owsley, *Plain Folk of the Old South* (Baton Rouge, 1949), in *Journal of Southern History*, XVI (November, 1950), 545–47.

12 Theodore Clarke Smith's reviews of Dwight L. Dumond, *Antislavery Origins of the Civil War in the United States* (Ann Arbor, 1939) and Arthur Y. Lloyd, *The Slavery Controversy, 1831–1860* (Chapel Hill, 1939), in *American Historical Review*, XLV (April, 1940), 663–64.

13 Richard S. Brownlee, *Gray Ghosts of the Confederacy, Guerrilla Warfare in the West, 1861–1865* (Baton Rouge, 1958).
14 Woodward, *Burden of Southern History,* x.
15 Sellers (ed.), *Southerner as American,* vi–vii.
16 Joseph C. Robert's review of Robert A. Warner, *New Haven Negroes: A Social History* (New Haven, 1940), appeared in the *Journal of Southern History,* VII (August, 1941), 417–18; W. E. B. Du Bois's appraisal was published in the *American Historical Review,* XLVII (January, 1942), 376–77.
17 John Hope Franklin, "As for Our History . . . ," Sellers (ed.), *Southerner as American,* 13–14.
18 Carl Becker's review of Marie Kimball, *Jefferson: The Road to Glory, 1743–1776* (New York, 1943), in *American Historical Review,* XLIX (October, 1943), 109–11.

CHAPTER XII

1 This paper was presented as the presidential address at the fifty-first annual meeting of the Mississippi Valley Historical Association, Minneapolis, April 24, 1958.

Index